The Jewish World
around the New Testament

Richard Bauckham

The Jewish World
around the New Testament

Baker Academic
a division of Baker Publishing Group
Grand Rapids, Michigan

Richard Bauckham, born 1946; 1973 PhD University of Cambridge, England; 1977–87 Lecturer in the History of Christian Thought, 1987–92 Reader in the History of Christian Thought, University of Manchester, England; 1992–2007 Professor of New Testament Studies, St Mary's College, St Andrews University, Scotland; now emeritus Professor, St Andrews University, and Senior Scholar, Ridley Hall, Cambridge.

© 2008 by Mohr Siebeck, Tübingen, Germany

Paperback edition published in North America in 2010 by Baker Academic
a division of Baker Publishing Group
P.O. Box 6287, Grand Rapids, MI 49516-6287
www.bakeracademic.com

ISBN 978-0-8010-3903-4

Originally published in 2008 in Tübingen, Germany, by Mohr Siebeck GmbH & C. KG Tübingen as *The Jewish World around the New Testament: Collected Essays I*, Wissenschaftliche Untersuchungen zum Neuen Testament 233.

Printed in the United States of America

Library of Congress Cataloging-in-Publication Data is on file at the Library of Congress, Washington, DC

Table of Contents

1. Introduction

Most New Testament scholars would now agree that the New Testament writings belong wholly within the Jewish world of their time. However much some may be in serious conflict with other Jewish groups, these disagreements take place within the Jewish world. Even New Testament works authored by and/or addressed to non-Torah-observant Gentile Christians still move within the Jewish world of ideas. Their God is unequivocally the God of Israel and of the Jewish Scriptures that they treat as self-evidently their own. Jesus for them is the Messiah of Israel and the Messiah also for the nations only because he is the Messiah of Israel. This is not to deny the obvious influence of the non-Jewish Greco-Roman world in which the New Testament writings also belong, but that influence was felt right across the Jewish world in varying ways and to varying degrees. The most profound influence of Hellenistic thought in the Jewish world of the first century CE is to be found, not in the New Testament, but in Philo of Alexandria, such that it was Philo, more than any of the New Testament writers, who prepared the way for the kind of profound engagement with Hellenistic philosophy that later Christian scholars, such as Clement of Alexandria and Origen, pursued.

The essays collected in this volume were written over the course of thirty years of study of the New Testament and early Judaism, and their topics are quite diverse, but they all share that basic perspective on the historical place of the New Testament writings within late Second Temple Judaism. In an essay I wrote to introduce students and beginning scholars to the relevance of extra-canonical Jewish literature to the study of the New Testament (chapter 14 in this volume) I said: 'The NT student and scholar must use the Jewish literature in the first place to understand Judaism. Only someone who understands early Judaism for its own sake will be able to use Jewish texts appropriately and accurately in the interpretation of the NT.' Accordingly the present volume includes some essays that make no or only passing reference to the New Testament but are intended as contributions to the understanding of Second Temple Judaism and its literature: these include chapters 15 (on Josephus), 16 (on Jewish beliefs about death and afterlife), 18 (on the Jewish apocalypses), and 23 (on the book of Tobit). Most of the essays in this volume relate some part or feature of the New Testament to the literature, religion or life of Jews in that period.

The main literary sources for late Second Temple Judaism are the Apocrypha, Old Testament pseudepigrapha, the Dead Sea Scrolls, and the works of Josephus and Philo. Rabbinic literature, though of much later date, can be relevant when used with caution, and we should not forget that the New Testament itself is evidence of the Judaism of its period, not only in the sense that the early Christian movement from which it comes was itself Jewish, but also in the sense that it refers to other forms and aspects of the Judaism of its period. As well as the literary sources, there is also documentary and epigraphic material, both from Palestine and from the Diaspora. Among these sources, these essays make most use (besides the New Testament) of the Apocrypha and pseudepigrapha, which have long been my special interest, though many of the essays do also refer to and discuss other sources. Among the sources, the most problematic as evidence for late Second Temple Judaism are the rabbinic literature, because of its date, and the so-called Old Testament pseudepigrapha. I do not say 'the Pseudepigrapha' because, unlike the Apocrypha, these are not a defined body of literature with even approximately agreed boundaries, but an indefinite category. While some of these writings can be conclusively shown to be early Jewish writings, the fact that most of them are known only from manuscripts of Christian provenance means that, not only is their date often hard to determine, but also whether they are of Christian or Jewish origin may be more debatable than some scholars have assumed. It is interesting that this issue of the Jewish or Christian provenance, either of Old Testament pseudepigrapha themselves or of traditions they transmit, is common to both the first and the last of the essays in this collection, showing that this is an issue of which I have long been aware. In chapter 21 I provide new arguments for the Jewish provenance of a text generally thought to be most likely of Christian origin.

The essays appear in the chronological order of their original publication, except that chapter 3 belongs so obviously with chapter 2 that I thought it best to place it out of chronological order. There is not much in these essays on which I have significantly changed my mind. Chapter 4 covers a large topic on which much has been written since I wrote it, but the most important point that would be different if I were to write it now is that I would not use the term 'apocalyptic' to refer to a kind of eschatology or a set of ideas, but only in a literary sense with reference to the literary genre apocalypse. To chapters 2 and 20 I have added appendices updating my treatments with reference to subsequently published information and discussion, but it would have been impractical to do this in other cases.

Special thanks are due to Patrick Egan, who compiled the indices.

2. The Martyrdom of Enoch and Elijah:
Jewish or Christian?*

From the standpoint of biblical theology "the establishment of the date of the apocalyptic tradition of the martyrdom of the returning of Elijah is of great importance" (J. Jeremias).[1] Almost all references to the martyrdom of the returning Elijah are to be found in early Christian literature and are references to the joint martyrdom of Elijah and Enoch at the hands of Antichrist:[2] the question of the origin of this Christian tradition of the martyrdom of Enoch and Elijah has, therefore, been regarded as a major line of inquiry in the search for a pre-Christian Jewish tradition of the martyrdom of Elijah. W. Bousset in 1895 sifted early Christian traditions about Antichrist to reconstruct a pre-Christian tradition which included the return of Enoch and Elijah to denounce Antichrist and to suffer martyrdom.[3] But texts of some importance to the question have come to light only since Bousset wrote, including the relevant section of the Coptic Apocalypse of Elijah, on which Jeremias's case for a pre-Christian tradition of Elijah's martyrdom depends heavily. This article is an attempt to reexamine the origins of the Christian tradition of the martyrdom of Enoch and Elijah. To facilitate this a diagrammatic analysis of the relevant texts is included.

The table lists only motifs which occur in more than one of the texts. The texts (which include several that were unavailable to Bousset) are:

(A) Rev 11:3–13.
(B) Coptic *Apocalypse of Elijah* (in G. Steindorff, *Die Apokalypse des Elias* [TU 17/3 a; Leipzig: Hinrichs, 1899]).
(C) Ethiopic *Apocalypse of Peter,* chap. 2 (tr. in E. Hennecke and W. Schneemelcher (eds.), *New Testament Apocrypha* [ed. R. McL. Wilson; London. Lutterworth, 1965], 2. 669).
(D) Tertullian, *De anima* 50.

---

* First publication: *Journal of Biblical Literature* 95 (1976) 447–458.
[1] *TDNT* 2 (1964) 941.
[2] Jeremias (*TDNT* 2 [1964] 941 n. 106) cites one rabbinic reference to Elijah's death. For the death of Elijah in Lactantius and Commodian, see n. 19 below.
[3] *The Antichrist Legend* (London: Hutchinson, 1896 [German original, Göttingen: Vandenhoeck & Ruprecht, 1895]) 203–11. – The term "Antichrist" is strictly anachronistic with reference to *Jewish* literature, but for convenience I have used it throughout this article with reference to both Jewish and Christian concepts of an eschatological adversary.

(E) Hippolytus, *De Antichristo* 43, 46–47; *In Danielem*, 35, 50.

(F) *Acts of Pilate* 25 (Greek text in L. F. K. Tischendorf, *Evangelia apocrypha* [Leipzig: Mendelssohn, 1876] 331; Latin text, ibid. 404–5).

(G) Ephraem Syrus, *Sermo de fine extremo* (in T. J. Lamy [ed.], *Sancti Ephraem Syri hymni et sermones* 3 [Mechlin: Dessain, 1889] 207–10).

(H) Ephraem "Graecus," *Sermo in adventum Domini* (in J. S. Assemani [ed.], *Sancti Ephraem Syri opera omnia quae exstant* [Rome: Salvioni, 1746], 3. 141–42).

(I) Ps.-Ephraem "Latinus," *Sermo de fine mundi* (in C. P. Caspari, *Briefe, Abhandlungen und Predigten* [Christiania: Malling, 1890] 219).

(J) Ps.-Hippolytus, *De consummatione mundi* 21 (in P. A. Lagarde [ed.], *Hippolyti Romani quae feruntur omnia graece* [Leipzig: Teubner, 1858] 104–5).

(K) Ps.-Hippolytus, *De consummatione mundi* 29 (ibid., 111).

(L) Ps.-Methodius, *Revelationes* 14 (Greek and Latin) (Greek text in A. Vassiliev, *Anecdota graeco-byzantina* [Moscow: Imperial University, 1893] 38; Latin text in E. Sackur, *Sibiyllinische Texte und Forschungen* [Halle: Niemeyer, 1898], 95–96).

(M) *Visio Danielis* (Greek) (in A. Vassiliev, *Anecdota*, 43).

(N) Ps.-Methodius, *Révélations* 6 (Syriac) (tr. in F. Naum, *Révélations et légendes* [Paris: Imprimerie Nationale, 1917] 31).

(O) Syriac (Clementine) *Apocalypse of Peter* (tr. in E. Bratke, "Handschriftliche Überlieferung und Bruchstücke der arabisch-aethiopischen Petrus-Apokalypse," *ZWT* 36/1 [1893] 471–72).

(P) Ethiopic (Clementine) *Apocalypse of Peter* (tr. in E. Bratke, "Handschriftliche Überlieferung," 483).

(Q) Latin *Tiburtine Sibyl* (in E. Sackur, *Sibyllinische Texte*, 186).

(R) Greek *Tiburtine Sibyl* (in P. S. Alexander, *The Oracle of Baalbek* [Dumbarton Oaks Studies 10; Washington: Dumbarton Oaks Research Library, 1967] 22).

(S) *Apocalypse of Ps.-Shenoute* (in E. Amélineau, *Mémoires publiés par les membres de la mission archéologique française au Caire (1885–1886)* 4/1 [Paris: Ernest Leroux, 1888] 345).

(T) Bohairic *History of Joseph* 31–32 (tr. in F. Robinson, *Coptic Apocryphal Gospels* [Texts and Studies 4/2; Cambridge: Cambridge University, 1896] 146–47; Arabic in J. K. Thilo, *Codex apocryphus Novi Testamenti* [Leipzig: Vogel, 1832] 58–61).

(U) *Apocalypse of Ps.-John* 8 (in L. F. K. Tischendorf, *Apocalypses apocryphae* [Leipzig: Mendelssohn, 1866] 77).

(V) Syriac *Apocalypse of Ezra* (tr. in F. Baethgen, "Beschreibung der syrischen Handschrift 'Sachau 131' auf der königlichen Bibliothek zu Berlin," *ZAW* 6 [1886] 209).

(W) Adso, *Libellus de Antichristo* (in E. Sackur, *Sibyllinische Texte*, 111–12).

(Y) Adso, *Libellus de Antichristo* (longer text) (in *PL* 90: 1186).

	A	B	C	D	E	F	G	H	I	J	K	L	M	N	O	P	Q	R	S	T	U	V	W	Y
Explicit quotation of Rev 11																				x				
Enoch and Elijah		x	x	x	x	x	x	x	x	x⁴	x	x	x	x	x	x	x	x	x	x⁵	x	x	x	x
Elijah and Enoch		x		x	x		x	x			x	x	x	x	x	x	x	x	x					
witnesses	x	x						x	x	x	x								x			x	x	x
prophets	x	x		x	x		x	x	x	x	x	x	x	x		x		x	x			x	x	x
descend		x												x										
fight Antichrist	x		x		x	x				x							x							
preach repentance	x		x		x					x														
plague enemies	x	x	x		x						x	x												
expose Antichrist	x	x	x				x	x	x	x	x	x	x	x	x	x	x	x	x		x	x	x	x
Antichrist enraged	x	x	x		x	x	x	x	x	x	x	x	x	x	x	x	x	x	x		x	x	x	x
fights them	x	x	x		x		x	x	x	x	x	x	x	x	x			x				x		x
conquers them	x	x	x		x			x	x	x	x	x	x	x	x			x		x		x		x
kills them	x	x	x	(x)⁶	x	x	x	x	(x)⁷	x	x	x	x	x	x	x	x	x	x		x	x	x	x
on the altar	x	x													x			x						
bodies lie unburied	x	x																x	x					x
3½ days	x	x			x⁸									x					x	x				x
3 days						x											x							
4 days														x	x			x						
in the streets of Jerusalem	x	x													x	x		x	x					x
the great city	x	x																	x					
everyone sees them	x	x																	x					
they rise	x	x			x			x						x	x	x		x	x		x			x
are raised by Michael and Gabriel							x									x								
renewed conflict with Antichrist		x																						x
ascend to heaven	x	(x)⁹				x								x				x						
in the sight of all														x										
destroy Antichrist	x	x		(x)⁶															x					

---

⁴ Ps.-Hippolytus 21 adds John.

⁵ *History of Joseph* (Arabic) adds "Schila" and Tabitha.

⁶ Tertullian: "They are reserved to die, so that they may extinguish Antichrist with their blood."

⁷ There is a gap in the MS.

⁸ Tischendorf's Latin text das 3½ days; his Greek text 3 days.

⁹ Is is not quite clear that the *Apocalypse of Elijah* intends to describe an ascension: "They will raise cries of joy towards heaven, they will shine, and all the people and the whole world will see them."

The date and interrelationships of many of these texts have not been established and cannot be on the basis of examining only this one element of the eschatological traditions they share. But it is important to notice that none of the texts F–Y may be dated before the fourth century[10] and many are much later. Undoubtedly, eschatological traditions in early and medieval Christianity were transmitted in relatively stable forms; the same apocalyptic texts were frequently updated and adapted to new circumstances, and late texts are therefore by no means worthless evidence of early tradition. But they must nevertheless be used with care in attempts to investigate the origins of traditions. Since it is rarely possible to prove that a tradition did *not* exist at an earlier date than the evidence attests, the temptations to project traditions further back than the evidence warrants must be painstakingly resisted.

Of the pre-fourth-century texts, there is, of course, no doubt of the date of Tertullian and Hippolytus. The *Apocalypse of Peter* dates from the early second century, but we shall see that the Ethiopic version's reference to Enoch and Elijah may not belong to the original apocalypse. The *Apocalypse of Elijah* is even more problematic. It has commonly been regarded as a third- or fourth-century Christian redaction of early Jewish material,[11] and most scholars have thought that its account of Enoch and Elijah is dependent on the account of the two witnesses in Revelation 11,[12] though perhaps also embodying independent Jewish tradition. Jeremias thought that a Jewish tradition of the martyrdom of Elijah could probably be discerned beneath the Christian redaction,[13] but much more confident of the Jewish provenience of the work is J.-M. Rosenstiehl.[14] He regards it as substantially an Essene work of the first century B.C., expanded in chap. 2 by another Jewish author of the third century A.D. Its account of the return of Enoch and Elijah he regards as wholly Jewish and pre-Christian, related to Revelation 11 only *via* a common source.

---

[10] An earlier date for the *Acts of Pilate* has sometimes been advocated, but G. C. O'Ceallaigh ("Dating the Commentaries of Nicodemus," *HTR* 56 [1963] 21–58) has demonstrated a *terminus post quem* at 555 for the earliest part (Part I) of the work. The Descent into Hell (which includes chap. 25) is later.

[11] E. Schürer, review of Steindorff's edition, *TLZ* 24 (1899) 7–8; W. Bousset, "Beiträge zur Geschichte der Eschatologie," *ZKG* 20 (1899) 103–12; H. Weinel, "Die spätere christliche Apokalyptik," ΕΥΧΑΡΙΣΤΗΡΙΟΝ: *Studien zur Religion und Literatur des Alten und Neuen Testaments* (Gunkel Festschrift; Göttingen: Vandenhoeck & Ruprecht, 1923), 2. 164–66.

[12] E. g., D. Haugg, *Die Zwei Zeugen: Eine exegetische Studie über Apok 11, 1–13* (NTAbh 17/1; Münster: Aschendorf, 1936) 94; M. Black, "Servant of the Lord and Son of Man," *SJT* 6 (1953) 10 n. 1; W. Wink, *John the Baptist in the Gospel Tradition* (SNTSMS 7; London/New York: Cambridge University, 1968) 14 n. 1.

[13] *TDNT* 2 (1964) 939–41.

[14] *L'Apocalypse d'Elie* (Paris: Geuthner, 1972).

Rosenstiehl's arguments do not carry complete conviction.[15] A final conclusion as to the date of the *Apocalypse of Elijah* can only be reached after a fuller study of the traditions it contains, and since the present inquiry is part of such study the question of date must be regarded as still open. Initially, however, we may notice from the table that the *Apocalypse of Elijah's* account of Enoch and Elijah obviously has close affinities not only with Revelation 11 but also with the Christian tradition of the fourth century onwards. These affinities provide the obvious indications of date, and we shall require strong evidence for dating as early as the first century B.C. a tradition which is otherwise attested for the fourth century and later but not before. It should also be noticed that the undoubtedly strongly Jewish character of the *Apocalypse of Elijah* need not mean that it always preserves *pre-Christian* Jewish tradition. Some of its striking points of contact with Jewish apocalyptic are not with extant pre-Christian apocalyptic but with the so-called Neo-Hebraic apocalyptic of the Christian era.[16] It is probable that a two-way traffic in apocalyptic traditions between Judaism and Christianity continued long after the first century,[17] and not beyond possibility that a Jewish tradition of the martyrdom of Enoch and Elijah could have resulted from the influence of Christian traditions based on Revelation 11.

J. Munck, in a survey of many of the texts included in the table, argued, against Bousset and Jeremias, that there was no Christian tradition of the return of Enoch and Elijah independent of Revelation 11 and therefore no evidence of a pre-Christian tradition of their martyrdom. Revelation 11, subjected to a mistaken exegesis by such writers as Hippolytus and Ps.-Hippolytus, gave rise to the whole Christian tradition of the return of Enoch and Elijah.[18] In his major contention that the *martyrdom* of Enoch and Elijah is a tradition deriving from exegesis of Revelation 11, we shall see that Munck was probably correct. But it is less likely that *all* aspects of the tradition derive from Revelation 11.

An expectation of the return of Enoch and Elijah is attested in pre-Christian Judaism, though much more rarely than the expectation of Elijah alone. 4 Ezra 6:26 expects the appearance of those who had not died (cf. 7:28; 13:52), but doubtless means not only Enoch and Elijah, for Jewish writers of this period exalted others (Moses, Baruch, Ezra) to the privilege of escaping death. But *1 Enoch* 90:31 does seem to refer to the return of

---

[15] See some critical comments in a review by P. M. Parvis, *JTS* 24 (1973) 588–89.

[16] This is especially true of the description of Antichrist: see J.-M. Rosenstiehl, "Le portrait de l'Antichrist," *Pseudépigraphes de l'Ancien Testament et manuscrits de la Mer Morte* (Paris: Presses Universitaires de France, 1967), 1. 45–60.

[17] Cf. M. Buttenwieser, *Outline of the Neo-Hebraic Apocalyptic Literature* (Cincinnati: Jennings and Pye, 1901) 1.

[18] *Petrus und Paulus in der Offenbarung Johannis* (Copenhagen: Rosenkilde og Bagger, 1950) 81–118.

Enoch and Elijah specifically, probably at a period when only these two were thought to have escaped death. The survival of this tradition in Christianity and its lack of attestation in Judaism ought perhaps to be associated with the popularity of the Enoch literature in some early Christian circles and its corresponding lapse from favor in Judaism. Certainly early Christian writers tended to regard Enoch and Elijah as the only two who had escaped death (Irenaeus, *Adv. haer.* 5.5.1; cf. 4 Ezra 1:39; *Apocalypse of Paul* 20).

If early Christian writers took over from Judaism the expectation that Enoch and Elijah would return to earth before the Judgment, it is not so clear that they took over specific functions that the two were to perform. In *1 Enoch* 90:31 they appear to have no function. Among Christian writers Hippolytus at least seems to have used no extra-scriptural traditions except the mere expectation of Enoch and Elijah's return. His accounts are closely dependent on Revelation 11 and he does little more than identify the two witnesses as Enoch and Elijah: his explanation that they are to be martyred "because they will not give glory to Antichrist" (*De Antichristo* 47) is surely an intelligent deduction from the text rather than a sign of the influence of independent tradition. But it is noteworthy that he apparently found it unnecessary to argue for his identification of the witnesses: he cites Mal 4:5–6 for the return of Elijah but seems to regard as unquestionable the identification of the second witness as Enoch. Arguably, once one witness had been identified as Elijah, Enoch's claim to be the other was obvious, for these were the two men who had not died. But it is more probable that an existing tradition of the return of Enoch with Elijah influenced Hippolytus' exegesis. Lactantius and Commodian show attempts to interpret Revelation 11 in the light of an alternative tradition of the return of Elijah alone,[19] and patristic authors who gave close attention to the text of Revelation 11 were quite capable, like modern scholars, of finding that the characteristics of the two witnesses in 11:5–6 recall Elijah and Moses and Jeremiah but not Enoch.[20] The identification with Elijah *and Enoch* was not obvious from the text, and its prevalence in the early church must probably be explained by reference to an independent tradition of the return of Enoch and Elijah in the light of which Revelation 11 was interpreted.

The tradition in most of the texts other than Hippolytus goes further than naming Enoch and Elijah in its divergence from Revelation 11. At least from the time of Ephraem Syrus, the tradition seems to assume an independent

---

[19] Lactantius (*Inst.* 7,17) and Commodian (*Carmen de duobus populis* 833–64) are both patently dependent on Rev 11:3–13, but Lactantius speaks only of one figure, Elijah, and Commodian speaks first of Elijah alone (833, 839, 850) and then of *prophetae* (856–62). The tradition of the return of Elijah alone also appears in Justin, *Dial.* 49; *Sib. Or.* 2:187; Tertullian, *De resurrectione* 22; *De anima* 25.

[20] Hilarius, *In Matt.* 20:10 (*PL* 9.1032); Victorinus, *In Apoc.* 11:5 (*PL* 5.334).

life of its own, so that the story as told in most of the texts bears little resemblance to the story of the two witnesses, and only in a few cases (J, W) does it appear that the writer himself made any reference to the text of Revelation 11. In terms of the motifs listed in the table, there are two accounts (C, N) which have no point of contact at all with Revelation 11, and one (H) which coincides only in describing the two as prophets. All the others agree with Revelation 11 at least in recounting the martyrdom, but six of these (D, L, M, T, U, V) coincide with Revelation 11 only at this point, and three (G, P, R) only at this point and at the resurrection. It is true that most of the accounts are much briefer than Rev 11:3–13; but this only highlights the significance in the tradition of recurrent motifs which are not found at all in Revelation 11. The idea that the purpose of Enoch and Elijah's mission is to expose Antichrist's deceits is found in sixteen of the texts (B, C, G, H, I, J, K, L, N, O, P, S, T, U, W, Y), while the motifs of Antichrist's rage against Enoch and Elijah occur in seven texts (B, G, L, M, O, R, S). Other features clearly not derived from Revelation 11 are found occasionally: Enoch and Elijah come to fight Antichrist (B, F, N, R), they are put to death on the altar (U, V), they are raised by Michael and Gabriel (G, P), their conflict with Antichrist continues after their resurrection (B, S), and they finally destroy Antichrist (B, N, S). The tradition is by no means uniform, and the omission of some motifs is doubtless often determined by the nature of the context or a desire for brevity; but most of the texts given in the table recount the return of Enoch and Elijah in the context of a sequential prophecy of the events of the last days and may, therefore, be expected to convey what was regarded as the main point of the tradition. Only a few of the texts (D, F, T) are in the nature of more incidental allusions. Therefore the degree of divergence from Relevation 11 and the recurrent prominence of motifs not derived from Revelation 11 is striking.

The point of most consistent divergence is the purpose of the mission of Enoch and Elijah. The two witnesses in Rev 11:3–13 are preachers of repentance; they are not represented as preaching against Antichrist specifically; they encounter Antichrist only when their witness is completed. In the Enoch and Elijah tradition, almost without exception,[21] the two prophets are sent against Antichrist, after his reign has begun. This may mean that they are the instruments of his destruction (B, D, N, S), but it most commonly means that they expose him as an imposter. They denounce him either to his face or to the people or both, and this is what provokes his rage and their

---

[21] The exceptions are Hippolytus, who follows Revelation 11 closely; the Latin *Tiburtine Sibyl* (Q), where the mission of Enoch and Elijah is "to announce the Lord's coming"; and the Syriac *Apocalypse of Ezra* (V), which has no reference to the purpose of their coming. Adso – and thence the whole Western medieval tradition – gives them the additional role of converting the Jews to Christianity.

martyrdom. The fact that some accounts (B, G, H, K, O) give details of the verbal exchange between Antichrist and the two prophets illustrates the prominence of this theme in the tradition. Sometimes the people at large are convinced by this exposure of the false Messiah (L), sometimes the faithful are encouraged or reclaimed (I, W, Y), sometimes "few believe" (H).

It is clear, therefore, that Bousset was correct in drawing attention to the characteristics of the Enoch and Elijah tradition which distinguish it from Revelation 11. But his conclusion, that such texts as K, L, U, V represent substantially a pre-Christian Jewish tradition uninfluenced by Revelation 11, was too hasty.[22] According to Bousset the pre-Christian tradition was that Enoch and Elijah would return to denounce Antichrist and would be slain by him. The motif of resurrection after three days he regarded as originating in Revelation 11 and appearing only in texts influenced by Revelation 11.[23] In fact, it is very doubtful whether the resurrection can be regarded as a secondary addition to a tradition which already included the martyrdom. It seems, on the contrary, that the resurrection has dropped out of the tradition in those texts which conclude the story with martyrdom, just as the ascencion has been omitted by almost all the texts which include the resurrection. There are some texts evidently dependent on Revelation 11 which omit both resurrection and ascension (E, J, W), and in many cases the motive for such an omission is clear. In most of the texts the account of the last days has been compressed so that the general resurrection follows swiftly upon the martyrdom of Enoch and Elijah, and their individual resurrection becomes redundant.[24] In other cases, (D, T) the allusion to the tradition is in order to make a particular point which depends on the martyrdom, not the resurrection.[25] If there was a pre-Christian tradition, it must either have included both martyrdom and resurrection or have included neither.

Those who, like Rosenstiehl, regard the account in the *Apocalypse of Elijah* as Jewish will argue that there was a Jewish tradition of both martyrdom and resurrection. It is much more probable that both features entered the tradition from Revelation 11. Apart from the debatable case of the *Apocalypse of Elijah* and the brief reference of Tertullian, the martyrdom is attested before the fourth century only in Hippolytus, who quite clearly derived it from Revelation 11. Thus two centuries before the texts from which Bousset constructed a pre-christian tradition, Christians were iden-

---

[22] *Antichrist Legend*, 208–9.

[23] Ibid., 209–10.

[24] It is interesting to note that in *Acts of Pilate* 25 the resurrection and ascension of Enoch and Elijah are related in the language of 1 Thes 4:17, thereby assimilating them to the general resurrection and rapture of the saints.

[25] Munck has argued at length that there was never a tradition of martyrdom without resurrection (*Petrus und Paulus*, 100–109).

tifying Enoch and Elijah with the two witnesses of Revelation 11. It would be surprising if the later tradition showed no influence from Revelation 11, and such influence is surely responsible for the near unanimity of the texts in expecting the martyrdom of Enoch and Elijah.

A more profitable approach to the question of pre-Christian tradition is to examine those three texts (C, H, N) which are remarkable for *not* mentioning the martyrdom.[26] These texts are the most dissimilar from Revelation 11 and the most likely to reflect entirely independent tradition. One of them, chap. 2 of the Ethiopic version of the *Apocalypse of Peter,* would be the earliest Christian reference to the return of Enoch and Elijah, if it could be shown to be part of the original early second-century apocalypse. But the Ethiopic text of chap. 2 is suspect. A general comparison of the Ethiopic of the *Apocalypse of Peter* with the Greek fragments and the patristic citations suggests that, while "on the whole the Ethiopic presents the original contents of the Apocalypse",[27] in detail it is scarcely a reliable witness to the original text. Moreover, the text of chap. 2 shows some degree of confusion. One part represents the "house of Israel" as following the false messiahs; another represents them as suffering martyrdom at the hands of the deceiver. The transition from the several false messiahs to the one Antichrist is oddly abrupt; and in favor of the originality of the former motif rather than the latter may be cited chap. 1 of the Ethiopic and vv. 1–2 of the Akhimimic text, which must represent at least a summary of this part of the apocalypse. In this case the *Apocalypse of Peter* belongs with 2 Peter and the synoptic apocalypse in knowing of false prophets and messianic pretenders of the last days, rather than of the single Antichrist of 2 Thessalonians. The parable of the fig-tree and its explanation would then have been introduced around an original prophecy of false messiahs who would lead the people astray. The introduction of Enoch and Elijah at the end of chap. 2 seems almost an afterthought, unnecessary to the interpretation of the parable and perhaps intended to clear up the difficulty of the preceding text: it is the preaching of Enoch and Elijah which will enlighten the Jews as to the true nature of Antichrist and so make them martyrs.

---

[26] Not only do all the other texts in the table refer to the martyrdom, but also other texts which were not sufficiently important to be included: Philippus Solitarius, *Dioptra* 3.10; John of Damascus, *De fide orthodoxa* 4.20; Honorius of Autun, *Elucidarium* 3.9. The only other example that I know of referring to the return of Enoch and Elijah without the mention of their martyrdom is in the Arabic (Clementine) *Apocalypse of Peter* (A. Mingana, *Woodbrooke Studies* [Cambridge: Heffer, 1931], 3. 359). But the martyrdom may be included in the section Mingana omits (p. 360), as it evidently is in the version described by Bousset (*Antichrist Legend*, 74).

[27] C. Maurer in E. Hennecke, New Testament Apocrypha (ed. R. McL. Wilson; London: Lutterworth, 1965), 2. 665.

This is a conjectural explanation of the text, but it illustrates the difficulty of using it as evidence that the tradition of Enoch's and Elijah's return to denounce Antichrist was already known in the early second century. On the other hand, the singular absence of reference to the martyrdom may indicate an early (though not necessarily second-century) tradition. It might be understood contextually, if the point of the reference to Enoch and Elijah is to explain how the Jews are to recognize Antichrist as an imposter. But even so the context of reference to martyrdom was one in which other writers would not be able to resist adding that Enoch and Elijah too would seal their witness in blood. The point is well illustrated by comparing this text with a parallel one in the later Ethiopic (Clementine) *Apocalypse of Peter* (P), which is certainly dependent on it:

(C)	(P)
... he will kill with the sword and there shall be many martyrs. Then shall the boughs of the fig-tree, that is the house of Israel, sprout, and there shall be many martyrs by his hand: they shall be killed and become martyrs. Enoch and Elijah will be sent to instruct them that this is the deceiver who must come into the world and do signs and wonders in order to deceive. And therefore shall they that are slain by his hand be martyrs and shall be reckoned among the good and righteous martyrs who have pleased God in their life.	... they will be beheaded and become martyrs. In that day will be fulfilled what is said in the Gospel: when the branches of the fig-tree are full of sap, know that the time of the harvest is at hand. Shoots of the fig-tree are those righteous men called, who become martyrs at his hand, and the angels will bring them to the joy, and no hair of their head will be lost. Then Enoch and Elijah will descend. They will preach and put to shame that tyrannical enemy of righteousness and son of lies. Then they will be beheaded, and Michael and Gabriel will raise them up and bring them into the garden of joy, and no drop of his *(sic)* blood will fall on the ground...

In the second text the preaching of Enoch and Elijah against Antichrist is retained, but no longer serves to make martyrs of anyone but Enoch and Elijah themselves. The parallelism of language between the account of the martyrs and the account of Enoch and Elijah shows the extent to which they are here portrayed as examples of martyrdom, the very last of all the martyrs. This was the dominant trend of the tradition.

The *Apocalypse of Peter* may thus be evidence that the tradition of the return of Enoch and Elijah to denounce Antichrist first existed independently of the tradition of the martyrdom. The same early tradition may also survive in Ephraem Graecus (H), where the martyrdom is not mentioned. The process of assimilation to Revelation 11 can be seen rather clearly in Ps.-Hippolytus: in chap. 21 (J) the motif of exposing Antichrist has been introduced into an account drawn from Hippolytus and dependent on Revelation 11; in chap. 29 (K) the motif of martyrdom has been added to an account of the mission of Enoch and Elijah very similar to that in Ephraem Graecus.[28]

The Syriac version of Ps.-Methodius (N) seems to represent another form of the tradition which did not include the martyrdom, a form in which Enoch and Elijah come to destroy Antichrist. It is a quite distinctive account:

... when he comes to Jerusalem, Enoch and Elijah will leave the land of life; they will rise up against him, they will withstand him and he will curse them. When he sees them, he will melt like salt in the presence of water, and he will be the first to be punished, before all men, together with the demons who entered into him...

The only close parallel to this account is at the end of the *Apocalypse of Elijah*, where Enoch and Elijah descend a second time from heaven, and "pursue the Son of Iniquity and kill him, without his being able to speak. In that day he will be destroyed before them like ice destroyed by the fire..." The destruction of Antichrist by Enoch and Elijah then reappears in the *Apocalypse of Ps.-Shenoute* (S), which is dependent on the *Apocalypse of Elijah*. Perhaps also to be connected with this tradition is Tertullian's statement that "they are reserved to die, so that they may extinguish Antichrist with their blood" (*morituri reservantur, ut Antichristum sanguine suo extinguant*). This is a reinterpretation of the destruction of Antichrist in terms of the martyrological idea that the death of the martyr rebounds in judgment on the persecutor and thereby secures his destruction. It is possibly a reinterpretation independent of Revelation 11 but more probably Tertullian, like Hippolytus, identified Enoch and Elijah with the two witnesses and understood their death in the light of Rev 12:11, 15:2 as a conquest of Antichrist.

This motif of the destruction of Antichrist by Enoch and Elijah is likely to be of Jewish origin, as is also the alternative tradition of his destruction by the archangel Michael, which found its way from Judaism into the Christian tradition:[29] the elimination of the last great enemy of the people of God was a messianic function in both Jewish and Christian apocalyptic.[30] A Christian author is unlikely to have originated a tradition in which Enoch and Elijah are permitted in this way to usurp the role of Christ.[31] But the messianic

---

[28] For the relationship of Ps.-Hippolytus to Ephraem Graecus, see W. Bousset, *Antichrist Legend*, 41–42.

[29] See W. Bousset, *Antichrist Legend*, 227–31; M. Buttenwieser, *Outlines*, 43; *Jewish Encyclopedia*, 8. 536–7.

[30] Jewish: *2 Apoc. Bar.* 40:1–2; M. Buttenwieser, *Outlines*, 31, 35, 38. Christian: 2 Thes 2:8; Rev 19:11–21; W. Bousset, *Antichrist Legend*, 224–25.

[31] This is undoubtedly why it appears rarely in the Christian sources. Ps.-Shenoute (S), which is dependent on the *Apocalypse of Elijah*, retains the motif, but the Greek *Ti-*

expectations of first-century Judaism were more varied and could easily have accommodated a tradition in which Enoch and Elijah were a pair of messianic figures appearing at the end to combat and destroy Antichrist. Such a tradition has not survived in extant Jewish texts, but a messianic role for Elijah is attested,[32] while Enoch in the Similitudes of Enoch assumes the messianic functions of the Son of Man.

We may now attempt a classification of the traditions:

Ia. The return of Enoch and Elijah (purpose unspecified): *1 Enoch* 90:31.

Ib. The return of Enoch and Elijah as the two witnesses of Revelation 11: Hippolytus (E).

Ia. The return of Enoch and Elijah to destroy Antichrist: Syriac Ps.-Methodius (N).

IIb. The return of Enoch and Elijah to destroy Antichrist by suffering martyrdom: Tertullian (D).

IIIa. The return of Enoch and Elijah to expose Antichrist: Apocalypse of Peter (C), Ephraem Graecus (H)

IIIb. The return of Enoch and Elijah to expose Antichrist and suffer martyrdom: Ps.-Hippolytus 29 (K) etc.

Ia and probably IIa are pre-Christian Jewish traditions. IIIa may also be a Jewish tradition, though we cannot be sure. The martyrdom appears only in the secondary development of each, probably in each case under the influence of Revelation 11. Certainly there is no *evidence* that this development had already taken place in Judaism. The majority of the texts belong to IIIb, with greater or less assimilation to Revelation 11.

The tendency of many of the texts is to emphasize the martyrological aspects of the tradition, not only by taking over the martyrdom motif itself from Revelation 11 but also by incorporating additional martyrological features such as Antichrist's rage (B, G, L, M, O, R, S)[33] and the sacrificial understanding of martyrdom attested by death on the altar (U, V).[34] The tendency to represent Enoch and Elijah primarily as exemplary martyrs of the last days is illustrated by the Ethiopic (Clementine) *Apocalypse of Peter* (P), quoted above, and is also to be seen in the account in the *Apocalypse of Elijah*, where Enoch and Elijah appear among a sequence of martyrs

---

burtine Sibyl (R), which is also dependent on the *Apocalypse of Elijah*, replaces it with the intervention of Christ himself, who raises Enoch and Elijah and then fights and destroys Antichrist.

[32] *TDNT* 2 (1964) 931; Str-B, 4. 782–84; J. A. T. Robinson, "Elijah, John and Jesus: An Essay in Detection," *NTS* 4 (1957–58) 263–81, esp. pp. 268–70.

[33] The rage of the persecutor is a stock feature of martyrdom stories: Dan 3:13, 19; 11:30; Bel 8; 2 Macc 7:39; 4 Macc 8:2; 9:10; Acts 7:54; H. Musurillo, *The Acts of the Christian Martyrs* (Oxford: Clarendon, 1972) 22, 26, 54, 66, 190.

[34] The same understanding is found in the Apocalypse of Elijah, when Antichrist throws the blood of the martyr Tabitha on the temple and when the Sixty Righteous Men are burned on the altar.

comprising Tabitha, Enoch, and Elijah, and the Sixty Righteous Men, and where the martyrological aspect of the tradition is strongly emphasized by the details of the narrative, including those which it shares with Revelation 11.

A narrative of idealized martyrs of the end-time can be paralleled from pre-Christian Jewish apocalyptic: the incident of "Taxo" and his seven sons in chap. 9 of the *Assumption of Moses*. But it was a Christian innovation to cast Enoch and Elijah in this role. Seen in the light of the rest of the evidence for the Enoch and Elijah tradition, the *Apocalypse of Elijah* has the characteristics of a relatively late version, taking up varied elements of eschatological tradition and elaborating them into an extended narrative of the reign of Antichrist. By means of incorporating two distinct forms of the tradition of Enoch and Elijah (IIIb and IIa), the *Apocalypse of Elijah* was able to relate two distinct comings of Enoch and Elijah: first to denounce Antichrist and suffer martyrdom and then a second time at the end to destroy him. Possibly the second belonged to an original Jewish *Apocalypse of Elijah*, but the first may be credibly attributed to the third- or fourth-century Christian redaction which was responsible for the present form of the work.[35]

To conclude: the Christian tradition of the return of Enoch and Elijah provides no evidence of a pre-Christian Jewish tradition of their martyrdom. The martyrdom is a Christian innovation deriving via Rev 11:3–13 from the Christian innovation of the martyrdom of the Messiah.

Additional Note A:
More texts

Since completing the article that is reprinted here as the above chapter, I have come across a variety of other Christian[36] apocalyptic works that contain the tradition of the martyrdom of Enoch and Elijah. They are all relatively late texts and they do not suggest that any modifications of my argument in the article are needed, but they are listed here and tabulated in the same way as the my original set of texts in order to supplement the evidence:

(A¹)   Arabic *Sibyl* A (E. Y. Ebied and M. J. L. Young, 'An Unrecorded Arabic Version of a Sibylline Prophecy,' *Orientalia Christiana Periodica* 43 [1977] 279–307).

(B¹)   Arabic *Sibyl* B (E. Y. Ebied and M. J. L. Young, 'A Newly-Discovered Version of the Arabic Sibylline Prophecy,' *Oriens Christiana* 60 [1976] 83–94).

---

[35] I have discussed the account of Enoch and Elijah in the Apocalypse of Elijah more fully in "Enoch and Elijah in the Coptic Apocalypse of Elijah" (chapter 3 below).

[36] The Falasha *Apocalypse of Ezra*, like other Falasha literature, is a de-christianized version of an originally Christian text.

(C¹) Greek *Apocalypse of Daniel (Diegesis Danielis)* 14:1–15/14:1–12 (Klaus Berger, *Die griechische Daniel-Diegese* [SPB 27; Leiden: Brill, 1976] 18, 144–148; G. T. Zervos, 'Apocalypse of Daniel [Ninth Century A. D.]: A New Translation and Introduction,' in James Charlesworth [ed.], *The Old Testament Pseudepigrapha*, vol. 1 [London: Darton, Longman & Todd, 1983] 755–770).³⁷

(D¹) *Apocalypse of Leo of Constantinople* 21 (Riccardo Maisano, *L'Apocalisse Apocrifa di Leone di Constantinopoli* [Nobiltà dello Spirito NS 3; Naples: Morano, 1975] 98–99).

(E¹) *Oracles of Leo the Wise* 5.36–39 (E. Legrand, *Les Oracles de Léon le Sage, La Bataille de Varna, La Prise de Constantinople: Poëmes en grecs vulgaires* [Collection de Monuments pour servir à l'étude de la langue néo-hellénique, NS 5; Paris: Maissonneuve/Athens: Coromilas, 1875] 49).

(F¹) *Andreas Salos Apocalypse*, 286–289 short text (L. Rydén, 'The Andreas Salos Apocalypse: Greek Text, Translation, and Commentary,' *Dumbarton Oaks Papers* 28 [1974] 197–261, here 212–213, 223–224).

(G¹) *Andreas Salos Apocalypse*, 286–289 long text (Rydén, 'The Andreas Salos Apocalypse,' 212, 223–224 n.).

(H¹) *Two Sorrows of the Kingdom of Heaven* 8 (Máire Herbert and Martin McNamara, *Irish Biblical Apocrypha* [Edinburgh: T. & T. Clark, 1989] 21).

(I¹) Karshuni *Testament of our Lord Jesus* 6 (J. Ziadé, 'Un testament de N. S. concernant les invasions des Mongols,' *ROC* 21 [1918–19] 261–273, 433–444, here 443; Juan Pedro Monferrer Sala, *Apócrifos Árabes Cristianos* [Madrid: Trotta, 2003] 240–241).

(J¹) Coptic *Vision of Daniel* 80–81 (Otto Meinardus, 'A Commentary on the XIVth Vision of Daniel: According to the Coptic Version,' *Orientalia Christiana Periodica* 32 [1966] 394–449, here 447).³⁸

(K¹) Falasha *Apocalypse of Ezra* (J. Halévy, *Tĕʾĕzâza Sanbat [Commandements du Sabbat] accompagnés de six autres écrits pseudo-épigraphiques admits par les Falachas ou Juifs d'Abyssinie* [BEHE.H 137; Paris, 1902] 195).

This list is still far from exhaustive. Like other apocalyptic traditions this one made its way far and wide in a variety of Christian traditions. For some further examples, see J. T. Milik, *The Books of Enoch: Aramaic Fragments of Qumrân Cave 4* (Oxford: Clarendon Press, 1976) 119–123; Berger, *Die griechische Daniel-Diegese*, table facing page 148; Richard Kenneth Emmerson, *Antichrist in the Middle Ages* (Manchester: Manchester University Press, 1981) 95–101, 136–140; David Dumville, 'Biblical Apocrypha and the Early Irish: A Preliminary Investigation,' *Proceedings of the Royal Irish Academy* 73C (1973) 299–338, here 308–311.

---

³⁷ On this apocalypse, see Lorenzo DiTommaso, *The Book of Daniel and the Apocryphal Daniel Literature* (SVTP 20; Leiden: Brill, 2005) 130–141, 356–359.

³⁸ On this apocalypse, see DiTommaso, *The Book of Daniel*, 179–184, 456–458.

	A¹	B¹	C¹	D¹	E¹	F¹	G¹	H¹	I¹	J¹	K¹
Explicit quotation of Rev 11											
Enoch and Elijah	(x)⁴¹	x	(x)⁴²	x	x³⁹		x⁴⁰		x	x	(x)⁴³
Elijah and Enoch						x⁴⁴		x			
witnesses											
prophets				(x)⁴⁵							x
descend											
fight Antichrist								x			
preach repentance											
plague enemies							x				
expose Antichrist	x	x	x	x		x	x		x		x
Antichrist enraged	x										
fights them				x							
conquers them											
kills them	x	x	x	x	x	x	x	x	x	x	x
on the altar	x	x	x					x			
bodies lie unburied				x			x				
3½ days		(2½)		x			x		x		
3 days											x
4 days											
in the streets of Jerusalem				x			x		x		
the great city									x		
everyone sees them							x				
they rise		x		x			x			x	x
are raised by Michael and Gabriel											
renewed conflict with Antichrist											
ascend to heaven				x			x				
in the sight of all											
destroy Antichrist											

---

[39] With John the evangelist.

[40] With John the evangelist.

[41] Two unnamed men.

[42] Two unnamed men from heaven (Enoch and Elijah) and one unnamed man from earth (John the evangelist).

[43] Two unnamed men.

[44] With John the evangelist.

[45] Here they are called 'preachers (κήρυκες) of the truth'.

Additional Note B:
A pre-Christian Jewish tradition
of the return of Enoch and Elijah?

In the first paragraph of the chapter I said that Wilhelm Bousset 'in 1895 sifted early Christian traditions about Antichrist to reconstruct a pre-Christian Jewish tradition which included the return of Enoch and Elijah to denounce Antichrist and to suffer martyrdom.' This statement was mistaken.[46] Bousset's purpose in the whole book was to reconstruct a tradition about Antichrist that early Christians inherited from Jewish sources.[47] I must have assumed that he considered 'the return of Enoch and Elijah to denounce Antichrist and to suffer martyrdom,' which he treats at some length in the course of working through the whole reconstructed narrative,[48] to be part of this pre-Christian Jewish tradition. In fact, however, at this point he draws some distinctions between the original Jewish tradition and the form in which it appears in early Christian literature. He states that the 'original Jewish expectation, as is still to be seen in the Gospels,[49] was for the return of Elias alone (Malachi iv.1).'[50] He notes that this expectation of Elijah alone is found also in the second book of the Sibylline Oracles (2.187), in Justin (*Dial.* 49, where it is attributed to the Jew Trypho), in Lactantius and Commodian,[51] and in the later Jewish apocalyptic literature. After showing the way in which the existing tradition about Enoch and Elijah was adapted by the author of Revelation 11, he concludes:

> Still, with all this, one point remains unexplained – the origin of the idea of the two witnesses. There can scarcely be a doubt that it cannot have emanated from a Jewish source. Here the return of Elias is expected, while the expectation of the two witnesses would seem to have never been more generally diffused, as is shown by the later Jewish tradition.[52]

Bousset's view seems to be that in Jewish tradition Elijah alone was expected, but that in a Christian version of the tradition, pre-dating Revelation, Enoch

---

[46] This was pointed out to me in a personal letter from Barry Blackburn, dated 23 May 1979.

[47] For recent critical assessments of Bousset's overall thesis about the Antichrist tradition, see Gregory C. Jenks, *The Origins and Early Development of the Antichrist Myth* (BZNW 59; Berlin/New York: de Gruyter, 1991) 5–13; G. W. Lorein, *The Antichrist Theme in the Intertestamental Period* (JSPSup 44; London/New York: T. & T. Clark International [Continuum], 2003) 1–7, 237.

[48] Wilhelm Bousset, *The Antichrist Tradition*, tr. A. H. Keane (London: Hutchinson, 1896) 203–11.

[49] Mark 9:11–13.

[50] Bousset, *The Antichrist Tradition*, 207.

[51] See n. 19 above.

[52] Bousset, *The Antichrist Tradition*, 210.

was added. In addition, he states clearly that the author of Revelation was 'personally responsible for the incident about the resurrection of the witnesses after the third day,' since this is clearly a Christian contribution[53] (but why should it not have been already part of the Christian tradition that added Enoch to Elijah?). What is wholly unclear is whether Bousset thinks that the role of denouncing Antichrist and consequent martyrdom at his hands were already to attributed to Elijah in Jewish tradition or belonged to that Christian redaction of the tradition that added the second figure, Enoch.

If Bousset's view were the latter, then he was in essential agreement with my own argument in the chapter above. However, he was mistaken in supposing that the idea of the eschatological return of Enoch and Elijah together had no non-Christian Jewish source. It is true that it is not to be found in rabbinic literature or in the medieval Jewish apocalypses that have parallels to many of the other traditions about Antichrist in the Christian apocalypses. Its absence from rabbinic literature may be due to the lack of a scriptural basis for expecting the return of Enoch, by contrast with the explicit prophecy relating to Elijah (Mal 4:1). The medieval Jewish apocalypses, on the other hand, reflect non-scriptural traditions abundantly. The absence of Enoch from them is perhaps to be attributed to the controversial nature of the figure of Enoch in Jewish tradition from the second century CE onwards. In any case, there is a pre-Christian Jewish reference to the return of Enoch and Elijah in a text Bousset neglected: 1 Enoch 90:31.[54]

This text deserves a little more attention than I gave it in the chapter above. It belongs to the Animal Apocalypse of 1 Enoch 85–90, which dates from the Maccabean period. In a work attributed to Enoch and in view of Enoch's assumption to heaven without dying (Gen 5:24; 1 Enoch 87:2–4), it is not very surprising to find this expansion of the already existing belief that Elijah would return at the end (Mal 4:1; Sir 48:10). 1 Enoch 90:31 reads:

> After that, those three who were clothed in white and who had taken hold of me [Enoch] by my hand, who had previously brought me up (with the hand of that ram also taking hold of me), set me down among those sheep before the judgment took place.[55]

The three are the angels who had taken Enoch up to heaven at the end of his earthly life (87:2–4). The ram is Elijah, whose assumption to paradise

---

[53] Bousset, *The Antichrist Tradition*, 210.

[54] There is a useful table of the sources used by Bousset and their contributions to his reconstructed Antichrist tradition in Jenks, *The Origins*, 8–9, while Jenks, *The Origins*, 10, lists Jewish works of the Second Temple period not used by Bousset, including 1 Enoch.

[55] Translation from George W. E. Nickelsburg and James C. VanderKam, *1 Enoch: A New Translation* (Minneapolis: Fortress, 2004) 134.

has also been described earlier in the Animal Apocalypse (89:52), which makes it clear that Elijah joined Enoch in paradise. No other assumption to paradise has been mentioned in this Apocalypse's grand review of biblical history. This makes very improbable the alternative suggestion: that the ram of 90:31 is Judas Maccabeus (depicted as a ram in 90:9–10).[56] Most scholars have agreed that the ram must be Elijah.[57]

The last phrase of 1 Enoch 90:31 ('before the judgment took place') is problematic. The judgment has already been recounted (90:20–27) and has been followed by an account of the New Jerusalem (90:28–30). No further judgment follows. It may be that the text is 'completely corrupt.'[58] If not, then according to Nickelsburg 'either the verse has been (accidentally?) transposed from its chronologically correct location between vv 19 and 20, or that "before the judgment took place" is a scribal gloss that ties Enoch's and Elijah's return to earth to the tradition of their participation in the judgment.'[59] It would seem easiest to suppose that, whatever the origin of the last phrase in the present Ethiopic text, the verse did not originally place the coming of Enoch and Elijah before the judgment. In that case, the significance of their return is not difficult to decide. They return in order to participate in the new age along with the rest of God's faithful people. What is clear is that they do not oppose an Antichrist figure or die at his hands. Those features of the later tradition are absent from this earliest reference to the return of Enoch and Elijah.

Additional Note C: A non-Christian Jewish tradition of the return and martyrdom of Enoch and Elijah?

In a brief response or addendum to my article,[60] Alexander Zeron pointed out the relevance of a passage I had not cited: Pseudo-Philo, *Biblical Antiq-*

---

[56] J. T. Milik, *The Books of Enoch: Aramaic Fragments of Qumrân Cave 4* (Oxford: Clarendon Press, 1976) 45.

[57] Matthew Black, 'The "Two Witnesses" of Rev. 11:3 f. in Jewish and Christian Apocalyptic Tradition,' in Ernst Bammel, C. Kingsley Barrett and W. D. Davies (ed.), *Donum Gentilicium: New Testament Studies in Honour of David Daube* (Oxford: Clarendon Press, 1978) 227–237, here 228 and n. 1; idem, *The Book of Enoch or 1 Enoch* (SVTP 7; Leiden: Brill, 1985) 279; Patrick A. Tiller, *A Commentary on the Animal Apocalypse of 1 Enoch* (SBL Early Judaism and Its Literature 04; Atlanta, Georgia: Scholars Press, 1993) 377–378; George W. E. Nickelsburg, *1 Enoch 1* (Hermeneia; Minneapolis: Fortress, 2001) 405.

[58] Tiller, *A Commentary,* 379.

[59] Nickelsburg, *1 Enoch 1,* 405.

[60] Alexander Zeron, 'The Martyrdom of Phineas-Elijah,' *JBL* 98 (1979) 99–100.

uities 48:1. This passage, probably from the late first century, is the earliest evidence of a tradition, later found in the Pseudo-Jonathan Targum to the Pentateuch (Exod 4:13; 6:18; 40:10; Deut 30:4; cf. Num 25:12) and occasionally in rabbinic literature (*Pirqe R. El.* 29), that identified Elijah with the high priest Phinehas, the grandson of Aaron.[61] We need not discuss the exegetical origins of the tradition here. What is important for our present purposes is that the version of the tradition in Pseudo-Philo refers to the death of the returning Elijah:

> And in that time Phinehas laid himself down to die, and the Lord said to him, 'Behold you have passed the 120 years that have been established for every man. And now rise up and go from here and dwell in Danaben on the mountain and dwell there many years. And I will command my eagle, and he will nourish you there, and you will not come down to mankind until the time arrives and you be tested at that time; and you will shut up the heaven then, and by your mouth it will be opened up. And afterward you will be lifted up into the place where those who were before you were lifted up, and you will be there until I remember the world. Then I will make you all come, and you [plural] will taste what is death (*Bib Ant.* 48:1).[62]

Here Phinehas is commanded to hide on a mountain, where God nourishes him, until the time – many centuries later – when he is to re-appear in the world as the prophet Elijah, unequivocally identified by the information that he will both conjure up a drought and put an end to it. Elijah's ascension is then predicted: 'you will be lifted up into the place where those who were before you (*priores tui*) were lifted up.' Presumably this is paradise, and there Elijah and the others remain until, at the end time, God brings them back to the earth. Only then will Phinehas-Elijah and the others die. This reference to the death of Phinehas-Elijah in the eschatological future seems to be unique among the texts that identify Phinehas and Elijah.

Who are the ones who had been lifted up to paradise before Phinehas-Elijah? Certainly they include Enoch, whose translation to heaven Pseudo-Philo has noted in its place, following Genesis 5:24 (*Lib. Ant.* 1:16). Perhaps Pseudo-Philo's statement that Enoch 'was not found' (*non inveniebatur*), where Genesis has 'was not,' is intended to assimilate Enoch's ascension to

---

[61] Martin Hengel, *The Zealots*, tr. David Smith (Edinburgh: T. & T. Clark, 1989) chap. IVB; Robert Hayward, 'Phinehas—the Same is Elijah,' *JJS* 29 (1978) 22–34; Richard Bauckham, 'Messianism According to the Gospel of John,' in John Lierman (ed.), *Challenging Perspectives on the Gospel of John* (WUNT 2/219; Tübingen: Mohr Siebeck, 2006) 34–68, here 36–37.

[62] Translation from D.J. Harrington, 'Pseudo-Philo,' in James Charlesworth (ed.), *The Old Testament Pseudepigrapha*, vol. 1 (London: Darton, Longman & Todd, 1983) 297–377, here 362. For the argument that Phinehas is here identified with Elijah, see Frederick J. Murphy, *Pseudo-Philo: Rewriting the Bible* (New York/Oxford: Oxford University Press, 1993) 184–185; Howard Jacobson, *A Commentary on Pseudo-Philo's Liber Antiquitatum Biblicarum*, vol. 2 (AGAJU 31; Leiden: Brill, 1996) 1060.

that of Elijah (cf. 2 Kgs 2:17).[63] Pseudo-Philo nowhere indicates that any other of his characters belong in the same category. According to 2 Baruch (13:3), Baruch does, and according to 4 Ezra (14:9), Ezra does, but these lived long after Elijah's ascension.[64] Later rabbinic literature supplies other names of 'those who entered paradise alive': Eliezer the servant of Abraham, Serah the daughter of Asher (Gen 46:17), Bithiah the daughter of Pharaoh (1 Chron 4:17, identified with the Egyptian princess who rescued Moses), Jabez (1 Chron 4:9–10), Hiram king of Tyre, Ebed-melech the Ethiopian (Jer 38:7–13; 39:15–18), Jonadab the Rechabite and his descendants (Jer 35), the servant of Rabbi Judah the Prince, Rabbi Joshua ben Levi, and the Messiah.[65] Of these, Eliezer, Serah, Bithiah, and perhaps Jabez, lived before the time of Phinehas, while Hiram lived before the time of Elijah's ascension. We have no evidence that precisely these persons were already, in the late first century CE, when Pseudo-Philo wrote, thought not to have died, but, in some cases at least, this idea about them was based in ingenious exegesis of the kind that certainly was employed in Pseudo-Philo's time and often presupposed by Pseudo-Philo's text. Some of these persons, therefore, may be those, besides Enoch, who had already been translated to paradise before Phinehas-Elijah was.

Pseudo-Philo's *Biblical Antiquities* has much in common, especially in its eschatological themes and language, with the two apocalypses of roughly the same date: 4 Ezra and 2 Baruch.[66] The notion of a group of people who had not died and whom God would bring to earth at the end-time is found in 4 Ezra (6:26; 7:28; 13:52; 14:9), which provides the closest parallel to the Biblical Antiquities in this respect. The group are defined as 'those who were taken up, who from their birth have not tasted death' (6:26). The following passage is especially illuminating for our purposes:

For my son the Messiah shall be revealed with those who are with him, and those who remain shall rejoice four hundred years. After those years my son the Messiah shall die, and all who draw human breath. Then the world shall be turned back to primeval silence for seven days, as it was at the first beginnings, so that no one shall

---

[63] Zeron, 'The Martyrdom,' 100.

[64] 2 Macc 15:13–16 is sometimes cited as evidence of a belief that Jeremiah had ascended without dying. This is not at all certain, but in any case, for our purposes, is not relevant, since Jeremiah lived after the ascension of Elijah.

[65] Louis Ginzberg, *The Legends of the Jews*, vol. 5 (Philadelphia: Jewish Publication Society of America, 1925) 95–96. The Messiah is included in the list of nine (including Enoch and Elijah) in Derek Ereṣ Zuta 1, because he was thought to have lived at some point in Israel's history and to have then been taken up to heaven, whence God will bring him to earth in the last days. This tradition is probably also presupposed in 4 Ezra 7:28.

[66] M.R. James, *The Biblical Antiquities of Philo* (London: SPCK, 1917) 46–58; Harrington, 'Pseudo-Philo,' 302.

be left. After seven days the world that is not yet awake shall be roused, and that which is corruptible shall perish (4 Ezra 7:28–31 NRSV).

In this passage those who are with the Messiah apparently share in the messianic kingdom, at the end of which both the Messiah and all living humans die. The latter must include those who had been taken up without dying and who return to earth with the Messiah at the beginning of the messianic kingdom. The idea seems to be that everything in this world must revert to nothing before it can be recreated in the world to come. No mortal being, not even the Messiah himself, can enter the new creation without dying and rising again. The issue seems to be the same as that with which Paul deals in 1 Corinthians 15:50–52, though the solution is rather different.[67]

It is not easy to parallel at all precisely these expectations of the death of the Messiah and the reversion of all creation to chaos (though cf. 2 Bar 44:9), but it is notable how closely the end of this passage and the following verses (4 Ezra 7:31–35) are paralleled by *Biblical Antiquities* 3:10, including the idea of another, everlasting world to come. In view of the close parallels at these and other points between the eschatological expectations of 4 Ezra and Pseudo-Philo, it is reasonable to find in 4 Ezra 7:28–31 an explanation of the expected death of the returning Elijah in *Biblical Antiquities* 48:1. Phinehas-Elijah will finally taste death because every human must; it is the only way into the new creation. But he will die, not be killed. Thus, while Zeron was right to find in *Biblical Antiquities* 48:1 an expectation that both Enoch and Elijah (along with others who ascended without dying) will eventually die, he was mistaken to call this death 'martyrdom.'[68] This expectation has little in common with the expectation found in the Christian apocalypses that Enoch and Elijah will come to denounce Antichrist and will be put to death by him. Both the manner of their death and the rationale for it are quite different.

Two studies that relate quite closely to the chapter above were published, coincidentally, around the same time. The first was the major work by Klaus Berger: *Die Auferstehung des Propheten und die Erhöhung des Menschensohn: Traditionsgeschichtliche Untersuchungen zur Deutung des Geschickes Jesu in frühchristlichen Texten* (SUNT 13; Göttingen: Vandenhoeck & Ruprecht, 1976). The second was a journal article: Johannes M. Nützel, 'Zum Schicksal der eschatologischen Propheten,' *BZ* 20 (1976) 59–94.

---

[67] Rabbinic literature often denies that either Enoch or Elijah escaped death. This may be due to a comparable sense that human nature as it exists in this world is mortal and there can be no exceptions to the universality of death. Denying that Enoch and Elijah ascended without dying deals with this concern in one way, affirming that they will die following their future return does so in another.

[68] Zeron, 'The Martyrdom,' 100.

Berger's book argues that there was a pre-Christian Jewish tradition in which a prophet (or prophets) would come in the last days, be put to death and be raised up by God prior to the general resurrection. This expectation of the pre-eschatological resurrection of a final prophet lies behind the early Christian accounts of the resurrection appearances of Jesus and the early Christian understanding of that event. For evidence of the pre-Christian Jewish tradition Berger relies on tradition-historical analysis of (1) Mark 6:14–16; (2) Rev 11:3–13; (3) the tradition of the eschatological return, martyrdom and resurrection of Enoch and Elijah in a large number of Christian texts, most of which are also the texts listed and analysed in my chapter above. The arguments deserve fuller discussion than can be given here, but what is most problematic about the whole argument is that Berger can cite no non-Christian Jewish text that speaks of the resurrection of a martyred eschatological prophet. Everything depends on distinguishing pre- or non-Christian elements from Christian elements in Christian texts. The lack of even a single unequivocally non-Christian Jewish text containing the pre-Christian Jewish tradition Berger constructs must throw serious doubt on the whole argument, especially as there are non-Christian Jewish texts that speak of final prophets (especially Elijah) without the element that is crucial for Berger's case: their pre-eschatological resurrection.

Nützel's article, written just before the publication of Berger's book, is nevertheless in a sense a reply to Berger's main argument. He is responding to a suggestion made by Rudolf Pesch, made first in a lecture in Tübingen in June 1972 and then in a published version of the lecture in 1973.[69] Between giving the lecture and publishing the article Pesch had read Berger's work in a version[70] earlier than the one Berger published in 1976.[71] It was primarily Berger's evidence that Pesch presented, briefly, in his 1973 article,[72] when he argued that there was, at the time of Jesus, a widespread Jewish expectation of the resurrection and ascension of the final prophet, prior to the general resurrection, and that this expectation lies behind the early Christian beliefs about Jesus. Nützel's article is an examination of the most important of the texts that both Berger and Pesch cite as evidence for this alleged expectation. He discusses, as of prime importance, the Apocalypse of Elijah and Revelation 11:3–11, and then, more briefly, the Apocalypse of Peter, the various Sibylline texts that contain the tradition about the return of Enoch

---

[69] Rudolf Pesch, 'Zur Entstehung des Glaubens an die Auferstehung Jesu: Ein Vorschlag zur Diskussion,' *ThQ* 153 (1973) 201–228.

[70] Berger's Habilitation dissertation, Hamburg.

[71] Klaus Berger: *Die Auferstehung des Propheten und die Erhöhung des Menschensohn* (SUNT 13; Göttingen: Vandenhoeck & Ruprecht, 1976) 5. Pesch's article generated a controversy among German scholars. Berger, *Die Auferstehung*, 5–6, lists contributions to this up to 1976, but not Nützel's article.

[72] Pesch, 'Zur Entstehung,' 222–226.

and Elijah, Lactantius (*Div. Inst.* 17.1–3), a reference to the return of Elijah in one version of the *Lives of the Prophets*, and the Arabic *Apocalypse of Schenoute*. Like Berger, he engages in tradition-historical and redactional analysis, especially of Rev 11:3–13 and Apocalypse of Elijah 3:7–20a,[73] and detects behind these two texts non-Christian Jewish traditions of the return, martyrdom and resurrection of two eschatological prophets, but insists that these traditions did not include the ascension of the prophets to heaven after resurrection. Moreover he argues that the time and place of these two instances of such a tradition (first century BCE, Egypt, and late first century CE, Asia Minor) make them of no value for establishing a tradition widespread in Palestine at the time of Jesus. Mark 6:16 provides only dubious evidence for such a tradition. Nützel's study comes considerably closer to Berger's view of the tradition than my own does, but he nevertheless rules it out as plausible or relevant background for early Christian beliefs about the resurrection and exaltation of Jesus.

---

[73] In the chapter and verse division used by Nützel, this is 3:7–21.

3. Enoch and Elijah
in the Coptic Apocalypse of Elijah*

The account of Enoch and Elijah in the Coptic Apocalypse of Elijah has come to light since W. Bousset in 1895 first attempted to reconstruct from the early Christian traditions about Antichrist a pre-Christian Jewish tradition which included the return of Enoch and Elijah to denounce Antichrist and suffer martyrdom at his hands.[1] Its relevance to this question has not gone unnoticed. The majority of scholars, noticing the close parallels between the Apocalypse of Elijah's account of Enoch and Elijah and the account of the two witnesses in Rev. 11: 3–13, have concluded that the Apocalypse of Elijah is dependent on Rev. 11, though perhaps also embodying independent Jewish tradition.[2] They have generally held the Apocalypse of Elijah to be a third- or fourth-century Christian redaction of earlier Jewish material.[3] J. Jeremias, arguing for a pre-Christian Jewish tradition of the martyrdom of the returning Elijah, thought that beneath the Christian recension of the Apocalypse of Elijah could probably be discerned a Jewish tradition attested also in Mk. 9: 12 and lying behind Rev. 11: 3–13.[4] J. Munck, in a careful treatment of most of the early Christian material about Enoch and Elijah on which Bousset's case rested and also of the Apocalypse of Elijah, argued, against both Bousset and Jeremias, that there was no Christian tradition of the return of Enoch and Elijah independent of Rev. 11 and therefore no evidence for a pre-Christian tradition of the

---

* First publication: Elizabeth A. Livingstone ed., *Studia Patristica*, vol. XVI Part II (Berlin: Akademie-Verlag, 1985) 69–76.

[1] W. Bousset, *The Antichrist Legend* (Eng. tr., London, 1896), pp. 203–11.

[2] E. g. D. Haugg, *Die zwei Zeugen: Eine exegetische Studie über Apok 11,1–13* (Neutestamentliche Abhandlungen 17. 1; Münster, 1936), p. 94: 'De Elias-Apok kennt und verwertet das 11. Kap. der Jo-Apok sehr reichlich, wenn sie sich auch verschiedene Änderungen erlaubt'; M. Black, 'Servant of the Lord and Son of Man', *SJT* 6 (1953), p. 10 n. 1: 'As the passage [in the Apocalypse of Elijah] is also drawing on Rev. 11, it is difficult to say which parts are Jewish, which are Christian'.

[3] E. Schürer, review of Steindorff's edition in *TLZ* 24 (1899), cols. 7 f.; W. Bousset, 'Beiträge zur Geschichte der Eschatologie', *Zeitschrift für Kirchengeschichte* 20 (1899), pp. 103–12; H. Weinel, 'Die spätere christliche Apokalyptik', in Εὐχαρήτριον: *Studien zur Religion und Literatur des Alten und Neuen Testaments II* (Gunkel Festschrift; Göttingen, 1923), pp. 164–6.

[4] *TDNT* 2, pp. 939–41.

martyrdom of either. Munck regarded Rev. 11, especially as interpreted by Hippolytus and Ps-Hippolytus, as the source of the whole Christian tradition on the subject.[5] Similarly W. Wink dismissed Jeremias' argument with the observation that the account in the Apocalypse of Elijah 'is obviously a haggadic expansion of Rev. 11: 3–12'.[6] On the other hand, J.-M. Rosenstiehl, in his recent edition of the Apocalypse of Elijah[7], has argued that the work is essentially an Essene work of the first century B.C., expanded in ch. 2 by another Jewish author of the third century A.D., and hardly at all affected by Christian editing. For Rosenstiehl, the Apocalypse of Elijah's account of the return of Enoch and Elijah is wholly Jewish and is related to Rev. 11 only *via* a common Jewish source.

Rosenstiehl's arguments, while demonstrating the strongly Jewish character of much of the material embodied in the Apocalypse of Elijah, are not wholly convincing.[8] Certainly it is not enough to show that a text could be pre-Christian in order to prove that it is, and Rosenstiehl's technique of providing many parallels from Jewish literature but few from Christian literature entails a distorted view of the work's affinities with other texts. We shall see that for its account of Enoch and Elijah the parallels in extant literature are all from Christian writers of the fourth century and later. Moreover, some of the Apocalypse of Elijah's most remarkable points of contact with extant Jewish apocalyptic are not with pre-Christian apocalyptic but with the so-called 'Neo-Hebraic' apocalyptic: this is true, for example, of its description of Antichrist.[9] In such cases we should not too readily suppose that there was no interaction between Jewish and Christian apocalyptic traditions after the first century: it is more likely, as Buttenweiser thought, that 'in the course of its development, the Christian apocalyptic drew freely from younger Jewish sources, and, on the other hand, the later Jewish writings were influenced directly or indirectly by the apocalyptic of the Church'.[10] While it seems beyond question that the Apocalypse of Elijah is in some degree a Christian recension of Jewish material[11], it need not therefore be the case that the Jewish traditions it preserves are pre-Christian. It is not even beyond possibility that

---

[5] J. Munck, *Petrus und Paulus in der Offenbarung Johannis* (Copenhagen, 1950), pp. 81–118.

[6] W. Wink, *John the Baptist in the Gospel Tradition* (Cambridge, 1968), p. 14 n. 1.

[7] J.-M. Rosenstiehl, *L'Apocalypse d'Elie* (Paris, 1972). In this paper I have employed Rosenstiehl's chapter and verse numbers.

[8] Cf. some criticisms in a review by P. M. Parvis in *JTS* 24 (1973), pp. 588 f.

[9] See J.-M. Rosenstiehl, 'Le portrait de l'Antichrist', in M. Philonenko *et al.*, *Pseudépigraphes de l'Ancien Testament et Manuscrits de la Mer Morte* I (Paris, 1967), pp. 45–60.

[10] M. Buttenweiser, *Outline of the Neo-Hebraic Apocalyptic Literature* (Cincinnati, 1901), p. 1.

[11] Clear examples of Christian editing are 1:2, 6 f., 19; 3:13, 10, 35, 66. For a longer list of possible allusions to the NT, see Schürer in *TLZ* 24 (1899), col. 7.

a Jewish tradition of the martyrdom of Enoch and Elijah resulted from the influence of Christian traditions based on Rev. 11.

I have attempted elsewhere to trace the development of the Christian tradition of the return of Enoch and Elijah.[12] The dominant Christian tradition from the fourth century onwards[13] is so far different from the account of the witnesses in Rev. 11 that it is difficult to accept Munck's argument that this was its sole source. I Enoch 90: 31 (cf. also IV Ezra 6: 26) is evidence that there was a Jewish tradition of the return of Enoch and Elijah, and two texts which were unavailable to Bousset (ch. 2 of the Ethiopic version of the Apocalypse of Peter; Syriac version of Ps.-Methodius) seem to preserve traditions uninfluenced by Rev. 11. But at least from the time of Hippolytus the two witnesses of Rev. 11 were identified as Enoch and Elijah, and the tradition of the martyrdom and resurrection of Enoch and Elijah is probably to be attributed wholly to this identification. A common tendency of the tradition was towards emphasizing this martyrological aspect. This paper attempts to place the account of Enoch and Elijah in the Apocalypse

---

[12] See my article, 'The Martyrdom of Enoch and Elijah: Jewish or Christian?' in *JBL* 95 (1976), pp. 447–58 (reprinted as chapter 2 above).

[13] The following list is of the Christian apocalyptic texts to which I refer by name only in the rest of the paper: Adso: *Libellus de Antichristo*, in E. Sackur, *Sibyllinische Texte und Forschungen* (Halle, 1898), pp. 111 f.; longer text in PL 90:1186. – Visio Danielis: in A. Vassiliev, *Anecdota Graeco-Byzantina* (Moscow, 1893), p. 43. – Ephraem Graecus: *Sermo in adventum Domini*, in J. S. Assemani ed., *Sancti Ephraem Syri opera omnia quae existant* III (Rome, 1746), pp. 141 f. – Ps.-Ephraem Latinus: *Sermo de fine mundi*, in C. P. Caspari, *Briefe, Abhandlungen und Predigten* (Christiana, 1890), p. 219. – Ephraem Syrus: *Sermo de fine extremo*, in T. J. Lamy ed., *Sancti Ephraem Syri Hymni et Sermones* III (Mechlin, 1889), pp. 207–10. – Syriac Apocalypse of Ezra: translated in F. Baethgen, 'Beschreibung der syrischen Handschrift "Sachau 131" aus der Königlichen Bibliothek zu Berlin', ZAW 6 (1886), p. 209. – Hippolytus: *De Antichristo*, 43, 46 f.; *In Danielem* 35, 50. – History of Joseph: Bohairic translated in F. Robinson, *Coptic Apocryphal Gospels* (Texts and Studies 4.2; Cambridge, 1896), pp. 146 f.; Arabic in J. K. Thilo, *Codex apocryphus Novi Testamenti* (Leipzig, 1832), pp. 58–61. – Ps.-Hippolytus: *De consummatione mundi* 21 and 29, in P. A. Lagarde ed., *Hippolyti Romani quae feruntur omnia graece* (Leipzig, 1858), pp. 104 f., 111. – Apocalypse of Ps.-John: in L. K. Tischendorf, *Apocalypses apocryphae* (Leipzig, 1866), p. 77. – Ps.-Methodius: *Revelationes*, Greek in Vassiliev, *op. cit.*, p. 38; Latin in Sackur, *op. cit.*, pp. 95 f. – Ps.-Methodius (Syriac): translated in F. Nau, *Révélations of légendes* (Paris, 1917), p. 31. – Apocalypse of Peter: Ethiopic version ch. 2, translated in E. Hennecke, *New Testament Apocrypha* II (ed. R. McL. Wilson; London, 1965), p. 669. – Arabic (Clementine) Apocalypse of Peter: in A. Mingana, *Woodbrooke Studies* III (Cambridge, 1931), p. 359. – Ethiopic (Clementine) Apocalypse of Peter: translated in E. Bratke, 'Handschriftliche Überlieferung und Bruchstücke der arabisch-aethiopischen Petrus-Apokalypse', *Zeitschrift für wissenschaftliche Theologie* 36.1 (1893), p. 483. – Syriac (Clementine) Apocalypse of Peter: translated in Bratke, *art. cit.*, pp. 471 f. – Apocalypse of Ps.-Shenoute: in E. Amélineau, *Mémoires publiés par les membres de la mission archéologique française au Caire* (1885–1886) IV.1 (Paris, 1888), p. 345. – Greek Tiburtine Sibyl: in P. S. Alexander, *The Oracle of Baalbek* (Dumbarton Oaks Studies 10; Washington, D. C., 1967), p. 22.

of Elijah within the broad context of the early Christian tradition of the return of Enoch and Elijah.

Twice in the Apocalypse of Elijah Enoch and Elijah descend from heaven. Their first appearance (3:25–39) is in the context of an extended narrative of the sufferings of the faithful during the tyranny of Antichrist. Antichrist encounters a series of opponents: the virgin Tabitha, who denounces him, suffers martyrdom, and rises to denounce him again (3: 16–24); Enoch and Elijah, whose rather similar career is described at greater length (3: 25–39); and the Sixty Righteous Men, who denounce Antichrist and are martyred (3: 51–4). Such a narrative of martyrs of the last days is not unknown in Jewish apocalyptic: the account of 'Taxo' and his seven sons in the Assumption of Moses is somewhat comparable.[14] A sequence of martyrs similar to that in the Apocalypse of Elijah is found in a Christian text, the Arabic version of the History of Joseph chs. 31–32, in which Antichrist is to slay not only Enoch and Elijah but also 'Schila' (= the Sibyl)[15] and Tabitha 'because of the rebukes with which they rebuked and exposed him while they lived'.

The portrayal of Enoch and Elijah in the Apocalypse of Elijah 3: 25–39 is as exemplary martyrs of the last days, following Tabitha in the vaguard of the resistance to Antichrist. Many of the features of the account, both those which have parallels in Rev. 11 and some which do not, are characteristic martyrological motifs, to be found in both Jewish and Christian literature. Thus the understanding of persecution and martyrdom in terms of warfare (3: 25, 31, 37, cf. 50 f.) is to be found in the popular IV Maccabees as well as in Revelation and later Christian literature. The rage of the persecutor is a stock theme in stories of the martyrs[16]; leaving the bodies of the martyrs unburied is a practice variously attested[17]; and the idea that the whole city or even the whole world witnesses the martyrs' conflict is again to be found in the Maccabean literature[18] as well as in Rev. 11. Even the resurrection and glorification of Enoch and Elijah find parallels in stories of the Christian martyrs, who are said to 'shine'[19] and who are seen in visions ascending to heaven or appearing alive after their martyrdom.[20] In Acts of Paul 11: 4 Paul tells Nero that, 'I will arise and appear to you in proof that I am not dead, but alive to my Lord Christ Jesus, who is coming to judge the world';

---

[14] On Taxo, see most recently J. J. Collins, 'The Date and Provenance of the Testament of Moses', in G. W. E. Nickelsburg ed., *Studies on the Testament of Moses* (SBL Septuagint and Cognate Studies 4; Cambridge, Mass., 1973), pp. 22–6.

[15] So W. E. Crum, 'Schila und Tabitha', *ZNW* 12 (1911), p. 352.

[16] Dan. 3:13, 19; 11:30; Bel 8; II Macc. 7:39; IV Macc. 8:2; 9:10; Acts 7:54; H. Musurillo, *The Acts of the Christian Martyrs* (Oxford, 1972), pp. 22, 26, 54, 66, 190.

[17] Musurillo, *op. cit.*, p. 80; I Macc. 7:17; Josephus, *BJ* 4:316 f.

[18] III Macc. 4:11; 5:24; IV Macc. 17:14.

[19] E. g. Musurillo, *op. cit.*, p. 234.

[20] *Ibid.*, pp. 182, 184; Hennecke, *New Testament Apocrypha* II, pp. 385 f.

and he does so, much as Tabitha and Enoch and Elijah rise up and prove to Antichrist that they 'live for ever in the Lord' (Apocalypse of Elijah 3: 23, 34, 36). The sacrificial understanding of martyrdom, while not present in the Apocalypse of Elijah's account of Enoch and Elijah, is emphasized in the stories of Tabitha, whose blood Antichrist is to 'throw on the temple' so that 'it will become salvation for the people' (3: 21 f., 24), and of the Sixty Righteous Men, whom Antichrist order to be burned on altars (3:54). In the Syriac Apocalypse of Ezra and the Apocalypse of Ps.-John Antichrist slays Enoch and Elijah on the altar, but in the Apocalypse of Elijah features drawn from the death of the witnesses in Rev. 11 are preferred.

The parallels with Rev. 11 are concentrated in 3: 31–33, 38, and are too close to be attributed to coincidence:

... The Shameless One will hear and be enraged and fight against them in the market-place of the great city. They will be three days and a half dead, in the market-place, and all the people will see them. But the fourth day they will arise... They will raise cries of joy towards heaven, they will shine, and all the people and the whole world will see them.

The parallels are all the more striking in view of the fact that the Apocalypse of Elijah shows little other evidence of dependence on Revelation.[21] But the author writes in general with relative independence of scriptural sources. He may have remembered details from Rev. 11 as he composed his narrative of Enoch and Elijah, or they may have already entered the tradition on which he depended.

Equally significant are the differences from Rev. 11. There the two witnesses are preachers of repentance who apparently come into conflict with Antichrist only at the end of their three-and-a-half year period of ministry. In the Apocalypse of Elijah, however, Enoch and Elijah 'descend' specifically to 'fight' Antichrist, which seems to mean primarily to denounce him (3:25). The verbal assault is also renewed after their resurrection (3: 33). This last feature, of renewed conflict with Antichrist after resurrection, is unparalleled elsewhere in the tradition, except in the Apocalypse of Ps.-Shenoute, which is almost certainly dependent on the Apocalypse of Elijah. But the idea that Enoch and Elijah's mission is to expose Antichrist by denouncing him as an imposter is found in most of the early Christian texts[22] and, along with the names Enoch and Elijah, constitutes the most

---

[21] 2:4, 24 are parallel to Rev. 9:6, but the context is entirely different and the saying may well be an apocalyptic commonplace. 1:9; 3:58 (the name on the forehead and the seal on the right hand) are somehow related to Rev. 7:3; 13:16; 14:1, 9, but in Rev. it is the beast, not God, who seals his servants on *both* the forehead and the right hand. 3:97, 99 are ultimately but not directly dependent on Rev. 20:4.

[22] Apocalypse of Peter, Ephraem Syrus, Ephraem Graecus, Ps.-Ephraem Latinus, Ps.-Hippolytus, Ps.-Methodius (Greek and Latin), *Visio Danielis*, Syriac (Clementine)

important point at which the tradition diverges from Rev. 11. Similarly in the motif of Antichrist's rage against the two (3: 31, 37, cf. 20, 40, 54), which is also absent from Rev. 11, the Apocalypse of Elijah aligns itself with the Christian tradition attested from Ephraem Syrus onwards.[23]

The tradition that Enoch and Elijah would return to expose Antichrist as a deceiver is one which probably antedates the tradition of their martyrdom. It is found without mention of the martyrdom in ch. 2 of the Ethiopic version of the Apocalypse of Peter (though this may be a later addition to the original early second-century Apocalypse of Peter), and also in Ephraem Graecus.[24] In this tradition Enoch and Elijah are preachers against Antichrist, a theme not incompatible with the motif of martyrdom by Antichrist which was commonly added to it under the influence of Rev. 11. But in the development of the tradition the portrayal of Enoch and Elijah as martyrs frequently became very much the dominant motif. A useful illustration of this development is a comparison of a passage from the Ethiopic (Clementine) Apocalypse of Peter with the Ethiopic version of the Apocalypse of Peter just mentioned, on which it is dependent:

Apocalypse of Peter (Ethiopic ch. 2)	*Later (Clementine) Apocalypse of Peter (Ethiopic)*
... he will kill with the sword and there shall be many martyrs. Then shall the boughs of the fig-tree, that is the house of Israel, sprout, and there shall be many martyrs by his hand: they shall be killed and become martyrs. Enoch and Elijah will be sent to instruct them that this is the deceiver who must come into the world and do signs and wonders in order to deceive. And therefore shall they that are slain by his hand be martyrs and shall be reckoned among the good and righteous martyrs who have pleased God in their life.	... they will be beheaded and become martyrs. In that day will be fulfilled what is said in the Gospel: when the branches of the fig-tree are full of sap, know that the time of the harvest is at hand. Shoots of the fig-tree are those righteous men called, who become martyrs at his hand, and the angels will bring them to the joy, and no hair of their head will be lost. Then Enoch and Elijah will descend. They will preach and put to shame that tyrannical enemy of righteousness and son of lies. Then they will be beheaded, and Michael and Gabriel will raise them up and bring them into the garden of joy, and no drop of his (sic) blood will fall on the ground ...

Apocalypse of Peter, Ethiopic (Clementine) Apocalypse of Peter, Apocalypse of Ps.-Shenoute, History of Joseph, Apocalypse of Ps.-John, Adso.

[23] Ephraem Syrus, Ps.-Methodius (Greek and Latin), Syriac (Clementine) Apocalypse of Peter, Greek Tiburtine Sibyl, Apocalypse of Ps.-Shenoute.

[24] The only other Christian texts I know which relate the return of Enoch and Elijah without mentioning their martyrdom are Ps.-Methodius (Syriac) (see below) and the Arabic (Clementine) Apocalypse of Peter.

Whereas in the first text the function of Enoch and Elijah is to expose Antichrist to those who are to be martyred by him, in the second text, while their preaching against Antichrist is retained, it no longer serves to make martyrs of anyone but Enoch and Elijah themselves. The parallelism of language in the references to the martyrs in general and to Enoch and Elijah in particular shows the extent to which they have here lost their unique role in the events of the last days and become merely the outstanding and final examples of martyrdom. A rather similar trend is revealed by the Apocalypse of Elijah, where Enoch and Elijah come second in a series of martyrs and it is apparently the later martyrdom of the Sixty Righteous Men which effectively convinces men that Antichrist is not the Messiah he claims to be (3: 54 f.).

The strongly martyrological character of the Apocalypse of Elijah's account is not an infallible indication of a late date. Tertullian's brief reference to the return of Enoch and Elijah is entirely to their martyrdom. But Tertullian does seem to allot them a distinctive role: 'they are reserved to die, so that they may extinguish Antichrist with their blood' (morituri reservantur, ut Antichristum sanguine suo extinguant) (*De Anima* 50). The Apocalypse of Elijah's series of martyrs seems rather to indicate a writer who is spinning a narrative of the reign of Antichrist out of various diverse traditional materials available to him.

The Apocalypse of Elijah is not an altogether coherent piece of work but nor does it altogether lack artistic skill. Antichrist's reign of terror builds up to a climax in the slaughter of the Sixty Righteous Men and his defeat then begins in earnest. The resurrections of Tabitha and of Enoch and Elijah had shown the limitations of his power: his victims rise from the grave, while he himself can perform all the miracles of the true Messiah *except* that of raising the dead (3: 10). But until the slaughter of the Sixty he is allowed to do his worst: then angelic interventions begin.

Eventually the angels 'come down and fight him in a battle of many swords' (3:81), and the cosmic conflagration of the last judgment begins (3: 82 f.). Oddly the destruction of Antichrist and the coming of Christ to inaugurate the millennium follow the last judgment (3: 91–7).

The destruction of Antichrist is accomplished by Enoch and Elijah appearing a second time (3: 91), as they had threatened (3: 35). This coming belongs in the series of angelic interventions, as the first belonged in the series of martyrs. They 'descend and lay aside the flesh (σάρξ) of the world (κόσμος), and put on their flesh (σάρξ) of spirit (πνεῦμα)' (3: 91). Presumably this means that while their first appearance was in mortal flesh, to die as martyrs, they come now in 'spiritual flesh' to oppose Antichrist with power. On their first appearance they fought him as the martyrs fight him, by words and suffering; now they fight him as the angels did (3: 81), with power to destroy him. 'In that day he will be destroyed before them like ice by the fire' (3: 93).

Two comings of Enoch and Elijah are not found in any other text. But the idea that they return in order to destroy Antichrist is found in the Syriac version of Ps.-Methodius:

... when he comes to Jerusalem, Enoch and Elijah will leave the land of life; they will rise up against him; they will withstand him and he will curse them. When he sees them, he will melt like salt in the presence of water, and he will be the first to be punished, before all men, together with the demons who entered into him ...

It is possible that Ps.-Methodius selected this one feature of the tradition represented by the Apocalypse of Elijah, but much more probable that he preserves a distinct tradition which the author of the Apocalypse of Elijah has combined with the more usual tradition that Enoch and Elijah come to denounce Antichrist and be martyred. It is a remarkable tradition to find in a Christian author, for the elemination of the last great enemy of the people of God is a task reserved for the Messiah both in Jewish and in Christian apocalyptic.[25] A Christian author is unlikely to have originated a tradition in which Enoch and Elijah are thus permitted to usurp the role of Christ[26], but it is quite conceivable in Judaism, where messianic expectations were more diverse and whence the alternative tradition of Antichrist's destruction by the archangel Michael found its way into Christian apocalyptic.[27] J. A. T. Robinson has questioned whether in first-century Jewish eschatology Elijah was as often the forerunner of the Messiah as he was himself a messianic figure[28], and we know that Enoch, exalted to the role of Son of Man, assumed messianic functions in the Similitudes of Enoch. It is entirely possible that a Jewish tradition portrayed Enoch and Elijah as a pair of Messiahs appearing at the End to combat and destroy Antichrist. That the author of the Apocalypse of Elijah preferred this tradition may perhaps be attributed to a desire to preserve, if somewhat artifically, the

---

[25] Jewish: II Bar. 40: 1 f.; Buttenweiser, *op. cit.*, pp. 31, 35, 38. Christian: II Thess. 2:8; Rev. 19:11–21; Bousset, *Antichrist Legend*, pp. 224 f.

[26] This is undoubtedly why it appears rarely in Christian sources. Ps.-Shenoute, which is dependent on the Apocalypse of Elijah, retains the motif, but the Greek Tiburtine Sibyl, which is probably also dependent on the Apocalypse of Elijah, replaces it with the intervention of Christ himself, who resurrects Enoch and Elijah and then fights and destroys Antichrist.

[27] See Bousset, *op. cit.*, pp. 227–31; Buttenweiser, *op. cit.*, p. 43; *Jewish Encyclopedia* VIII, pp. 536 f.

[28] J. A. T. Robinson, 'Elijah, John and Jesus', *NTS* 4 (1957–8), pp. 268–70. Also for Elijah as a messianic figure, see Jeremias in TDNT II, p. 931; for rabbinic traditions of Elijah as a military deliverer of the last days, see Strack-Billerbeck, *Kommentar* IV, pp. 782–4. L. Ginzberg, *The Legends of the Jews* (Philadelphia, 1913–38) IV, p. 235, cites a late tradition in which Elijah slays Samael (thereby assuming the role of Michael).

link Tertullian made between the martyrdom of Enoch and Elijah and the destruction of Antichrist. The martyrs' 'victory' over Antichrist (3: 50) is finally actualized when the greatest of the martyrs return in heavenly power to destroy him.

Additional Note

Important publications on the Apocalypse of Elijah that have appeared since the chapter above was written include:

Wolfgang Schrage, 'Die Elia-Apokalypse,' in Werner Georg Kümmel et al. (ed.), *Apokalypsen* (JSHRZ 5/3; Gütersloh: Gütersloher Verlagshaus, 1980) 195–288;

Albert Pietersma, Susan Turner Comstock and Harold W. Attridge (ed. and trans.), *The Apocalypse of Elijah based on P. Chester Beatty 2018* (SBL Texts and Translations Pseudepigrapha Series 9; Chico, California: Scholars Press, 1981);

O. S. Wintermute, 'Apocalypse of Elijah (First to Fourth Century A.D.): A New Translation and Introduction,' in James Charlesworth (ed.), *The Old Testament Pseudepigrapha,* vol. 1 (London: Darton, Longman & Todd, 1983) 721–753;

K. H. Kuhn, 'The Apocalypse of Elijah,' in H. F. D. Sparks (ed.), *The Apocryphal Old Testament* (Oxford: Clarendon Press, 1984) 753–773;

David T. M. Frankfurter, 'Tabitha in the Apocalypse of Elijah,' *JTS* 41 (1990) 13–26;

David T. M. Frankfurter, *Elijah in Upper Egypt: The Apocalypse of Elijah and Early Egyptian Christianity* (Minneapolis: Fortress, 1993);

Albert-Marie Denis, *Introduction à la littérature religieuse judéo-hellénistique,* vol. 1 (Turnhout: Brepols, 2000) 618–628.

Frankfurter, 'Tabitha,' argues that the figure of Tabitha is a combination of the Egyptian goddess Tabithet and Bithiah, the daughter of Pharaoh who rescued Moses. In some Jewish traditions the latter is regarded as one of those, like Enoch and Elijah, who ascended to heaven without dying.

I published the following review of Frankfurter, *Elijah,* in *Journal of Ecclesiastical History* 46 (1995) 488–490:

Elijah in Upper Egypt: The Apocalypse of Elijah and Early Egyptian Christianity. By David Frankfurter. (Studies in Antiquity and Christianity.) Pp. xviii + 380. Minneapolis: Fortress Press, 1993. n. p. ISBN 0–8006–3106–4.

The *Apocalypse of Elijah,* which was composed in Greek but survives only in Coptic (a Sahidic and an Achmimic version), has been widely recognized, by scholars who have studied it, to have originated – or, at least, reached its present form – in late third-century Egypt. But the interest of most scholars who have studied it has been in identifying an earlier Jewish source or at least Jewish traditions within it. This interest goes back to a period of scholarship when source criticism was the dominant method of study of the so-called Pseudepigrapha (Jewish and Christian works written under Old Testament pseudonyms), but it persists into the treatment of the *Apocalypse of Elijah* in volume 1 of *The Old Testament Pseudepigrapha,* ed. J. H. Charlesworth (London: Darton, Longman & Todd, 1983), a collection of works supposed either to have been written by Jews before 200 C. E. or to preserve Jewish traditions from that period. A work such as the *Apocalypse of Elijah,* which belongs to the tradition of Jewish and Christian apocalyptic literature that goes back to the second century B. C. E., certainly does need to be placed and studied within that tradition, but it also needs to be placed and studied within the context of its composition (final redaction). The classification of such works as Pseudepigrapha unfortunately has a tendency to isolate them from this context. David Frankfurter's book is a very welcome attempt to reverse this tendency and to study the *Apocalypse of Elijah* as evidence of late third-century Egyptian Christianity. Whatever sources the author may have used (and Frankfurter makes some important fresh contributions to this question, discounting any notion of a Jewish *Urtext*), clearly the composition of the work as we have it needs to be explained from its Egyptian Christian context. While Frankfurter handles the Jewish apocalyptic background of the work competently, he is also fully at home in the literature and history of Roman Egypt, Christian and non-Christian. His exploration of the relation of the *Apocalypse of Elijah* to that Egyptian context constitutes a massive advance in study of the *Apocalypse of Elijah,* as well as a significant contribution to the history of Egyptian Christianity. It is a model of the kind of work which needs to be done on many of the Christian apocalypses (both those bearing Old Testament pseudonyms and those bearing New Testament and other Christian pseudonyms). (He quite correctly points out, incidentally, that the *Apocalypse of Elijah* is not generically an apocalypse, though it bears this title in the Achmimic recension. Didymus the Blind called it the *Prophecy of Elijah,* distinguishing it from an *Apocalypse of Elijah* which he also knew. But it is nevertheless closely related to the tradition of apocalyptic literature.)

The *Apocalypse of Elijah* has usually been dated by reading chapter 2 (a narrative prophecy of the reigns of a series of kings of Egypt) as *vaticinia ex eventu,* and attempting to identify the historical persons and events to which cryptic reference is made. Frankfurter convincingly shows that this approach is mistaken. The chapter paints a picture of the eschatological future in traditional Egyptian mythological and prophetic colours. It employs very traditional Egyptian motifs, deriving especially from Egyptian priestly circles in which very ancient Egyptian traditions were preserved and adapted for conservative nationalist ends. This is one of the points where Frankfurter postulates a certain syncretism in which native Egyptian traditions are integrated into a Christian apocalyptic outlook. At some other such points it could be questioned whether his zeal to find native Egyptian resonances for the imagery may not go too far, privileging Egyptian over more obvious Jewish and Christian backgrounds to particular motifs. But in general he has established that the *Apocalypse of Elijah* has its roots not only in the Jewish and Christian apocalyptic tradition, but also in native Egyptian prophetic literature.

Since he does not accept earlier arguments for the late third-century date based on alleged *vaticinia ex eventu,* his case for this date rests on establishing more general correlations between the text and the historical and social conditions of Egypt in that period. He sees in the text's rigorist treatment of martyrdom a millennialist (a term which he uses in its social scientific sense as characterizing a kind of popular movement, not just religious ideas) response to the Decian and Valerian edicts, which is all the more intelligible when set against the background of socio-economic decline in third-century Egypt and the evidence of 'nationalistic' revolts by a variety of groups during the century. His case for seeing the *Apocalypse of Elijah* as a Christian manifestation of wider nationalistic oppositional sentiments is strengthened by some evidence for Christian millennialism in rural Egypt at this time (the account by Dionysius of Alexandria of how he had to refute a literalist interpretation of Revelation current in Arsinoe). Finally, he rightly draws attention to the way the *Apocalypse of Elijah* places its apocalyptic expectation in the context of a contemporary dispute about fasting, and reconstructs a possible scenario in which the extreme fasting characteristic of the milieu of the work came under criticism from ecclesiastical authorities who associated it with Manicheanism. It is a little disappointing to find that, in his thorough account of evidence on attitudes to fasting in Egyptian Christianity, there is actually no real evidence for the case that opposition to Manicheanism affected attitudes to fasting and led to condemnation of extreme fasting by Christian groups. It should also be said that the use of cross-cultural evidence of millennialism in reconstructing the context of the *Apocalypse of Elijah* sometimes comes close to the hazardous method of using social scientific models to fill in gaps in the evidence, rather than to interpret the evidence. Inevitably, Frankfurter's reconstruction of the context, while making full use of all the evidence there is, involves a certain amount of conjecture, but he paints a very plausible picture.

In arguing for a relative difference between the *Apocalypse of Elijah* and the Jewish and Christian apocalyptic literature in general, Frankfurter stresses not only the work's native Egyptian affinities, but also its relatively popular and rural background, distinguishing it from apocalypses whose background is highly literate and learned. There is certainly something in this contrast (the *Apocalypse of Elijah* is a far less sophisticated literary work than many of the apocalypses), but the rural context is very insecurely based in the text (as Frankfurter really acknowledges in n.51 on p. 98). That the text is designed for oral performance is probably true, but then so was the book of Revelation, which is nevertheless a work of immense learning and literary complexity. That the author's relationship to Jewish and Christian traditions is predominantly oral rather than textual I do not think he has proved. The fact that allusions to Scripture are not distinguished, as quotations, from the rest of the author's words is not an indication of orality, but a literary feature of almost all the Jewish and Christian apocalypses. Pseudepigraphy requires it (Elijah cannot quote the New Testament!). But finally I wonder if Frankfurter's full and useful discussion of the significance of attribution to Elijah should not have taken more seriously the possibility that the text was not originally attributed to Elijah at all. The facts that 1:5–6 refers to the incarnation as a past event (with only a partial attempt to correct this in the Sahidic recension), and that 4:7–19; 5:32–34 refer to Elijah in the third person, are features inconsistent with the pseudonym (and such inconsistency is rare in works employing biblical pseudonyms), while no aspect of the implied author is at all specific to Elijah.

These are questions which do not detract from the value of this most impressive study, which succeeds in integrating a remarkably wide range of evidence into an illuminating historical reconstruction of the origin of a text.

4. The Rise of Apocalyptic*

Apocalyptic is currently a growth area in biblical studies. Fresh study, more reliable texts, new editions, even hitherto unpublished documents are enriching our understanding of the intertestamental apocalyptic literature. In addition, there has been fresh debate over the origins of apocalyptic and its relation to Old Testament prophecy, while in the wake of E. Käsemann's notorious claim that 'apocalyptic is the mother of all Christian theology'[1] the importance of apocalyptic as the intellectual matrix of primitive Christianity is increasingly recognized. More and more, apocalyptic must be seen as a crucial historical bridge between the Testaments.

All this raises serious theological questions. Is apocalyptic a legitimate development of Old Testament religion? The historical investigation of apocalyptic origins cannot avoid a theological assessment, which has its implications also for New Testament theology to the extent that apocalyptic was a formative factor in early Christian theological development. In this way the question of the theological continuity between the two Testaments themselves is involved in the problem of the status of apocalyptic. Moreover, as James Barr points out,[2] the status of apocalyptic raises the question of the status of the canon in which it is only marginally represented. Can an *intertestamental* development be seen as providing theological continuity between the Testaments?

In this article we shall be concerned primarily with the rise of apocalyptic up to he flowering of Hasidic apocalyptic in the mid-second century BC. We shall be asking (in Part I) the *historical* question of the origins of apocalyptic, in the light of some recent studies, and (in Part II) the *theological* question of the theological legitimacy of apocalyptic as a development of Old Testament religion.

---

* First publication: *Themelios* 3/2 (1978) 10–23; reprinted in: Carl R. Trueman, Tony J. Gray, Craig L. Blomberg ed., *Solid Ground: 25 Years of Evangelical Theology* (Leicester: Inter-Varsity Press, 2000) 43–68.

[1] 'The beginnings of Christian theology', *JTC* 6 (1969), p. 40 (= E. Käsemann, *New Testament Questions of Today*, London: SCM, 1969, p. 102).
[2] 'Jewish apocalyptic in recent scholarly study', *BJRL* 58 (1975–6), pp. 28–29.

I. Origins

Apocalyptic in the prophets

The most important recent investigation of the origins of apocalyptic in Old Testament prophecy is that of Paul D. Hanson.[3] Hanson argues that apocalyptic eschatology developed in the early post-exilic period (late sixth and early fifth centuries) as a development rooted in the prophetic tradition. The extent of the development of apocalyptic in this period, as he estimates it, is indicated by his revision of the usual terminology: he uses the term 'proto-apocalyptic' for Second Isaiah, since he points in the apocalyptic direction; Third Isaiah and other prophetic material from the early Persian period (Zech. 9–13; Is. 24–27) he calls 'early apocalyptic'; Zechariah 14, which he dates in the mid-fifth century and thinks marks the point at which apocalyptic eschatology is fully developed, is 'middle apocalyptic'; Daniel, from the mid-second century, is already 'late apocalyptic'.[4] (To avoid confusion, in this article I shall use the term 'apocalyptic prophecy' to designate apocalyptic material within the Old Testament prophetic books, i.e. Hanson's 'early' and 'middle' apocalyptic.) Hanson admits a chronological gulf between Zechariah 14 and 'late' apocalyptic, but the special characteristic of his thesis is that he considers apocalyptic eschatology to have already developed in all essentials *before* this gulf. This enables him to stress the continuity between prophecy and apocalyptic to an unusual degree, and to deny the importance of the non-Israelite influences (Iranian and Hellenistic) which have so often been regarded as contributing significantly to the development of apocalyptic. Such influences, he argues, enter the pictures only at a late stage when apocalyptic's essential character was already developed.

Of course such a thesis can only be maintained if an appropriate definition of apocalyptic is used. Hanson's focuses on apocalyptic *eschatology* and relates it to prophetic eschatology, distinguishing the two in terms of the kind of balance which each maintains between myth and history. The characteristic of classical prophecy is he dialectic it maintains between the cosmic vision of Yahweh's plans and the prophet's responsibility to

---

[3] *The Dawn of Apocalyptic* (Philadelphia: Fortress Press, 1975). See also Hanson's articles: 'Jewish apocalyptic against its Near Eastern environment', *RB* 78 (1971), pp. 31–58; 'Old Testament apocalyptic re-examined', *Int* 25 (1971), pp. 454–479; 'Zechariah 9 and the recapitulation of an ancient ritual pattern', *JBL* 92 (1973), pp. 37–59; 'Apocalypticism', *Interpreter's Dictionary of the Bible: Supplementary Volume* (Nashville, Tennessee; Abingdom, 1976), pp. 28–34.

[4] In this article I accept, as Hanson does, the usual critical conclusions as to the unity and date of the books of Isaiah, Zechariah and Daniel. Readers who maintain the traditional conservative views on these issues will naturally have to differ very radically from both Hanson's and my own reconstructions of the rise of apocalyptic.

translate that vision into concrete historical terms. Prophetic eschatology is 'a religious perspective which focuses on the prophetic announcement to the nation of the divine plans for Israel and the world which the prophet has witnessed unfolding in the divine council and which he translates into terms of plain history, real politics and human instrumentality'.[5] What apocalyptic lacks is that last clause. The balance between vision and history is lost. Despairing of the realization of the vision in the historical sphere, the apocalyptists were increasingly content to leave it in the realm of myth. Apocalyptic eschatology is 'a religious perspective which focuses on the disclosure... to the elect of the cosmic vision of Yahweh's sovereignty – especially as it relates to his acting to deliver his faithful – which disclosure the visionaries have largely ceased to translate into terms of plain history, real politics, and human instrumentality'.[6]

This apocalyptic eschatology developed among the disciples of Second Isaiah (to whose tradition belong not only Is. 56–66 but also Zech. 9–14) in the post-exilic Palestinian community. Second Isaiah's prophecies of glorious restoration remained unfulfilled, and in the bleak conditions of the early Persian period the visionary group which maintained his eschatological hope increasingly presented it in purely mythical terms, in images of sheer divine intervention and cosmic transformation. To the possibility of fulfilment through human agency and favourable historical conditions they became indifferent.

As the sociological context for the development of apocalyptic eschatology Hanson postulates an intra-community struggle between this visionary group on the one hand, and on the other hand the hierocratic group, a Zadokite priestly group which adopted a pragmatic approach to restoration. By contrast with the visionary programme of Second Isaiah and his followers, this latter group were at first inspired by the more pragmatic restoration programme of Ezekiel, and through the preaching of Haggai and Zechariah they succeeded in harnessing eschatological enthusiasm to their policies. After the rebuilding of the temple they won control in the community and thereafter discouraged all eschatological expectation as a threat to the stability of their achievement. The visionary group, on the other hand, consistently opposed the rebuilding of the temple in the name of their transcendent eschatology and waged the most bitter polemic against the hierocratic party. Their own political powerlessness encouraged their visionary indifference to the sphere of political responsibility.

Hanson's reconstruction of this community struggle is speculative at best and probably the weakest part of his thesis. In particular it leads him

---

[5] Hanson, *The Dawn of Apocalyptic,* p. 11.
[6] Ibid.

to a polarization of the prophetic tradition of Second Isaiah, Third Isaiah and Zechariah 9–14 on the one hand, and on the other hand the tradition of Ezekiel and Zechariah 1–8. The former he regards as the tradition in which apocalyptic emerged, while the latter only used apocalyptic motifs to legitimate a pragmatic political programme. Such a polarization does far less than justice to the significance of Ezekiel and Zechariah 1–8 in the development of apocalyptic,[7] as Hanson himself has begun to recognize in a subsequent modification of his treatment of Zechariah.[8] To treat Zechariah 9–14 as belonging to the tradition of Third Isaiah *rather than* to the tradition of Ezekiel and Zechariah 1–8 is to ignore the evidence that these chapters are quite heavily dependent on Ezekiel and relatively little dependent on Isaiah 40–66.[9] This in itself suggests that the emergence of apocalyptic must be reconstructed according to a less rigid classification of prophetic traditions.

This is not the place to attempt an alternative reconstruction in detail, but what seems needed is greater recognition of the common features of the various post-exilic prophecies. Despite the varying emphases there is a common conviction that the eschatological promises of restoration in Second Isaiah and Ezekiel remained largely outstanding despite the restored city and temple. In all of these prophecies there is therefore a degree of dependence on and reinterpretation of the earlier prophecies, and all are more or less apocalyptic (according to Hanson's definition) in the extent to which they depict the coming salvation in terms of Yahweh's direct intervention and radical transformation of historical conditions. The distinctive aspect of Haggai and Zechariah (1–8) is that they focused these apocalyptic hopes on the rebuilding of the temple and the leadership of Joshua and Zerubbabel. But these historical realities soon proved incapable of measuring up to the hopes aroused, and so those who subsequently kept alive the eschatological expectation were not opponents of Haggai and Zechariah but successors who sought to remain faithful to their prophecy.

There is, however, a great deal of value in Hanson's analyses of Isaiah 56–66 and Zechariah 9–14. He shows convincingly how various features of apocalyptic eschatology emerge in these passages. Thus, judgment and salvation are no longer prophesied for the nation as a whole but respectively for the faithless and the faithful within Israel.[10] The doctrine of a *universal*

---

[7] For the contrary view that apocalyptic arises in the tradition of Ezekiel and Zechariah, cf. H. Gese, *ZTK* 70 (1973), pp. 20–49; R. Noth, 'Prophecy to apocalyptic via Zechariah', *VTSup* 22 (Congress Volume, Uppsala 1971), pp. 47–71.

[8] *Interpreter's Dictionary of the Bible: Supplementary Volume*, pp. 32, 982–983.

[9] M. Delcor, *RB* 59 (1952), pp. 385–411: contacts with Ezekiel listed, p. 386, relation to Third Isaiah discussed, pp. 387–390. R. A. Mason, *ZAW* 88 (1976), pp. 227–238, claims that continuity of themes shows that Zech. 9–14 stands in the tradition of Zech. 1–8.

[10] E. g. *Dawn*, pp. 143 f., 150–151.

judgment is adumbrated in Isaiah 63:6, 66:16,[11] and eschatology takes on cosmic dimensions. Beyond the judgment lies a new age radically different from the present age and inaugurated by a new act of creation: this idea has its background in Second Isaiah and is already developed in such passages as Isaiah 65:17–25; Zechariah 14:6–9.[12] These elements compose the transcendent eschatology of divine intervention and cosmic transformation which forms the central core of apocalyptic belief.

Hanson also shows how this development entails the revivification of ancient mythical material, especially the Divine Warrior myth, to depict the coming eschatological triumph of Yahweh.[13] Here Hanson follows the pioneering work of his teacher F. M. Cross, whose studies of Canaanite myth in relation to the Old Testament revealed the extent to which 'old mythological themes rise to a new crescendo' in apocalyptic.[14] Other studies have shown the extent to which Canaanite myth continues to be used even in Daniel and Enoch,[15] while the apocalyptic assimilation of myth extended also to Babylonian, Iranian and Hellenistic material. This 'remythologization' of Israelite religion was not, however, a reversion to an ahistorical worldview, but serves to represent an eschatological future which is now understood to transcend the categories of ordinary history.

Hanson has succeeded in demonstrating that the transcendent eschatology which characterizes apocalyptic emerged in post-exilic prophecy as an internal development in the Israelite prophetic tradition in response to the historical conditions of the post-exilic community. This is an important conclusion. On the other hand, there remains a significant gulf, which is not only chronological, between this apocalyptic prophecy of the fifth century and the Hasidic apocalyptic of the second century. Apocalyptic prophecy is not pseudonymous, though it is often anonymous. It does not include extensive surveys of history in the form of *vaticinia ex eventu*. Its angelology is relatively undeveloped. The temporal dualism of two ages is emerging, but the spatial dualism of heaven and earth, which also characterized intertestamental apocalyptic, is not yet apparent. Moreover, the transcendent

---

[11] Ibid., pp. 185, 207.

[12] Ibid., pp. 155–161, 376–379, 397.

[13] On the Divine Warrior myth: ibid., pp. 300–323, 328–333.

[14] F. M. Cross, *Canaanite Myth and Hebrew Epic* (Cambridge, MA: Harvard University Press, 1973), p. 90, cf. pp. 144, 170, 343–346.

[15] *Daniel:* J. A. Emerton, *JTS (NS)* 9 (1958), pp. 225–242; Cross, op. cit., p. 17; M. Delcor, *VT* 18 (1968), pp. 290–312; idem, *Le livre de Daniel* (Paris: Gabalda, 1971), pp. 32, 210–211. *Enoch:* M. Delcor, *RHR* 190 (1976), pp. 3–53; R. J. Clifford, *The Cosmic Mountain In Canaan and the Old Testament* (Cambridge, MA: Harvard University Press, 1972), pp. 182–189; J. T. Milik, *The Books of Enoch* (Oxford: Clarendon Press, 1976), pp. 29, 39.

eschatology of apocalyptic prophecy does not yet include the transcendence of death, so central to later apocalyptic belief.[16]

In other words, although Hanson has demonstrated the continuity between prophecy and the apocalyptic prophecy of the early Persian period, there still remains a problem of continuity between this apocalyptic prophecy and the later apocalyptic of Daniel and the intertestamental literature.

To the origins of this later apocalyptic we now turn. We shall see that it is really the heir of post-exilic prophecy and owes its transcendent eschatology to that source. But we shall also see that this is not the whole story, for the alternative derivation of apocalyptic from wisdom has some validity, and there is moreover a significant discontinuity between the self-understanding of apocalyptic prophecy and that of the later apocalyptists.

Daniel and mantic wisdom

The most radical rejection of the derivation of apocalyptic from prophecy is that of Gerhard von Rad, who argued that apocalyptic is not the child of prophecy but the offspring of wisdom.[17] This proposal has been widely criticized,[18] as being at least one-sided. In this section and the next, we shall argue that, while von Rad's thesis was too generalized and cannot be treated as an *alternative* to the derivation from prophecy, it does have some validity in relation to the background of the books of Daniel and Enoch. In both cases, however, the wisdom background needs more careful definition than von Rad gave it.

An important attempt to refine von Rad's argument is H. P. Müller's proposal to derive apocalyptic not from proverbial but from *mantic* wisdom.[19] For alongside the wise men whose type of wisdom is represented by the book of Proverbs, the ancient Near East had also mantic wise men,

---

[16] Probably a doctrine of resurrection appears in Is. 26:19, which Hanson considers 'early apocalyptic' (op. cit., pp. 313 f.), but he does not discuss it.

[17] G. von Rad, *Old Testament Theology* 2 (ET Edinburgh and London: Oliver and Boyd, 1965), pp. 301–308, is the original version of his argument; this was completely revised for the fourth German edition: *Theologie des Alten Testaments* 2 (Munich: Kaiser, 1965), pp. 316 ff. (not in ET); and developed again in *Wisdom in Israel* (ET London: SCM, 1972), pp. 263–282.

[18] For criticism see P. Vielhauer in *New Testament Apocrypha* 2, ed. W. Schneemelcher and R. McL. Wilson (London: Lutterworth, 1965), pp. 597–598; W. Zimmerli, *Man and his Hope in the Old Testament* (London: SCM, 1971), p. 140; K. Koch, *The Rediscovery of Apocalyptic* (London: SCM, 1972), pp. 42–47; W. Schmithals, *The Apocalyptic Movement* (Nashville, TN: Abingdon, 1975), pp. 128–131; J. Barr, art. cit., p. 25.

[19] 'Mantische Weisheit und Apokalyptik', *VTSup* 22 (Congress Volume, Uppsala 1971), pp. 268–293. Müller's argument takes up von Rad's in the sense that, although von Rad failed to distinguish mantic from proverbial wisdom, his thesis did in the end concentrate on the mantic aspect of wisdom: *Wisdom in Israel*, pp. 280–281. Cf. also J. J. Collins, *JBL* 94 (1975), pp. 218–234.

whose function was to divine the secrets of the future by various methods including the interpretation of dreams, omens, mysterious oracles, and the stars.[20] There is little trace of a class of mantic wise men in Israel, but two Old Testament figures who rose to prominence in foreign courts did so by virtue of their successful competition with the court diviners in the practice of the mantic arts: Joseph at the court of Pharaoh and Daniel at the court of Nebuchadnezzar. It is the case of Daniel which suggests that one of the roots of apocalyptic lies in mantic wisdom.

Daniel was not a prophet in the sense of classical Israelite prophecy.[21] His activity in chapters 2, 4, and 5 consists in the interpretation of Nebuchadnezzar's dreams and of the mysterious message on Belshazzar's palace wall. In each case he is called in after the failure of the other diviners at court. Clearly he belongs among them (2:18), and as a result of his success becomes their chief (2:48; 4:9; 5:11). His *function* is exactly theirs: the disclosure of the secrets of the future. Of course the source of his supernatural knowledge is the God of Israel, and his success is designed to bring glory to the God of Israel as the God who is sovereign over the political future. Daniel is the representative of the God of Israel among the magicians and astrologers of the Babylonian court, but he represents him *in the practice of mantic wisdom* (cf. 5:12).

It is, moreover, this aspect of the Daniel of chapters 1–6 which most plausibly accounts for the ascription to him of the apocalypse of chapters 7–12. We must therefore take seriously the claim that apocalyptic has roots in mantic wisdom.

There are strong formal resemblances between the symbolic dream with its interpretation in mantic wisdom and the apocalyptic dream or vision with its interpretation. The latter also has roots in prophecy (especially Ezekiel and Zech. 1–6), but the connection with mantic wisdom is hard to deny in the case of Daniel, where Nebuchadnezzar's dream and its interpretation in chapter 2 corresponds so well to Daniel's dream-visions and their interpretation in chapters 7 and 8. Besides their dream-interpretation, the mantic wise men were doubtless responsible for the literary prophecies of the ancient east, such as the Mesopotamian 'apocalypses' which have

---

[20] Old Testament references to mantic wise men: Gen. 41:8; Est. 1:13; Is. 44:25; 47:10–13; Jer. 50:35–36; Dan. 2:2, 48; 4:4–5; 5:7, 11. On mantic wisdom in Mesopotamia, see A.L. Oppenheim, *Ancient Mesopotamia* (Chicago: University of Chicago Press, 1964), pp. 206–227; on interpretation of dreams in particular, see idem, *The Interpretation of Dreams in the ancient Near East: With a Translation of an Assyrian Dream-book* (Philadelphia: American Philosophical Society, 1956).

[21] In later times he could be loosely called a prophet (Mark 13:14), as could David (Acts 2:30), in the sense that they gave inspired predictions.

been compared with Jewish apocalyptic in certain respects.[22] These provide precedent, which cannot be found in Israelite prophecy, for the long reviews of history in the form of predictions from a standpoint in the past, such as we find in Daniel 11 and other Jewish apocalypses.[23] The astrological aspect of mantic wisdom is naturally less well represented in Jewish parallel material, but it is noteworthy that interest in astrological prediction recurs at Qumram.

The argument about the date of Daniel may have been conducted too simply in terms of a choice between the sixth and second centuries. We may now be able to recognize the book's dual affinities, with Babylonian mantic wisdom on the one hand and with Hasidic apocalyptic on the other, which indicate the probability of a developing Daniel tradition,[24] which has its roots as far back as the exile in Jewish debate with and participation in mantic wisdom, developed in the Eastern diaspora, and finally produced Daniel apocalypses on Palestinian soil in the time of Antiochus Epiphanes.[25] This is all the more probable in view of the similar chronological development which the Enoch tradition underwent (see below).

The key to the emergence of apocalyptic in such a tradition is undoubtedly a growing concern with eschatology. Apocalyptic, like mantic wisdom, is the revelation of the secrets of the *future,* but in its concern with the *eschatological* future apocalyptic moves beyond the scope at least of *Babylonian* mantic wisdom.[26] Thus, while Daniel's interpretations of the dream of chapter 4 and the oracle of chapter 5 belong to the typical activities of the Babylonian diviners, his *eschatological* interpretation of the dream of chapter 2 is already in the sphere of apocalyptic. Hence it is chapter 2 which provides the point of departure for the apocalypse of chapters 7–12, which

---

[22] A. K. Grayson and W. G. Lambert, *JCS* 18 (1964), pp. 7–30; W. W. Hallo, *IEJ* 16 (1966), pp. 231–242; R. D. Biggs, *Iraq* 29 (1967), pp. 117–132; W. W. Hallo and R. Borger, *BibOr* 28 (1971), pp. 3–24; H. Hunger and S. A. Kaufman, *JAOS* 95 (1975), pp. 371–375. Note that Hunger and Kaufman (p. 374) suggest that their text dates from the reign of Amel-Marduk, son of Nebuchadnezzar II.

[23] The device of *vaticinia ex eventu* is used in the texts published by Grayson and Lambert, Hunger and Kaufman, and in Hallo and Borger's Sulgi text. Most of these texts are probably anonymous, but Hallo and Borger's (like the Jewish apocalypses) are pseudonymous.

[24] The products of the Daniel tradition are not limited to our book of Daniel: to the 'court-tales' of Dan. 1–6 must be added 4Q *Prayer of Nabonidus* and the LXX *Additions to Daniel;* and to the 'apocalypse' of Dan. 7–12 must be added the (still unpublished) fragments of a Daniel apocalypse from Qumran: 4QpsDan^a–c.

[25] That Dan. 1–6 originated in circles of Jewish mantic wise men in the eastern diaspora, and Dan. 7–12 in the same circles after their return to Palestine, is argued by Collins, art cit. (n. 19).

[26] Mesopotamian 'apocalyptic' (n. 22 above) has no properly eschatological features, at most a cyclical view of history: cf. Hallo, art. cip., p. 241.

interprets the future according to the pattern of the four pagan empires succeeded by the eschatological kingdom. But even this contrast between mantic wisdom and apocalyptic may be too sharply drawn. If Nebuchadnezzar's prognosticators would not have given his dream an eschatological sense, the Zoroastrian magi who succeeded them at the court of Darius might well have done.[27] Precisely the four-empires scheme of chapter 2, with its metals symbolism and its eschatological outcome, has close parallels in the Iranian material which has been plausibly suggested as its source.[28] We touch here on an old debate about apocalyptic origins: the question of the influence of Iranian eschatology.[29] Whatever the extent of the *influence*, it is clear that there are *parallels*, of which the Jews of the diaspora cannot have been unaware. Not even eschatology decisively differentiates Jewish apocalyptic from the products of mantic wisdom, insofar as eschatology developed also to some extent in non-Jewish mantic circles.

It becomes increasingly clear that apocalyptic, from its roots in mantic wisdom, is a phenomenon with an unusually close relationship to its non-Jewish environment. At every stage there are parallels with the oracles and prophecies of the pagan world. This is equally true as we move from the Persian to the Hellenistic age. Hellenistic Egypt has an 'apocalyptic' literature of its own: pseudonymous oracles set in the past, predicting political events, eschatological woes, and a final golden age.[30] There is an extensive Hellenistic literature of heavenly revelations and celestial journeys sometimes remarkably similar in form to those of the apocalyptic sees.[31] It is not surprising that H. D. Betz concludes that 'we must learn to understand apocalypticism as a peculiar manifestation within the entire course of Hellenistic-oriental syncretism'.[32]

Nevertheless this close relationship of Jewish apocalyptic to its non-Jewish environment is misunderstood if it is treated merely as syncretistic. Undoubtedly there is considerable borrowing of motifs, symbols, literary

---

[27] For the mantic activity of the magi at the courts of Media and Persia, cf. S. K. Eddy, *The King is Dead* (Lincoln, NB: University of Nebraska Press, 1961), pp. 65–71.

[28] D. Flusser, *Israel Oriental Studies* 2 (1972), pp. 148–175. The Iranian sources are late, but are based on a lost passage of the *Avesta* and the parallels are too close to be fortuitous. Note how the passage from the *Zand-i Vohuman Yasn* (p. 166) incorporates precisely the connection between mantic wisdom and apocalyptic in terms of symbolic dream / vision: Ahuramazda gives Zarathustra a vision of a tree with branches of four metals, which he explains as four periods. M. Hengel, *Judaism and Hellenism* 1 (London: SCM, 1974), pp. 182–183, prefers to trace Dan. 2 to Hellenistic Greek sources.

[29] Cf. Hengel, op. cit., p. 193; J. J. Collins, *VT* 25 (1975), pp. 604–608.

[30] C. C. McCown, *HTR* 18 (1925), pp. 357–411; Hengel, op. cit., pp. 184–185.

[31] Ibid., pp. 210–218.

[32] 'On the problem of the religio-historical understanding of apocalypticism', *JTC* 6 (1969), p. 138.

forms – not only by Jew from Gentile but also *vice versa*.[33] Undoubtedly Judaism after the exile, especially in the diaspora but increasingly also in Palestine, was not immune from the moods and concerns of the international religious scene. The relationship, however, was not one of passive absorption of alien influence, but of creative encounter and debate in which the essence of Israelite faith was reasserted in new forms.

This element of debate is already in evidence in the encounter with Babylonian mantic wisdom. Daniel, as we have seen, practises it among but also in competition with the Babylonian diviners, to show that it is the God of Israel who is sovereign over the future and gives real revelation of the secrets of destiny (2:27f., 46). Such a tradition of debate found one of its most natural expressions in the Jewish *Sibylline Oracles,* in which an internationally known pagan form of prophetic oracle was adopted as a vehicle for a Jewish eschatological message. The message, drawn from Old Testament prophecy, of God's judgment on idolatry and his purpose of establishing his kingdom, was attributed to the ancient prophetesses, the Sibyls, largely, it seems, with an apologetic aim, to gain it a hearing in the non-Jewish-world. Of course the bulk of Jewish apocalyptic was written for an exclusively Jewish audience, but behind it lay a close but critical interaction with its non-Jewish environment such as the *Sibyllines* bring to more deliberate expression. This kind of relationship is hazardous. The appropriation of pagan forms and motifs can become insufficiently critical and the voice of authentic Jewish faith can become muffled or stifled. We cannot suppose that the Jewish apocalyptists never succumbed to this danger, but on the whole the risk they took was justified by the achievement of an expression of prophetic faith which spoke to their own age.

From its potentially ambiguous relationship with paganism, apocalyptic emerged in the crisis of hellenization under Antiochus, *not* as the expression of hellenizing syncretism, but as the literature of the Hasidic movement, which stood for uncompromising resistance to pagan influence. How did apocalyptic succeed in retaining its Jewish authenticity and avoiding the perils of syncretism? This is the point at which the derivation of apocalyptic from mantic wisdom fails us, and needs to be supplemented with the derivation from Old Testament prophecy. The two are after all not entirely dissimilar. While Jewish practitioners of mantic wisdom were entering into competition with the Babylonian fortune-tellers, Second Isaiah, the father of apocalyptic prophecy, was also engaged, at a greater distance, in debate with his pagan counterparts, exposing the impotence of the Babylonian gods and their prognosticators (Is. 44:25; 47:13) by contrast with Yahweh's

---

[33] Hengel, op. cit., p. 185: 'It is not improbable that Egyptian "apocalypticism"... and its Jewish counterpart had a mutual influence on each other.'

sovereignty over the future revealed to his servants the prophets (Is. 44:26; 46:9–11). The apocalyptic heirs of Jewish mantic wisdom were not prophets, but their concern with God's revelation of the future made them students of Old Testament prophecy, and the more they concerned themselves with the *eschatological* future, the more they sought their inspiration in the prophets. With the cessation of prophecy in Israel, the apocalyptists became the interpreters of Old Testament prophecy for their own age. So while the *form* of their work was stamped by its continuity with pagan oracular literature, its *content* was frequently inspired by Old Testament prophecy. Again we can see this in Daniel. His eschatological dream-interpretation in chapter 2 is, if not inspired by, at least congruous with the eschatological hope of the prophets. Taken as the fundamental idea of the apocalypse of chapters 7–12, it is then filled out by means of the interpretation of Old Testament prophecy. Thus the Hasidic apocalyptists stood in a tradition with its origins in mantic wisdom, but filled it with their own dominant concern to achieve a fresh understanding of prophecy for their own time. In that sense they were also the heirs of post-exilic apocalyptic prophecy.

Enoch and consmological wisdom

We have traced the emergence of apocalyptic between the exile and the Maccabees, between prophecy and mantic wisdom, in the tradition which produced our book of Daniel. We must now look at the emergence of apocalyptic in another tradition which spans the same period, the Enoch tradition.

The discovery of the Aramaic fragments of *Enoch* at Qumran, now available in J. T. Milik's edition,[34] is most important for the study of apocalyptic origins. With the exception of the *Similitudes* (*1 Enoch* 37–71), fragments of all sections of *1 Enoch* have been found: the *Book of Watchers* (1–36), the *Astronomical Book* (72–82), the *Book of Dreams* (83–90), and the *Epistle of Enoch* (91–107). There are also fragments of a hitherto unknown *Book of Giants*.

These discoveries clarify the issue of the relative dates of the parts of the Enoch corpus.[35] The generally accepted date of the *Book of Dreams* (165 or 164 BC) may stand, but the pre-Maccabean date of the *Astronomical Book* and the *Book of Watchers*, hitherto disputed, is now certainly established on palaeographic evidence. The *Astronomical Book* (now known to have been much longer than the abridged version in *Ethiopic Enoch* 72–82) cannot be later than the beginning of the second century, and Milik would date it in the

---

[34] *The Books of Enoch* (Oxford: Clarendon, 1976).
[35] On the relative dates, cf. also P. Grelot, *RB* 82 (1975), pp. 481–500.

early Persian period.[36] The *Book of Watchers* cannot be later than c. 150 BC, and Milik thinks it was written in Palestine in the mid-third century.[37] He is almost certainly correct in regarding chapters 6–19 as an earlier written source incorporated in the *Book of Watchers;* these chapters he regards as contemporary with or older than the *Astronomical Book.*[38] While Milik's very early dating of the *Astronomical Book* and chapters 6–19 is uncertain, the important point for our purpose is their relative age as the earliest part of the Enoch corpus. This means that apocalyptic was not originally the dominant concern in the Enoch tradition, for the apocalyptic elements in these sections are not prominent.[39] The expansion of chapters 6–19 with chapters 1–5, 21–36 to form the *Book of Watchers* had the effect of adding much more eschatological content to this part of the tradition. Then in the Maccabean period a full-blown Enoch apocalypse appeared for the first time in the *Book of Dreams.* So we have a development parallel to that in the Daniel tradition.

Also like the Daniel tradition, the Enoch tradition has its roots in the Jewish encounter with Babylonian culture, but in this case over a wider area than mantic wisdom.[40] The circles which gave rise to the tradition had an encyclopedic interest in all kinds of wisdom, especially of a cosmo-logical kind: astronomy and the calendar, meteorology, geography, and the mythical geography of paradise. In all these areas of knowledge they were indebted to Babylonian scholarship,[41] while the picture of Enoch himself as the initiator of civilization, who received heavenly revelations of the secrets of the universe and transmitted them in writing to later generations, is modelled on the antediluvian sages of Mesopotamian myth.[42]

But, once again as in the Jewish involvement in mantic wisdom, this Jew-ish encyclopedic wisdom is not only indebted to but also in competition with its pagan counterpart. Civilization is represented as an ambiguous phe-nomenon, with its sinful origins in the rebellion of the fallen angels (*1 Enoch* 7:1; cf. 69:6–14) as well as an authentic basis in the divine revelations to

---

[36] Milik, op. cit., pp. 7–9.

[37] Ibid., pp. 22–25, 28.

[38] Ibid., pp. 25, 31.

[39] Eschatological material appears only in 10:12–11:2 (which may have been expanded when chs. 6–19 were incorporated in the *Book of Watchers*); 16:1; 72:1; 80.

[40] The debate with mantic wisdom is reflected in *1 Enoch* 7:1; 8:3.

[41] Milik, op. cit., pp. 14–18, 29–31, 33, 37–38, 277; P. Grelot, *RB* 65 (1958), pp. 33–69.

[42] P. Grelot, 'La Légende d'Hénoch dans les apocryphes et dans la Bible: origine et signification', *RSR* 46 (1958), pp. 5–26, 181–210; R. Borger, *JNES* 33 (1974), pp. 183–196. Grelot, 'Légende', p. 195, concludes that the Babylonian exile was the *Sitz im Leben* of the origin of the Enoch legend, whence a continuous tradition reached the Hasidim of the Maccabean age. It is not always easy to distinguish Canaanite and Babylonian sources: cf. Grelot, 'Légende', pp. 24–26; *RB* 65 (1958), p. 68; and n. 15 above.

Enoch.[43] The true astronomy which Enoch learns from the archangel Uriel is not known to the pagan astrologers who take the stars to be gods (80:7) and distort the calendar (82:4f.). The true wisdom which Enoch teaches is inseparably connected with the worship of the true God. So the scientific curiosity of the Enoch circle retains a genuinely Jewish religious core.

Von Rad's derivation of apocalyptic from wisdom relied heavily on the evidence of *1 Enoch*, but he was mistaken to generalize from this evidence. Only in the Enoch tradition was encyclopedic wisdom (as distinct from the mantic wisdom of the Daniel tradition) the context for the development of apocalyptic. Von Rad explained this development simply from the wise men's thirst for knowledge, which led them to embrace eschatology and the divine ordering of history within the sphere of their wisdom. There may be some truth in this, but the increasing dominance of eschatology in the Enoch tradition demands a more specific explanation. Perhaps the most promising is that the Enoch tradition shows from the start a preoccupation with *theodicy,* with the origin and judgment of sin. The myth of the Watchers, the fallen angels who corrupted the antediluvian world, is a myth of the origin of evil. Though the Watchers were imprisoned and the antediluvian world annihilated in the flood, the spirits of their offspring the giants became the evil spirits who continue to corrupt the world until the last judgment (15:8–16:1). Already in the earliest section of the *Book of Watchers* (6–19), eschatology emerges in this context: the judgment of the antediluvian world prefigures the final judgment[44] when the wickedness of men will receive its ultimate punishment (10:13 = 4Qn^{c}1:5:1 f.) and supernatural evil be entirely eliminated (16:1; 19:1). With the expansion of the *Book of Watchers,* the emphasis on the final judgment increases. Enoch, who in chapters 6–19 was primarily the prophet of God's judgment on the Watchers at the time of the flood, now becomes, naturally enough, the prophet of the last judgment (1–5). Also, for the first time in Jewish literature, a doctrine of rewards and punishments for all men after death is expounded (22 = 4QEn^{c}1:22):[45] this

---

[43] So the Enoch writings do not *identify* Enoch with an antediluvian sage of pagan myth. They present Enoch *in opposition to* the pagan heroes and sages, who are identified rather with the fallen angels and their offspring the giants: cf. Milik, op. cit., pp. 29, 313.

[44] In 10:20, 22 it is clear that the deluge and the final judgment are assimilated; cf. also the description of the deluge as 'the first end' in 93:4 *(Epistle of Enoch).*

[45] On this passage see Milik, op. cit., p. 219. In view of the mention of Cain's descendants (22:7), 'the souls of all the children of men' (22:3) must mean all men, not just all Israelites, as R. H. Charles thought: *The Book of Enoch* (Oxford: Clarendon, 1912), p. 46. So a doctrine of general rewards and punishments after death was already developed in pre-Maccabean apocalyptic tradition. This is a decisive refutation of the thesis of G. W. E. Nickelsburg Jr, *Resurrection, Immortality, and Eternal Life in Intertestamental Judaism* (Harvard Theological Studies 26: Cambridge, MA: Harvard University Press, 1972), who argues that a doctrine of rewards and punishments after death developed at the time of the Antiochan crisis with reference only to the martyrs and persecutors of the

too expresses a concern with the problem of evil, the problem of the suffering of the righteous at the hands of the wicked (22:5–7,12).

So the Enoch tradition included a strong interest in the problem of evil, which was first expressed in the antediluvian legends of chapters 6–13, but also gave rise to increasing preoccupation with eschatology. This was its point of contact with apocalyptic prophecy, which therefore began to provide the content of Enoch's prophecies of the end.[46] Apocalyptic prophecy was also much concerned with theodicy, specifically with the problem of Israel's continued subjection to the Gentile powers, but this specific problem does not (at least explicitly) appear in the Enoch tradition until the *Book of Dreams,* in which the tradition at last related itself to the prophetic concern with Israelite salvation history. The special mark of the Enoch tradition, linked as it was to prehistoric universal history, was its treatment of theodicy as a cosmic problem. This proved a reinforcement of a general tendency in apocalyptic to set the problem of God's dealings with Israel within a context of universal history and cosmic eschatology.

The pre-Maccabean Enoch tradition left a double legacy. On the one hand, much as in the Daniel tradition, the tradition became a vehicle for the interpretation of Old Testament prophecy. In the Hasidic *Book of Dreams* and the (probably later) *Epistle of Enoch,* we have classic expressions of the apocalyptic view of history and eschatology inspired by Old Testament prophetic faith. On the other hand, however, Enoch's journeys in angelic company through the heavens and the realms of the dead, discovering the secrets of the universe, are the first examples of another aspect of later apocalyptic literature. We need to distinguish two types of apocalypse. There are those which reveal the secrets of *history:* the divine plan of history and the coming triumph of God at the end of history. These could be called 'eschatological apocalypses'. But there are also apocalypses which reveal the mysteries of the *cosmos:* the contents of heaven and earth, or the seven heavens, or heaven and hell. These could be called 'cosmological apocalypses'.[47] The Hasidic apocalypses – Daniel, the Enochic *Book of Dreams,* the *Tetament of*

---

time. His discussion of *1 Enoch* 22 assumes a post-Maccabean date (p. 134 n. 15, p. 143), which the 4QEn fragments now render impossible. *1 Enoch* 22 (cf. also 10:14; 27:2–3) is therefore of crucial importance for the origins of Jewish beliefs about the afterlife, as is the fact that the Enoch tradition, unlike other apocalyptic traditions, never expresses belief in bodily resurrection, but rather the doctrine of spiritual immortality which is also found in Jubilees and probably at Qumran. This is a striking instance of the continuing distinct identity of the various apocalyptic traditions.

[46] The apocalyptic passages of the pre-Maccabean parts of *1 Enoch* are especially indebted to Third Isaiah: 5:6 (cf. Is. 65:15); 5:9 (cf. Is. 65: 19–20, 22); 10:17 (cf. Is. 65:20); 10:21 (cf. Is. 66:23; Zech. 14:16); 25:6 (cf. Is. 65:19f.); 27:3 (cf. Is. 66:24); 72:1 (cf. Is. 65:17; 66:22); 81:9 (cf. Is. 57:1).

[47] This distinction, in different terminology, is made by I. Willi-Plein, *VT* 27 (1977), p. 79.

Moses[48] – are eschatological apocalypses. But the cosmological interest did not die out, and was by no means divorced from eschatological apocalyptic, since the secrets of heaven were believed to include the preexisting realities of the eschatological age. Cosmology really came into its own in the late Hellenistic apocalypses of the Christian era, such as *2 Enoch* and *3 Baruch*, in which the eschatological hope has disappeared and apocalyptic is well on the way to the pure cosmology of Gnosticism. As the revelation of cosmic secrets the apocalypse became the typical literary form of Gnosticism.

So we see once more how apocalyptic, from its origins in the Jewish encounter with the Gentile cultures of the diaspora, retained a somewhat ambiguous position between Jewish and Gentile religion. Its continuity with Old Testament prophetic faith cannot be taken for granted. Each apocalyptist had to achieve this continuity by creative reinterpretation of prophecy in apocalyptic forms. His success depended on the vitality of his eschatological hope inspired by the prophets, and when this hope faded apocalyptic easily degenerated into cosmological speculation of a fundamentally pagan character.

Apocalyptic as interpretation of prophecy

The continuity between prophecy and apocalyptic occurred when the apocalyptists assumed the role of interpreters of prophecy. They did not always do this nor always to the same extent, for as we have seen there are other aspects of apocalyptic literature, but this was the dominant aspect of the major tradition of eschatological apocalypses. In this tradition the transcendent eschatology of post-exilic prophecy was taken up and further developed in a conscious process of reinterpreting the prophets for the apocalyptists' own age.

The apocalyptists understood themselves not as prophets but as inspired interpreters of prophecy.[49] The process of reinterpreting prophecy was already a prominent feature of post-exilic prophecy, but the post-exilic prophets were still prophets in their own right. The apocalyptists, however, lived in an age when the prophetic spirit was quenched (1 Macc 4: 46). Their inspiration was not a source of new prophetic revelation, but of interpretation of the already given revelation. There is therefore a decisive difference of self-understanding between prophets and apocalyptists, which implies also a difference of authority. The authority of the apocalyptists' message is only derivative from that of the prophets.

---

[48] For the date of the *Testaments of Moses*, see n. 52 below.
[49] This is argued most recently by Willi-Plein, art. cit. Cf. also D.S. Russell, *The Method and Message of Jewish Apocalyptic* (London: SCM, 1964), ch. 7.

So when Jewish writers with a background in the mantic wisdom of the Daniel tradition or the cosmological wisdom of the Enoch tradition inherited the legacy of post-exilic prophecy, they did so as non-prophetic interpreters of the prophetic tradition which had come to an end. There may course have been other groups without a wisdom or diaspora background who stood in greater *sociological* continuity with the prophetic tradition, maintaining the eschatological hope of the disciples of Second Isaiah and influencing the Enoch and Daniel traditions. The strong influence of Isaiah 49–66 on the apocalyptic of the *Book of Watchers*[50] and Daniel[51] is suggestive in this respect. To such a group we might attribute the eventual compilation of the book of Isaiah. But even in such a tradition a *theological* discontinuity occurred (perhaps gradually) when consciousness of independent prophetic vocation disappeared.

The puzzling apocalyptic device of pseudonymity is at least partly connected with this apocalyptic role of interpreting prophecy. The *Testament of Moses*, which may well be a Hasidic work contemporary with Daniel,[52] is the least problematic example: as an interpretation of Deuteronomy 31–34 it puts its interpretation of Moses' prophecies into Moses' mouth. Similarly Daniel 7–12 has been attributed to Daniel because its fundamental idea is the scheme of the four empires followed by the eschatological kingdom, which derives from Daniel's prediction in chapter 2. Of course the apocalyptist does not interpret only the prophecies of his pseudonym, but the pseudonym indicates his primary inspiration.[53] Pseudonymity is therefore a device expressing the apocalyptist's consciousness that the age of prophecy has passed: not in the sense that he fraudulently wishes to pass off his work as belonging to the age of prophecy, but in the sense that he thereby acknowledges his work to be mere interpretation of the revelation given in the prophetic age. Similarly the *vaticinia ex eventu* are not a fraudulent device to give spurious legitimation to the apocalyptist's work; they are his interpretation of the prophecies of the past, rewritten in the light of their fulfilment in order to show how they have been fulfilled and

---

[50] See n. 46 above.

[51] For Daniel's (and general Hasidic) dependence on Third Isaiah, cf. Nickelsburg, op. cit., pp. 19–22.

[52] There are two possible dates for the *Testament of Moses* (also called *Assumption of Moses*): c. 165 BC (with ch. 6 as a later interpolation) or early first century AD. The former is supported by J. Licht, *JJS* 12 (1961), pp. 95–103; Nickelsburg, op. cit., pp. 43–45, and in *Studies on the Testament of Moses*, ed. G. W. E. Nickelsburg (Cambridge, MA: SBL, 1973), pp. 33–37; J. A. Goldstein in ibid., pp. 44–47.

[53] In later apocalypses, such as those attributed to Ezra and Baruch, there is no longer any question of interpreting the pseudonym's prophecies. The authors of *4 Ezra* and *2 Baruch* doubtless chose their pseudonyms because they identified with the historical situation of Ezra and Baruch after the fall of Jerusalem.

what still remains to be fulfilled. In pseudonymity and *vaticinia ex eventu* the apocalyptists adopted a form which was common in pagan oracular literature and made it a vehicle of their self-understanding as interpreters of Israelite prophecy.

II. Theological issues

The problem of theological evaluation

Discussion of the origins of apocalyptic cannot really be isolated from a theological evaluation of apocalyptic. Implicitly or explicitly, much recent discussion has involved the judgment that apocalyptic is a more or less degenerate form of Israelite faith. Von Rad, for example, was clearly led to deny the connection between prophecy and apocalyptic because he believed the apocalyptic understanding of history compared so badly with the prophetic, and even Hanson, despite his strong argument for the continuity of prophecy and apocalyptic, still treats pre-exilic prophecy as the high point of Old Testament theology, from which apocalyptic is a regrettable decline, however much it may be an understandable development in post-exilic circumstances.

Moreover, the general theological outlook of the scholar can determine which new theological developments in the rise of apocalyptic he selects as the really significant ones. An older generation of scholars regarded the development of Jewish belief in life after death as a major landmark in the history of revelation, and so, however unsympathetic they may have been to other aspects of apocalyptic, this feature alone guaranteed the positive importance of apocalyptic. Recent scholarship in this area has paid remarkably little attention to this central apocalyptic belief, so that von Rad barely mentions it, and Hanson can argue that apocalyptic eschatology was in all essentials already developed before the introduction of a doctrine of immortality or resurrection.

Almost all modern attempts either to denigrate or to rehabilitate apocalyptic focus on its attitude to history. So discussion of Wolfhart Pannenberg's evaluation of apocalyptic in his systematic theology has centred on whether he is correct in supposing that apocalyptic gave real significance to universal history as the sphere of God's self-revelation.[54]

To a large extent recent discussion has rightly concentrated on the apocalyptic view of history in relation to eschatology, since this takes us to the heart of the problem. The real issue is whether theology may seek the

---

[54] E.g. H.D. Betz, *JTC* 6 (1969), pp. 192–207; W.R. Murdock, *Int* 21 (1967), pp. 167–187.

ultimate meaning of human life and the ultimate achievement of God's purpose *beyond* the history of this world. For many modern scholars, pre-exilic prophecy is the Old Testament theological norm partly because it did not do this, while apocalyptic is a serious decline from the norm, even a relapse into paganism, because it did. Thus for Hanson the transcendent eschatology of apocalyptic prophecy is 'myth' not merely in the literary sense (which is undeniable) but in a sense akin to Bultmann's. In their literal expectation that Yahweh was going to establish his kingdom by direct personal intervention rather than human agency, and in a way which involved radical transformation of this world beyond the possibilities of ordinary history, the disciples of Second Isaiah were *mistaken*. Such language of divine intervention and cosmic transformation could only be valid as a mythical way of illuminating the possibilities of ordinary history. So when the apocalyptists did not translate it into pragmatic political policies but took it to mean that ordinary history would really be transcended with the arrival of salvation, they were engaged in an illusory flight from the real world of history into the timeless realm of myth.

For the Christian the validity of transcendent eschatology is in the last resort a problem of New Testament theology. While the apocalyptic hope was certainly modified by the historical event of Jesus Christ, the New Testament interprets this event as presupposing and even endorsing a transcendent eschatology of divine intervention, cosmic transformation and the transcendence of death. The final achievement of God's purpose and the ultimate fulfilment of humanity in Christ really do lie beyond the possibilities of this world of sin and suffering and death, in a new creation such as apocalyptic prophecy first began to hope for on the strength of the promise of God. Of course the new creation is the transformation of *this world* – *this* distinguishes Christian eschatology from the cosmological dualism of Gnosticism – but it transcends the possibilities of ordinary history. So it seems that a serious commitment to the New Testament revelation requires us to see apocalyptic eschatology as essentially a theological advance in which God's promises through the prophets were stirring his people to hope for a greater salvation than their forefathers had guessed. This must be the broad context for our evaluation of apocalyptic.

It still remains, however, a serious question whether the apocalyptists in fact abandoned the prophetic faith in God's action *within* history, and the prophetic demand for man's free and responsible action in history. Have they in fact *substituted* transcendent eschatology for history, so that history itself is emptied of meaning, as a sphere in which God cannot act salvifically and man can only wait for the End? To answer this we must look more closely at the apocalyptic attitude to history in the context of the post-exilic experience of history to which it was a response.

The negative view of history

The apocalyptic attitude to history is commonly characterized by a series of derogatory terms: radically dualistic, pessimistic, deterministic. The apocalyptists are said to work with an absolute contrast between this age and the age to come. This age is irremediably evil, under the domination of the powers of evil, and therefore all hope is placed on God's coming intervention at the end, when he will annihilate the present evil age and inaugurate the eternal future age. In the history of this age God does not act salvifically; he has given up his people to suffering and evil, and reserved the blessings of life in his kingdom wholly for the age to come. So the apocalyptists were indifferent to the real business of living in this world, and indulged their fantasy in mere escapist speculation about a transcendent world to come. It is true that they engage in elaborate schematizations of history and emphasize God's predetermination of history, but this is purely to show that God is bringing history to an end, while their extreme determinism again has the effect of leaving man with no motive for responsible involvement in the course of history.

This is the wholly negative view of history commonly attributed to the apocalyptists. Like so much that is said about apocalyptic, it suffers from hasty generalization. It would not be difficult to make it appear plausible by quoting a secondhand collection of proof-texts, and especially by preferring later to earlier apocalyptic, and emphasizing texts which are closer to Iranian dualism at the expense of those most influenced by Old Testament prophecy. We have seen that the apocalyptic enterprise, with its potentially ambiguous relationshipi to its non-Jewish environment, was hazardous, and the above sketch has at least the merit of illustrating the hazard. But it does no justice to the apocalyptists to draw the extreme conclusions from a selection of the evidence.

The apocalyptic view of history must be understood from its starting-point in the post-exilic experience of history, in which the returned exiles remained under the domination of the Gentile powers and God's promises, through Second Isaiah and Ezekiel, of glorious restoration, remained unfulfilled. Those who now denigrate apocalyptic rarely face the mounting problem of theodicy which the apocalyptists faced in the extended period of contradiction between the promises of God and the continued subjection and suffering of his people. The apocalyptists refused the spurious solution of a realized eschatology accommodated to Gentile rule and the cult of the second temple: they insisted on believing that the prophecies meant what they said, and undertook the role of Third Isaiah's watchmen, who are to 'put the Lord in remembrance, take no rest, and give him no rest until he establishes Jerusalem' (Is. 62:6f., RSV).

So the apocalyptists did not begin with a dogma about the nature of history: that God cannot act in the history of this world. They began with an empirical observation of God's relative absence from history *since the fall of Jerusalem*. It did not appear to them that he had been active on behalf of his people during this period. Consequently the common apocalyptic view, which goes back to Third Isaiah,[55] was that the exile had never really ended.[56] Daniel 9 therefore multiplies Jeremiah's seventy years of exile into seventy weeks of years to cover the whole period since 586. It was of the history of this period that the apocalyptists took a negative view. Daniel's four world empires are not a scheme embracing all history, but specifically history since Nebuchadnezzar and the exile. The Enochic *Book of Dreams* contains an allegorical account of the whole history of the world since creation (*1 Enoch* 85–90), but again the negative view characterizes only the period since the end of the monarchy. In this period (89:59–90:17) God is represented as no longer ruling Israel directly but as delegating his rule to seventy 'shepherds', angelic beings who rule Israel successively during the period from the fall of Jerusalem to the end. The number seventy indicates that the author is reinterpreting the seventy years of exile of Jeremiah's prophecy. God in the vision commands the shepherds to punish the apostates of Israel by means of the pagan nations which oppress Israel during the whole of the post-exilic period, but in fact they exceed their commission and allow the righteous also to be oppressed and killed. God is represented as repeatedly and deliberately refusing to intervene in this situation. Evidently this is a theologically somewhat crude attempt to explain what the author felt to be God's absence from the history of his people since the exile. Later the idea of angelic delegates developed into the idea of Israel's being under the dominion of Satan during this period. It was the 'age of wrath' (CD 1:5) in which Satan was 'unleashed against Israel' (CD 4:12).

This view of post-exilic history came to a head in the crisis of Jewish faith under Antiochus Epiphanes. This was the climax of the age of wrath, 'a time of trouble, such as never has been' (Dan. 12:1; cf. *Testament of Moses* 8:1). The Hasidic movement, which produced the apocalypses of this period, was therefore a movement of repentance and suffering intercession,[57] seeking the promised divine intervention to deliver the faithful. This was not a retreat from history but precisely an expectation that God would vindicate his people and his justice on the stage of history, though in such a way as to transcend ordinary historical possibility.

---

[55] C. Westermann, *Isaiah 40–66* (London: SCM, 1969), pp. 348–349.

[56] M. A. Knibb, *HJ* 17 (1976), pp. 253–272.

[57] Hengel, op. cit., pp. 179–180; cf. Dan. 9; 11:33, 12:3; *1 Enoch* 83 f.; *Testament of Moses* 9; 12:6.

The apocalyptists faced not only the absence of God's saving activity from history since the exile, but also the silence of God in the period since the cessation of prophecy. 'There is no longer any prophet, and there is none among us who knows how long' (Ps. 74:9). Behind apocalyptic lurks a fear that God had simply abandoned his people, and against that fear apocalyptic is a tremendous reassertion of the prophetic faith. In apocalyptic God's silence was broken by the renewal of his past promises in their relevance to the present. God had not abandoned his people; his promised salvation was coming. Sometimes, perhaps, the apocalyptists broke God's silence with speculations of their own, forced too much contemporary relevance out of the prophecies, answered too precisely the unanswerable 'how long?'[58] But their work ensured the survival of hope.

It is true that the act of divine deliverance for which the apocalyptists looked far transcended the great events of the salvation-history of the past. So the image of a new exodus is less common in apocalyptic than the image of a new creation. In the Enoch literature the dominant type of the end is the deluge, in which a whole universe was destroyed.[59] This universalization of eschatology resulted in part from the historical involvement of post-exilic Israel in the destiny of the world empires, and in part from the pressure of a universal theodicy which looked for the triumph of God over every form of evil: we saw how this developed in the Enochic *Book of Watchers*. The apocalyptists dared to believe that even death would be conquered. So they expected an act of God within the temporal future which would so far transcend his acts in past history that they could only call it new creation.

This is the expectation which gives rise to the temporal dualism of apocalyptic: its distinction between this age and the age to come which follows the new creation. The terminology of the two ages does not emerge in apocalyptic until a late stage, becoming popular only in the first century AD, as the New Testament evidences.[60] This is significant because it shows that apocalyptic did not begin from a dualistic dogma, but from an experience of history. For this reason the contrast between the two ages is never absolute. There is no denial that God has been active in the past history of Israel, and this can even be emphasized, as in the Enochic *Book of Dreams*. His coming eschatological intervention transcends, but is not wholly different in kind

---

[58] In fact the apocalyptists were less addicted to setting dates for the end than is often thought: L. Hartman, *NTS* 22 (1975–6), pp. 1–14.

[59] *1 Enoch* 83 makes the flood a cosmic catastrophe; cf. n. 44 above.

[60] In *1 Enoch* the terminology of the two ages appears only in the *Similitudes*, now almost universally admitted to be no earlier than the first century AD. The classic statement of the doctrine of the two ages, from the end of the first century AD, is 4 Ezra 7:50: 'The Most High has made not one age but two.' For possible rabbinic examples from the first century BC, see M. Delcor, *Le Testament d'Abraham* (Leiden: Brill, 1973), pp. 41–42.

from his past acts.[61] Even in late apocalyptic where the dualism is sharpened, this world remains God's world. It is not totally given over to the powers of evil. So the temporal dualism of apocalyptic is not cosmological dualism.

Apocalyptic eschatology does not therefore arise from an abandonment of the prophetic faith that God acts in history. It would be better to say that the apocalyptists held on to this in the face of the doubt which the universal experience of history provokes. Because they believed he had acted in the past they hoped for his action in the future. But they saw the world in terms which demanded the hope of total transformation as the only appropriate expression of faith in a God who rules history.

In a sense, then, the prophetic faith could only survive the post-exilic experience by giving birth to eschatological faith. We may be grateful for that. Nevertheless, there was surely a danger. The apocalyptists might be so intent on eschatology that they could forget that God does act in history before the end .They might despair of history altogether, and the experience of God's absence from their own history might become the dogma of his absence from all history.

So the Hasidic apocalyptists have often been contrasted with their contemporaries the Maccabees. The former are said to have deduced from their eschatology a quietist attitude of waiting for divine intervention, so that they held aloof from the Maccabean revolt and were unable to see the hand of God in the Maccabean victories. We can see how this might have happened, but it is not really clear that it did. It is true that the book of Daniel refers to the Maccabees only as 'a little help' for the martyred Hasidim (11:34), but this need not be as disparaging a reference as is often thought. More probably it indicates that Daniel was written when the Maccabean resistance had only just begun. The Enochic *Book of Dreams,* written a year or so later, regards the Maccabean victories as the beginning of God's eschatological victory and Judas Maccabaeus as a practically messianic agent of God's eschatological intervention (*1 Enoch* 90:8–18). The truth would seem to be that the apocalyptic hope mobilized support for the Maccabees. Of course the Maccabean revolt did not turn out actually to be the messianic war, though it was a notable deliverance, but it does not follow that the apocalyptists must have concluded that their expectations of it were entirely misplaced. The fact that the Hasidic apocalypses were preserved without modification, and Daniel was even canonized, suggests otherwise. An historical event like the Maccabean deliverance could be regarded as a provisional realization of God's promises, an act of God within history

---

[61] A typological view of history is still quite clear in *2 Baruch,* a late first-century AD work which reflects growing dualism. *2 Baruch* 63 tells of the deliverance of Jerusalem from Sennacherib in terms which prefigure the end.

which anticipated and kept alive the hope of the greater deliverance still to come. Transcendent eschatology need not empty history of divine action; it can on the contrary facilitate the recognition and interpretation of God's action in history.

Again I do not wish to say that this was always the case. In this as in other respects the apocalyptists were walking a theological tightrope, and there was no guarantee that they would keep their balance, other than their study of Old Testament prophecy. It seems that in the end they did not. The overwhelming disappointment of Jewish apocalyptic hopes in the period AD 70–140 proved too great for the healthy survival of the apocalyptic hope. The great apocalypses of that period – the *Apocalypse of Abraham, 2 Baruch,* and *4 Ezra* – are the last great eschatological apocalypses of Judaism. In *4 Ezra* in particular we can see the strain under which the apocalyptic theodicy was labouring. There is a deepening pessimism, an almost totally negative evaluation of the whole history of this age from Adam to the end, a stark dualism of the two ages. This apocalyptist does not surrender his eschatological faith, but we can see how short a step it now was to cosmological dualism and outright Gnosticism.

Apocalyptic eschatology at its best spoke to a contemporary need. It was not identical with the faith of the pre-exilic prophets, but nor was the experience of history in which it belonged. Perhaps it is true that transcendent eschatology was gained at the cost of a certain loss of awareness of the significance of present history. This loss was recovered in the New Testament revelation, but it is worth noticing that it was recovered in a way which, so far from repudiating the apocalyptic development, took it for granted. The significance of present history was guaranteed for the New Testament writers by their belief that in the death and resurrection of Jesus God had *already* acted in an *eschatological* way, the new age had invaded the old, the new creation was under way, and the interim period of the overlap of the ages was filled with the eschatological mission of the church. So it is true that the apocalyptic tendency to a negative evaluation of history is not to be found in New Testament thought, but this is not because the New Testament church reverted to a pre-apocalyptic kind of salvation history.[62] It is because the apocalyptic expectation had entered a phase of decisive fulfilment.

Apocalyptic determinism

We have still to answer the charge of determinism against the apocalyptic view of history. Von Rad made this a major reason for denying apocalyptic

---

[62] *Contra* W. G. Rollins, *NTS* 17 (1970–71), pp. 454–476.

an origin in prophecy.[63] He correctly stresses the apocalyptic doctrine that God has determined the whole course of the world's history from the beginning: 'All things which should be in this world, he foresaw and lo! it is brought forth' (*Testament of Moses* 12:5). This is the presupposition of the comprehensive reviews of future history and of the conviction that the end can come only at the time which God has appointed (Dan. 11:27, 29, 35 f.). It is the secrets of the divine plan, written on the heavenly tablets of destiny, which the apocalyptist is privileged to know: 'what is inscribed in the book of truth' (Dan. 10:21); 'the heavenly tablets... the book of all the deeds of mankind, and of all the children of flesh that shall be upon the earth to the remotest generations' (*1 Enoch* 81:2). Von Rad correctly points out that this differs from the prophetic conception, in which Yahweh makes continually fresh decisions, and issues threats and promises which are conditional on men's sin or repentance (Jer. 18:7–10). Granted that the apocalyptists share the prophetic concern for Yahweh's sovereignty over history, is their deterministic way of expressing it a denial of human freedom and responsibility and so a retreat from human involvement in history?

Determinism certainly belongs more obviously in the context of apocalyptic's continuity with the pagan oracles than it does in the context of its debt to Old Testament prophecy. Pagan divination was generally wedded to a notion of unalterable fate. There are no threats or promises calling for an ethical response, simply the revelation that what will be will be. The forms of oracle which apocalyptic shares with its pagan neighbours, including the *vaticinia ex eventu,* tend to reflect this outlook. Their popularity in the centuries when apocalyptic flourished may partly reflect the fact that the nations of the Near East had lost the power to shape their political future. A genre which made the seer and his audience mere spectators of the course of history corresponded to the mood of the time.

Again we can see the hazardous nature of apocalyptic's relationship to its environment. In its attempt to express in this context the sovereignty of the personal and ethical God of Israel there was the risk of confusing him with fate. The avoidance of this risk depended on the apocalyptists' ability to place alongside a passage like Daniel 11, with its deterministic emphasis, a passage like Daniel's prayer in Daniel 9, with its conviction that God judges his people for their rebellion and responds in mercy to their repentance and to the prayers of intercessors like Daniel. It is no solution to this paradox to excise Daniel's prayer as later interpolation,[64] for the conviction that God would respond to repentance and intercession was at the heart of the Hasidic movement and appears in all their apocalypses. All their

---

[63] *Wisdom in Israel,* pp. 268–277.
[64] As von Rad does: *Old Testament Theology* 2, p. 309 n. 19.

pseudonymous seers were noted intercessors: Daniel (Dan. 9; *Testament of Moses* 4:1–4), Enoch (*1 Enoch* 83 f.), Moses (*Testament of Moses* 11:14, 17; 12:6).[65] Belief in the divine determination of all events clearly exists in tension with the conviction that the covenant God responds to his people's free and responsible action. The former does not result in fatalism because it is only one side of the apocalyptic faith.

Positively, the apocalyptic belief in divine determination of history functioned to support eschatological faith in the face of the negative experience of history. In an age when it was tempting to believe that God had simply abandoned the historical process and with it his promises to his people, the need was for a strong assertion of his sovereignty. This functions, first, to relativize the power of the pagan empires in stressing that it is God 'who removes kings and sets up kings' (Dan. 2:21). So his purpose of giving the kingdom to his own people is assured of success at its appointed time. Secondly, the apocalyptic belief emphasizes that in the last resort the promise of eschatological salvation is unconditional, as it was also for the prophets. For their sins, Moses predicts, Israel 'will be punished by the nations with many torments. Yet it is not possible that he should wholly destroy and forsake them. For God has gone forth, who foresaw all things from the beginning, and his covenant is established by the oath' (*Testament of Moses* 12:11–13). Similarly Second Isaiah had met the despair of the exiles with the message of Yahweh's sovereignty over the nations and his irrevocable purpose of salvation for his people.

So the determinism of apocalyptic must be judged not as an abstract philosophy, but by its function within its context, which is precisely to counter fatalistic despair, to lay open to men the eschatological future, and call men to appropriate action. In terms of that function the gulf between the prophetic and apocalyptic concepts of history is by no means so unbridgeable as von Rad assumes.[66]

Apocalyptic and the canon

We have defended the apocalyptists as interpreters of prophecy for their own generation. A literature as varied as the apocalyptic literature must be evaluated with discrimination rather than generalization, and we have recognized the theological hazards which the apocalyptists did not always avoid. But they lived in an age whose dominant mood encouraged just such a flight from historical reality as eventually issued in Gnosticism. So if their hold on the full reality of Old Testament salvation history seems sometimes

---

[65] On the significance of this theme in *Testament of Moses*, see A.B. Kolenkow in *Studies on the Testament of Moses*, pp. 72–74.

[66] *Wisdom in Israel*, p. 270.

precarious we should not be surprised. It is more surprising that they kept hold of it as well as they did. They faced the problem of believing in the God of the prophets against the evidence of history. Their transcendent eschatology was both a solution, in that the problem of history demands a solution which transcends history, and an aggravation of the problem, as apocalyptic hopes remained unfulfilled. But with New Testament hindsight, we can see that this was their theological role between the Testaments: to keep Jewish faith wide open to the future in hope.

The apocalyptists occupy an essentially intertestamental position. They interpret the prophets to an age when prophecy has ceased but fulfilment is still awaited. They understand their inspiration and their authority to be of a secondary, derivative kind. Their transcendent eschatology, which is apocalyptic's theological centre, is already developed in post-exilic prophecy,[67] and the apocalyptists' role is to intensify it and enable their own generation to live by it. It was by means of apocalyptic that the Old Testament retained its eschatological orientation through the intertestamental age. In this sense apocalyptic is the bridge between the Testaments, and it corresponds to the character of apocalyptic that it is represented, but not extensively represented, in the Old Testament canon.

---

[67] Probably even resurrection: Is. 26:19. But the development of this doctrine remains a very significant development in the intertestamental period.

5. The Delay of the Parousia*

Early Christianity was both continuous and discontinuous with first-century Judaism. Its theology shared many features of contemporary Jewish thought, though these were given a distinctively Christian character by their relationship to Christianity's unique faith in Jesus Christ. As in the case of many other issues, an adequate account of the understanding of the delay of the *parousia* in early Christianity must reflect both the continuity and the discontinuity with Judaism.

In some respects the problem[1] of the delay of the *parousia* was the same problem of eschatological delay which had long confronted Jewish apocalyptic eschatology; in other respects it was a new and distinctively Christian problem, in that the End was now expected to take the form of the *parousia* of Jesus Christ in whose death and resurrection God had already acted eschatologically. Our subject therefore needs to be approached from two angles: from its background in Jewish apocalyptic and in terms of its distinctively Christian characteristics. Within the limits of this lecture, I can attempt only one of these approaches, and I have chosen the former, both because almost all previous study has entirely neglected this approach,[2] treating the delay of the *parousia* as a uniquely Christian issue,[3] and also because it is only when we relate the Christian understanding of the delay

---

* The Tyndale Biblical Theology Lecture 1979. First publication: *Tyndale Bulletin* 31 (1980) 3–36.

[1] By using the word 'problem' I do not mean to endorse the hypothesis (now generally abandoned) of a *crisis* of delay in early Christianity. I mean simply that the delay raised questions which had to be answered.

[2] The only significant exception is the important work of A. Strobel, *Untersuchungen zum eschatologischen Verzögerungsproblem auf Grund der spätjüdisch-urchristlichen Geschichte von Habakuk 2.2ff.* (Supplements to Novum Testamentum 2. Leiden: E. J. Brill, 1961).

[3] E. g. O. Cullmann, *Christ and Time* (ET, London: SCM, 1951) 86–90; *Salvation in History* (ET, London: SCM, 1967) 236–47; H. Conzelmann, *An Outline of the Theology of the New Testament* (ET, London: SCM, 1969) 307–17. It is remarkable that the school of 'Consistent Eschatology', for which the interpretation of Jesus and the early church by reference to Jewish apocalyptic was a methodological principle and which postulated a major crisis of delay in early Christianity, seems not to have asked how Jewish apocalyptic coped with the problem of delay: cf. M. Werner, *The Formation of Christian Dogma* (ET, London: A. & C. Black, 1957).

to its Jewish apocalyptic background that we shall be able to appreciate its distinctively Christian features in their true significance. So if this lecture on biblical theology seems to linger rather long over Jewish extracanonical literature, I hope you will find that this procedure is justified by its contribution to an understanding of the New Testament.

I. Eschatological delay in Jewish apocalyptic

The problem of eschatological delay was familiar to Jewish apocalyptic from its earliest beginnings. It could even be said to be one of the most important ingredients in the mixture of influences and circumstances which produced the apocalyptic movement. In the face of the delay in the fulfilment of the eschatological promises of the prophets, the apocalyptic visionaries were those who believed most fervently that the promises remained valid and relevant. Despite appearances, God had not forgotten his people. His eschatological salvation, so long awaited, was coming, and now at last it was very close at hand. In almost all the apocalypses there is no mistaking both a consciousness, to some degree, of the problem of delay, in that the prophecies had so long remained unfulfilled, and also the conviction of their imminent fulfilment. It goes only a little beyond the evidence to say that in every generation between the mid-second century BC and the mid-second century AD Jewish apocalyptists encouraged their readers to hope for the eschatological redemption in the very near future. At the same time there is very little evidence to suggest that during that long period the continued disappointment of that expectation discredited the apocalyptic hope or even diminished the sense of iminence in later generations. The apocalypses of the past were preserved and treasured; and passages whose imminent expectation had clearly not been fulfilled were nevertheless copied and by no means always updated. Each apocalyptist knew that his predecessors had held the time of the End to be at hand, but this knowledge seems to have encouraged rather than discouraged his own sense of eschatological imminence. Clearly the problem of delay was an inescapable problem at the heart of apocalyptic eschatology, but the tension it undoubtedly produced was not a destructive tension. It was a tension which the apocalyptic faith somehow embraced within itself. The problem was felt but it did not lead to doubt.

The question we need to ask, then, is: how did Jewish apocalyptic manage to cope with the problem of delay? The key to this question – and the theme of much of this lecture – is that alongside the theological factors which promoted the imminent expectation there were also theological factors accounting for the fact of delay. These two contrary sets of factors were held in tension in apocalyptic. They were not harmonized to produce a kind of compromise: expectation of the End in the fairly near future but not just yet. The factors promoting imminence and the factors accounting for delay (or even, as we shall see, promoting an expectation of delay) are held in paradoxical tension, with the result that the imminent expectation can be maintained in all its urgency in spite of the continuing delay.

Strobel has shown that many of the apocalyptic references to the delay allude to the text Habakkuk 2:3, which seems to have been the *locus classicus* for reflecting on the problem of delay.[4] 'The vision is yet for the appointed time. It hastens to the end and will not lie. If it tarries, wait for it, for it will surely come and will not be late.' This text and the history of its interpretation contain the basic apocalyptic 'explanation' of the delay, insofar as it may be called an explanation. It appeals to the omnipotent sovereignty of God, who has determined the time of the End. Even though it is longer in coming than the prophecies seem to have suggested, this apparent delay belongs to the purpose of God. It will not be 'late' according to the timescale which God has determined.

Now it cannot be said that this explanation explains very much. The delay remains incomprehensible to men, but is attributed to the inscrutable wisdom of God. But it is important to notice that the effectiveness of this explanation derived not so much from its power as an intellectual explanation, but rather from its quality as an affirmation of faith in God which calls for an appropriate response. Acknowledging the sovereignty of God and the truth of his promises, the apocalyptic believer is called therefore to wait patiently, persevering in obedience to God's commandments in the meantime. As the Qumram commentary on Habakkuk 2:3 puts it: 'Interpreted, this concerns the men of truth who keep the Law, whose hands shall not slacken in the service of the truth when the final age is prolonged. For all the ages of God reach their appointed end as he determines for them in the mysteries of his wisdom.'[5] Thus the apocalyptic 'solution' to the problem of delay was practical as much as theological. The believer's impatient prayer that God should no longer delay was balanced by the attitude of patient waiting while, in his sovereignty, God did delay. And these two attitudes remained in tension: the apocalyptists maintained both. On the one hand the impatient prayer was met by the assurance that God would bring salvation at the appointed time and therefore with an exhortation to patience; on the other hand the believer's patient waiting was encouraged and supported by the assurance that there would be only a short time to wait and therefore

---

[4] Strobel, *op. cit.*, chs. 1 and 2.
[5] 1QpHab 7:10–12; trans. in G. Vermes, *The Dead Sea Scrolls in English* (Harmondsworth: Penguin, 1968) 239.

by an exhortation to hope. In this way the tension of imminence and delay was maintained and contained within the apocalyptist's faith.

Essentially this is why the problem of delay did not discredit or destroy the apocalyptic hope. From the beginning apocalyptic faith incorporated the problem of delay. It was a real problem creating a real tension: there is genuine anguish in the apocalyptists' prayers 'Do not delay!' (Dn. 9:19; 2 Baruch 21:25) and 'How long?' (Dn. 12:6; 2 Baruch 21:19). But the tension was held within a structure of religious response which was adequate to contain it.

I have admitted that the basic apocalyptic response to the problem of delay – the appeal to the sovereignty of God – provided little in the way of explanation. Later we shall see how some apocalyptists, especially in the later period, filled out this explanation with some attempts at more positive understanding of the meaning of the delay. For much of the period when apocalyptic flourished, however, it would seem that the problem of delay was contained mainly by the appeal to the sovereignty of God to balance the urgency of the imminent expectation. It is necessary to ask whether this was theologically legitimate. In other words, it may be that the fact of delay *ought* to have discredited the apocalyptic hopes, if only it had been squarely faced in the cool light of reason. What I have called the structure of religious response by which apocalyptic contained the problem may have been no better than a psychological means of maintaining false expectations. History could supply many examples of unfulfilled prophecies which managed to maintain their credibility long after they deserved to do so, often because believers who have staked their lives on such expectations are not easily disillusioned. Is there any reason to put the apocalyptists in a different category?

I believe there is a good reason at least to take the apocalyptic faith very seriously indeed. The problem of delay in apocalyptic is no ordinary problem of unfulfilled prophecy. The problem of delay is the apocalyptic version of the problem of evil. The apocalyptists were vitally concerned with the problems of theodicy, with the demonstration of God's righteousness in the face the unrighteousness of his world. They explored various possibilities as to the origins of evil and the apportioning of responsibility for evil,[6] but of primary and indispensable significance for the apocalyptic approach to the problem of evil was the expectation of the End, when all wrongs would be righted, all evil eliminated, and God's righteousness therefore vindicated. The great merit of the apocalyptic approach to theodicy was that it refused to justify the present condition of the world by means of an abstract exon-

---

[6] Cf. the survey in A. L. Thompson, *Responsibility for Evil in the Theodicy of IV Ezra* (SBL Dissertations Series 29. Missoula, Montana: Scholars Press, 1977) ch. 1.

eration of God from responsibility for the evils of the present. Only the overcoming of present evil by eschatological righteousness could vindicate God as righteous, and only the hope of such a future triumph of righteousness could make the evils of the present bearable.

Of course, this was no armchair theodicy, but was produced by concrete situations of injustice and oppression in which the apocalyptists lived and suffered: the continued oppression of Israel by the Gentiles, and / or the sufferings of the righteous remnant of Israel with whom the apocalyptists often identified themselves. It is not always easy for us to appreciate the apocalyptists' concern for righteousness in these situations: the desire for Israel's vindication and her enemies' condemnation can seem to us like mere narrow nationalism, and the apocalyptists' conviction of belonging to the righteous remnant which is unjusty suffering while sinners prosper can seem to us like arrogant self-righteousness. Undoubtedly those defects sometimes mar the apocalypses, but it is important to realize that the genuinely ethical character of the apocalyptic hope is far more dominant. What is at stake in the sufferings of God's people is the righteousness of God, which, as often in the Old Testament, means at the same time justice *for* the oppressed and *against* the oppressor. It is true that the apocalyptists often fail to see that the problem of evil extends to the sinfulness of the righteous themselves, but they have an agonizingly clear grasp of the problem of innocent suffering. When the problem of theodicy is posed in that form I think we still have much to learn from them. Moreover, the special characteristic of the apocalyptists' grasp of the problem is that, out of their own situation, they were able to see the universal dimensions of the problem of evil, the universal dominance of evil in 'this present evil age', as they came to call the present. This universal challenge to the righteousness of God demanded a universal righting of wrongs, an elimination of evil on a universal, even cosmic, scale.

I have dwelt on this aspect of apocalyptic because I hope it will enable us to see the real meaning of the problem of eschatological delay. The *imminent* expectation expresses the extremity of the situation, the intensity of the apocalyptists' perception of the problem of evil, in its sheer contradiction of the righteousness of God. Surely God can no longer tolerate it. Yet he does: there is the problem of *delay*. What is greatly to the credit of the apocalyptists is that in this dilemma they abandoned neither the righteousness nor the sovereignty of God, which make up the theistic form of the problem of evil. Their belief in the powers of evil was not dualistic: God remained in ultimate control. And so in the face of the delay, they continued to hold that God is righteous – his eschatological righteousness *is* coming – and that he remains sovereign – the delay belongs to his purpose and the End will come at the time he has appointed. This is the tension of imminence and delay, the tension experienced by the theistic believer who, in a world of injustice, cannot give up his longing for righteousness. Thus we do not, I think, have the right to ask the apocalyptist to *explain* the delay in any complete sense, because the problem of evil is not susceptible to complete theoretical explanation. The tension which apocalyptic faith contained within itself is the tension which all forms of theism must somehow contain if they take the problem of evil seriously. It is a tension which cannot be resolved by explanation but only by the event of the final victory of God's righteousness.

I conclude, therefore, that the apocalyptists rightly maintained the tension of imminence and delay, and that in some degree that tension must remain a feature of Christian theology. The promise of God's eschatological righteousness presses in upon the present, contradicting the evils of the present, arousing our hopes, motivating us to live towards it. Because the righteousness of God himself is at stake in this expectation it demands immediate fulfilment. That the fulfilment is delayed will always contain a hard core of incomprehensibility: the greatest saints have protested to God against his toleration of evil, and have done so in faith, because of their conviction of his righteousness. But must the delay remain *completely* incomprehensible? The difficulty of the mere appeal to God's sovereignty is that it is in danger of evacuating the present in which we live of all meaning. The present becomes the incomprehensible time in which we can only wait, and it must be admitted that the apocalyptists do sometimes approach this bleakly negative view of the present.

This danger, however, was partially met in the Jewish apocalyptic tradition itself in attempts to find some positive meaning in the delay. Such attempts become particularly evident in the later period of Jewish apocalyptic, especially after the fall of Jerusalem in AD 70, and they have parallels in the Christian literature of the same period. I think this fact must correspond to a certain intensification of the problem of delay in late first-century Judaism. This was not due to the mere continuing lapse of time; it is a mistake to suppose the problem of delay necessarily increases the longer the delay. The problem is itensified not by the mere lapse of time, but by the focusing of expectation on specific dates or events which fail to provide the expected fulfilment. In the case of Jewish apocalyptic, the Jewish wars of AD 66–70 and 132–135 were disappointments of the most extreme kind, for so far from being the onset of eschatological salvation, they proved to be unprecedented contradictions of all the apocalyptists had hoped for. Consequently the apocalyptic writers of the late first century are engaged in a fresh and agonizing exploration of the issues of eschatological theodicy. The imminent expectation seems if anything to be heightened, but it seems to require that on the other hand some meaning be found in the interval of delay.

So we will turn to four specific examples of the problem of delay in the late first century, two Jewish examples and then for comparison two Christian examples which are relatively close to the Jewish discussion. In all of them we shall be looking especially for attempts to understand the delay.

II. Four examples from the late first century AD

(a) A Rabbinic Debate

There is a well-known rabbinic tradition of a debate about the delay of eschatological redemption[7] between R. Eliezer b. Hyrcanus and R. Joshua b. Hananiah.[8] If authentic, this debate will date from the late first century AD. Unfortunately its authenticity cannot be assumed as uncritically as it has generally been.[9] Neusner, in his classification of the traditions of R. Eliezer according to the reliability of the attestation, places this tradition in his least well attested category, 'The Poor Traditions':[10] this means not only that the attestation of the tradition is late, but also that its content is largely unrelated to earlier traditions. Traditions in this category are not thereby shown to be inauthentic, but their authenticity is very difficult to establish with any degree of certainty. There are, however, some things to be said in favour of our tradition: (1) It belongs to a group of traditions which together form a coherent set of opinions on issues which were certainly matters of concern to the rabbis in the period immediately after AD 70. In other words, they are historically appropriate to Eliezer's historical situation, and they are mutually consistent.[11] (2) Neusner also concludes that this group of traditions represent in substance what we should have expected Eliezer to have thought about these topics, on the basis of the best attested sayings of Eliezer.[12] (3) Furthermore, there is a passage in the *Apocalypse of Ezra* (c. AD 100) which proves that the contrasting views of R. Eliezer and R. Joshua, as represented in our tradition, were held and debated during their lifetimes: in *4 Ezra* 4:38–42, Ezra puts forward as a suggestion the attitude to the problem of eschatological delay which our tradition attributes to R. Eliezer, while the angel's reply maintains the position attributed to R. Joshua. Thus, even if we cannot be quite sure that R. Eliezer and R. Joshua themselves held

---

[7] For the sake of simplicity, in this and the following section I am ignoring the problems of the distinction between expectation of the messianic kingdom and expectation of the age to come. They do not greatly affect our topic.

[8] *Midrash Tanhuma Behuqotai* 5; *y Taʿan.* 1:1: *b Sanh.* 97 b–98 a. The text's are given in translation in J. Neusner, *Eliezer ben Hyrcanus* (Leiden: E. J. Brill, 1973) I 477–79.

[9] E. g. Strobel, *op. cit.* 23–26.

[10] Neusner, *op. cit.* II 235, no. 57.

[11] *Ibid.* II 417–21.

[12] *Ibid.* II 421.

the opinions attributed to them, we can at least be sure that those opinions were debated in the late first century.

In the briefest version of the debate the issue is succinctly stated as follows:

> R. Eliezer says, 'If Israel repents, they will be redeemed'.
> R. Joshua says, 'Whether or not they repent, when the end comes, they will forthwith be redeemed, as it is said, "I the Lord in its time will hasten it" (Is. 60:22).'[13]

R. Joshua maintains the traditional apocalyptic appeal to the sovereignty of God, who has determined the time of the End. When the appointed time arrives, the eschatological redemption will come as God's sovereign grace to Israel, in no way dependent on Israel's preparation. R. Eliezer, on the other hand, makes the coming of redemption conditional on Israel's repentance.

The idea of Israel's repentance before the End was not new,[14] but the view that it is a condition for the arrival of redemption is at least rare in the earlier literature,[15] though it subsequently became a common rabbinic view. It seems probable that Eliezer's saying represents a reaction to the disaster of AD 70, when hopes of redemption were dashed and Israel experienced instead a catastrophe which could only be interpreted as divine punishment. The conclusion must be that Israel was unworthy of redemption. Only when Israel repented would redemption come.

Eliezer's position could mean that the divinely appointed date for the End had actually been postponed because of Israel's sins,[16] as some late Rabbis certainly held.[17] Alternatively it could mean that there is no such thing as a fixed date for the End,[18] or, finally, it could mean that Israel's repentance is itself part of God's predetermined plan. This is the view suggested by a longer version of the debate:

> R. Eliezer says, 'If Israel does not repent, they will never be redeemed...'
> R. Joshua said to him, 'If Israel stands and does not repent, do you say they will never be saved?'.

---

[13] *Midrash Tanḥuma Beḥuqutai* 5 (Neusner, *op. cit.* I 479). The use of Is. 60:22 with reference to this issue is well attested for this period: Ecclus. 26:8; *2 Baruch* 20:1 f; 54:1; 83:1; *Ep. of Barnabas* 4:3; cf. Ps-Philo, *Lib. Ant. Bib.* 19:13; 2 Pet. 3:12. Cf. further rabbinic references in Strobel, *op. cit.* 92 n. 6.

[14] Cf. *Testament of Moses* 1:18. It is presupposed in the message of John the Baptist, but his teaching in Mt. 3:7–10 par. Lk. 3:7–9 seems to run counter to any suggestion that Israel's redemption was a necessary condition for the coming of the Kingdom. Similarly Lk. 13:6–9 embodies the idea of delay in order to give time for repentance, but explicitly not *until* repentance.

[15] But *cf. Testament of Dan* 6:4; Acts 13:19–21.

[16] This is how Eliezer is understood by Strobel, *op. cit.* 23–26.

[17] b Sanh. 97 b; *b ʻAbodah Zarah* 9 a.

[18] This is how Eliezer is understood by E. E. Urbach, *The Sages: Their Concepts and Beliefs* (ET, Jerusalem: Magnes Press, 1975) I 669.

R. Eliezer said to him, 'The Holy One, blessed be he, will raise up over them a king as harsh as Haman, and forthwith they will repent and be redeemed'.[19]

In other words redemption cannot be indefinitely postponed by Israel's failure to repent, because God himself will stir Israel to repentance.

The importance of this debate is that R. Eliezer's view is an attempt to understand the delay. The meaning of the delay is not totally hidden in God's mysterious sovereign purpose. It is the time in which God graciously waits for his people to repent and chastises them until they repent.

(b) The Apocalypse of Baruch

The *Apocalypse of Baruch* dates from the late first or early second century AD. The pseudonym Baruch and the historical setting immediately following the fall of Jerusalem in 586 BC are transparent vehicles for the author's own reactions to the tragedy of AD 70.

The note of imminent expectation pervades the book (20: 1 f,6; 23:7; 48:39; 54:17; 82:2; 83:1; *cf.* 48:32), most memorably expressed in the often-quoted lines:

The youth of the world is past,
the strength of creation is already exhausted.
The advent of the times is very close,
yea, they have passed by.
The pitcher is near to the well,
and the ship to the port.
The course of the journey is reaching its destination at the city,
and life approaches its end (85:10).[20]

The events of AD 70 have not dampened but inflamed the expectation of redemption, but it is clear that the delay, while Israel is humiliated and the Gentiles triumph, is an agonizing problem, especially as Baruch sees God's own honour at stake in the fate of his people (5:1; 21:21). The problem of delay is focussed in Baruch's question, 'How long will these things endure for us?' (81:3; *cf.* 21:19), and his prayer that God may 'now, quickly, show thy glory, and do not delay the fulfilment of thy promise' (21:25).

---

[19] *y Ta'an.* 1:1 (Neusner, *op. cit.* I 477). I follow Neusner (I 479, *cf.* II 418) in preferring this version to that in *b Sanh.* 97 b, which attributes the saying about the cruel king like Haman to R. Joshua. (Urbach, *op. cit.* I 669 f., II 996 n. 63, prefers the latter.) Neusner, *op. cit.* II 419 f, also finds evidence in *Pesigta Rabbati* 23:1, that Eliezer did believe in a fixe date at which redemption must come.

[20] Quotations from *2 Baruch* are adapted from the translation by R. H. Charles (in R. H. Charles and W. O. E. Oesterley, *The Apocalypse of Baruch* (London: SPCK, 1917)), with reference to the French translation in P. Bogaert, *Apocalypse de Baruch* (Sources Chrétiennes 144. Paris: Éditions du Cerf., 1969) I 463–528.

Alongside the imminent expectation, Baruch recognizes theological factors which account for the delay. First among these is the traditional appeal to the divine sovereignty. Baruch has a strong sense of the qualitative difference between God and man, the majesty and sovereignty of God over against the dependence and frailty of man (14:8–11; 21:4–10; 48:2–17; 54:1–13). One aspect of this is the eternity of God (21:10; 48:13) contrasted with the transitoriness of man (14:10f, 48:12). Unlike man, who cannot even foresee the outcome of his own brief life, God surveys the whole course of the world and is sovereign over all events, determining their times (48:2f; 54:1; 56:2f). Consequently only God knows in advance the time of the End which he has appointed (21:8; 48:3; 54:1). Baruch's repeated use of the phrase 'in its time' (5:2; 12:4; 13:5; 20:2; 51:7; 54:1; cf. 42:8) stresses that the End will come only at the time which the eternal sovereign God has appointed. This theme therefore provides a certain counterbalance to the urgency of the imminent expectation.

A minor attempt to fill out this appeal to the divine sovereignty over the times is the idea that God has determined a fixed number of people to be born into this world, so that the End cannot come until that number is complete (23:2–5). (A similar idea, of a predetermined number of the *righteous*, is found in *4 Ezra* 4:36.) This scarcely constitutes an *explanation* of the delay: it simply appeals again to the inscrutable divine decree.[21]

Baruch, however, has something more substantial to contribute to the understanding of delay. I observed earlier that the imminent expectation in apocalyptic is connected with the apocalyptic perception of the character of God, in particular his righteousness. It is the contradiction between the righteousness of God and the unrighteousness of present conditions which fires the expectation of God's immediate coming in judgment. It is therefore of the greatest interest that Baruch's understanding of the delay is also related to the character of God, in this case to his longsuffering (patience, forbearance). As Baruch himself is reminded by the angel (59:6), this quality belongs to the central Old Testament revelation of God's character, to Moses on Mount Sinai: 'The Lord, the Lord, a God merciful and gracious, *slow to anger*, and abounding in steadfast love and faithfulness…' (Ex. 34:6): the description of God to which the Old Testament frequently refers (Nu. 14:18; Pss. 86:15; 103:8; Joel 2:13; Jon. 4:2; Wisdom 15:1; cf. CD 2:4). In Baruch's words, Moses was shown 'the restraint of wrath and the abundance of longsuffering' (59:6).[22] God's longsuffering is that quality by which he bears with sinners, holds back his wrath, refrains from intervening in judg-

---

[21] Cf. Ezra's (unanswered) queries in *4 Ezra* 5:43–45: why could not all the predetermined number of men have lived as a single generation?

[22] Baruch refers to the other characteristics of God according to Ex. 34:6 in 77:6 (merciful, gracious, faithful) and 75:5 (merciful, gracious).

ment as soon as the sinner's deeds deserve it, though not indefinitely.[23] As Baruch correctly sees, it is this quality of God which accounts for the whole history of this sinful world: 'the longsuffering of the Most High, which has been throughout all generations, who has been long-suffering towards all who are born, sinners and righteous' (24:2).[24]

Baruch's use of this theme is unlikely to be original; his references to it are too casual (12:4; 21:20f; 24:2; 48:29; 59:6; 85:8). The related and nearly contemporary *Apocalypse of Ezra* also employs the theme of God's patience (3:30; 7:33,74; *cf.* 9:21), and includes it in a formal meditation on the character of God according to Exodus 34:6f (7:132–139).[25] Evidently the apocalyptic tradition had already related its eschatological concerns to the classic features of the character of God, and seen not only God's sovereignty but also his longsuffering in the delay.

The attribution of delay to God's patience does not always enable Baruch to take a positive view of it. In his grief over the fall of Jerusalem and the contrasting prosperity of her enemies, Baruch, like Jeremiah before him (Je. 15:15; *cf.* Jon. 4:2), reproaches God for his patience, for restraining his wrath while his people's enemies triumph (11:3; *cf.* Is. 64:12; *4 Ezra* 3:30). And in his impassioned plea for God to hasten the judgment, Baruch prays:

> How long will those who transgress in this world be polluted with their great wickedness? Command them in mercy, and accomplish what thou saidst thou wouldst bring, that thy might may be known to those who think that thy longsuffering is weakness (21:19f).

It is worth noticing in that passage how God's *mercy* is opposed to his longsuffering. His mercy here means his mercy to the righteous who suffer; the coming of God in judgment is at the same time mercy to the righteous and condemnation to the wicked (82:2).[26] In other words Baruch asks that God in his mercy to the righteous should put an end to his longsuffering towards the wicked. He is aware, then, that his plea that God should no longer delay, while it is founded, as prayer must be, on the character and promises of God, appeals only to one aspect of God's dealings with men *against* another. Baruch knows that if the *imminence* of the judgment is demanded by God's mercy to the righteous (which goes hand in hand with

---

[23] Note Strobel's remark (*op. cit.* 31): 'der für unsere Begriffe anscheinend nur psychologische Begriff der "Landmut" im hebräischen Sprachgebrauch einen ausgesprochen *chronologischen* Bedeutungsgehalt hat' (my italics).

[24] Like Paul (Rom. 2:4), Baruch can also sometimes connect this slightly negative quality of long-suffering with the more positive quality of kindness (48:29; *cf.* 13:12; 82:9).

[25] On this passage, see Thompson, *op. cit.* 202f, 301–3.

[26] Baruch holds the common Jewish view of this period, that God will show mercy to the righteous and strict justice to the wicked; *cf.* E. P. Sanders, *Paul and Palestinian Judaism* (London: SCM, 1977) 421.

his judgment on the wicked), the *delay* in jugdment is also founded on the character of God, on his longsuffering, which restrains his wrath towards the wicked (but therefore also delays his mercy to the righteous).

Baruch's attitude to God's forbearance varies according to the aspect of the fall of Jerusalem which he considers. When he laments the humiliation of Israel at the hands of her godless enemies, God's tolerance of the situation seems incomprehensible to Baruch. When, however, he considers God's patience with *Israel* it becomes a more positive concept (85:8). For Baruch interprets the fall of Jerusalem as God's chastisement of his people for their sins (1:5; 4:1; 13:10; 78:6; 79:2): 'They were chastened then so that they might be forgiven' (13:10). Although the fall of Jerusalem was God's judgment on Israel, it was a judgment which manifested God's patience with them. It was a warning judgment, designed to bring them to repentance, whereas when the final judgment comes there will no longer be any time left for repentance (85:12). In this way the delay gains the positive aspect of a respite, in which God's people, who would perish if the final judgment came sooner, are graciously granted the opportunity of repentance.[27] In the paraenetic sections of the book Baruch urges this lesson on his readers (44:2–15; 46:5 f; 77:2–10; 78:3–7; 83:1–8; 84:1–85:15).

Finally we must notice the initially puzzling statement in which God says: 'Therefore have I now taken away Zion, so that I may hasten to visit the world in its time' (20:2).[28] The meaning of this verse must be that because God wills the repentance of his people before the End, he has stirred them to repentance by destroying Jerusalem. The fall of Jerusalem brings the End nearer, in that it brings about a precondition of the End, the repentance of Israel. The thought is similar to R. Eliezer's saying about the cruel king like Haman. Here it is even clearer than in R. Eliezer's case that there is no contradiction between this thought and the idea, which Baruch stresses, that the End will come at the time God has determined. That God will 'hasten to visit the world in its time' does not mean that he will advance the date of the End, but that, now Jerusalem has fallen, the appointed time of the End is fast approaching. The present time of delay retains in the *Apocalypse of Baruch* a predominantly negative character: Baruch's expressions of the miseries and worthlessness of this life have often been cited as prime examples of apocalyptic pessimism.[29] In the shadow of the tragedy of AD 70 this aspect is hardly surprising. More remarkable, for our purposes, are the traces of a positive theological understanding of the delay in terms of God's longsuffering and his desire for his people's repentance. Here Baruch fills out the

---

[27] Baruch's hints that the delay can also benefit Gentiles are less explicit, but *cf.* 1:4; 41:4; 42:5.

[28] This verse is dependent on Is. 60:22; *cf.* n. 13 above.

[29] 21:13 f; 83:10–21; but *cf.* 52:6: 'Rejoice in the sufferings which you now endure.'

reported sayings of R. Eliezer.[30] The urgency of the imminent expectation is not diminished by this recognition of the positive character of the delay: the two are held in tension.

(c) 2 Peter 3

2 Peter 3 contains the most explicit treatment of the delay of the *parousia* in the New Testament. It is also, as we shall see, the most thoroughly Jewish treatment, reproducing exactly the arguments we have been studying in the Jewish literature. In fact the passage 3:5–13 contains nothing which could not have been written by a non-Christian Jewish writer, except perhaps the use of the simile of the thief, derived from Jesus' parable, in verse 10. It is possible that the author is closely dependent on a Jewish apocalyptic writing in this chapter, just as he depends on the epistle of Jude in chapter 2.[31]

The problem of delay has been raised by false teachers, who so far as we can tell from the letter combined eschatological scepticism with ethical libertinism (ch. 2), apparently supporting the latter by appeal to Paul's teaching on freedom from the Law (2:19; 3:15). Whether, as has often been thought, both these features were connected with a Gnostic or proto-Gnostic form of over-realized eschatology[32] is less certain, since there is no clear hint of this in 2 Peter, but it is certainly a real possibility.[33]

The allegation of the 'scoffers' that the delay of the *parousia* disproves the expectation of the *parousia* is met in verses 8 and 9, with what I take to be two distinct arguments. The first reads: 'But do not ignore this one fact, beloved, that one day before the Lord is as a thousand years, and a thousand

---

[30] Strobel, *op. cit.* 32 f, thinks that Baruch agrees with R. Joshua rather than R. Eliezer, because he holds that R. Eliezer thought the date of the End was postponed on account of Israel's sins, while Baruch held to God's unconditional determination of the End.

[31] D. von Allmen, 'L'apocalyptique juive et le retard de la parousie en II Pierre 3:1–13' *Revue de Théologie et de Philosophie* 16 (1966) 255–74, attempts to identify specific verses as quoted from a Jewish apocalypse but, in view of the way he uses Jude, it is unlikely that the author of 2 Peter would quote without adaptation. It is possible that he is using the apocryphal writing quoted in *1 Clement* 23:3 f and *2 Clement* 11:2 f.

[32] E. g. C. H. Talbert, 'II Peter and the Delay of the Parousia,' *Vigiliae Christianae* 20 (1966) 137–45, who holds that their realized eschatology was the real basis of their denial of the *parousia*: 'it seems that their question about the delay of the parousia, just as their appeal to the stability of the universe, is but an argument used to justify a position held on other grounds' (p. 143). *Cf.* also E. Käsemann, *Essays on New Testament Themes* (ET, London: SCM, 1964) 171.

[33] In parallel passages where the reality of future eschatology is defended against over-realized eschatology, it is the reality of future resurrection which is usually given special attention (1 Cor. 15; *1 Clement* 23–26; *2 Clement* 9–12; '*3 Corinthians*' 3: 24–32), but it is quite possible that the author of 2 Peter deliberately preferred to deal with the question of future judgment because for him the ethical implications of traditional eschatology were paramount and he clearly regarded the eschatology of the 'scoffers' as an excuse for their immoral behaviour (*cf.* also Polycarp, *Philippians* 7).

years as one day.' Precisely what this argument is intended to prove is a matter of debate among the exegetes, who divide into two schools: (1) those who interpret the verse according to parallels in contemporary Jewish and Christian literature, and conclude that it is not intended to meet the problem of delay;[34] (2) those who interpret the verse as an answer to the problem of delay, and conclude that the author has here produced an original argument which has no known precedent or parallel in the literature.

The first school point to the many rabbinic and second-century Christian texts in which an eschatological chronology is based on the formula 'A day of the Lord is a thousand years'. This seems to have been a standard exegetical rule, derived from Psalm 90:4 ('a thousand years in thy sight are but as yesterday when it is past'), but existing as an independent formulation. The procedure is to quote a biblical text in which the word 'day' occurs; then the rule 'A day of the Lord is a thousand years' is cited, with or without a further quotation of Psalm 90:4 to support it; the conclusion is therefore that where the text says 'day' it means, in human terms, a thousand years. The rule was sometimes applied to the creation narrative, in order to yield the notion that the history of the world is to last six thousand years, six 'days' of a thousand years each, followed by a millennial Sabbath: this calculation lies behind the widespread millenarianism of the second century.[35] Or, similarly, the rule could be applied to texts which were thought to mention the day or days of the Messiah (Is. 63:4; Ps. 90:15): in another tradition of debate between R. Eliezer and R. Joshua, R. Eliezer concluded that the messianic kingdom would last a thousand years, but R. Joshua argued that 'days' (plural, Ps. 90:15) implies two thousand years.[36] The application of the rule was not always to eschatological matters:[37] it was also very commonly used to interpret Genesis 2:17 in accordance with the length of Adam's life.[38] But all of these instances are chronological calculations: the point is not, as originally in Psalm 90:4, to contrast God's everlasting life with the transience of human life, but simply to yield the chronological information that one of God's days, when Scripture mentions them, is equal to a thousand of our years.

---

[34] F. Spitta, *Der zweite Brief des Petrus und der Brief des Judas* (Halle: Buchhandlung des Waisenhauses, 1885) 251–257; Strobel, *op. cit.* 93 f; von Allmen, *art, cit.* 262.

[35] *Ep. of Barnabas* 15:4; Irenaeus, *Adv. Haer.* 5:28:3; *cf. b Sanh.* 97 a.

[36] *Midrash on Psalms* on Ps. 90:4; *Pesiqta Rabbati* 1:7 (where R. Eliezer is the later R. Eliezer b. R. Jose the Galilean). There are further calculations on a similar basis in *Pesiqta Rabbati* 1:7; *b Sanh.* 99 b; Justin, *Dial.* 81.

[37] As von Allmen, *art. cit.* 262 n. 1; *cf.* Strobel, *op. cit.* 93.

[38] *Jubilees* 4:30 (the earliest example of this use of Ps. 90:4); *Gen. R.* 19:8; 22:1; *Midrash on Psalms* on Ps. 25:6; Justin, *Dial.* 81; Irenaeus, *Adv. Haer.* 5:23:2; *Pirge de R. Eliezer* 18. *Gen. R.* 8:2 uses the rule to prove from Pr. 8:30 that the Torah preceded the creation of the world by 2000 years.

If these parallels are to govern the interpretation of 2 Peter 3:8, then the verse means that the 'day of judgment', mentioned in verse 7, will last a thousand years. Verse 8 is then not a contribution to the debate about the delay, but an explanation of the eschatological expectation set out in verse 7.

Now it is true that 2 Peter 3:8 appears to cite the current exegetical rule in the first half of the saying ('one day before the Lord is as a thousand years')[39] and then, in the second half, to back it up by citing Psalm 90:4. It is also a sound hermeneutical principle to expect a writer to follow the exegetical methods of his contemporaries.[40] In this case, the resulting exegesis of verse 8 is very hard to sustain in context: (1) The introductory words ('But do not ignore this one fact, beloved') formally signal a fresh line of thought, not an explanatory footnote to verse 7. (2) If verse 8 means that the day of judgment will last a thousand years, it contributes nothing to the argument against the 'scoffers'. It is hard to believe that in such a brief section the author would have allowed himself this entirely redundant comment. (3) There is actually no parallel to the idea that the day of *judgment* would last a thousand years, and it is difficult to see how it could fit into the eschatology of 2 Peter 3.

Must we then conclude, with the majority of exegetes, that the author's use of Psalm 90:4 in this verse is entirely unprecedented?[41] Not at all, for there are in fact two relevant Jewish parallels which, so far as I can tell, the commentators have not noticed, presumably because Strack and Billerbeck missed them.

The first is a piece of rabbinic exegesis which belongs to the tradition of apocalyptic interpretation of the revelation to Abraham in Genesis 15. It is ascribed to the early second-century Rabbi Eleazar b. Azariah, and although the attestation is late, the fact that it seems closely related to the traditions embodied in the Apocalypse of Abraham[42] perhaps permits us to consider

---

[39] This is closer to Ps. 90:4 than the usual formulation of the rule, but, for παρὰ Κυρίῳ, see *Ep. of Barnabas* 15:4 (παρ’ αὐτῷ), and, for ὡς, see Justin, *Dial.* 81; Irenaeus, *Adv. Haer.* 5:23:2; 5:28:3.

[40] Von Allmen, *art. cit.* 262 n. 1.

[41] E.g. J.N.D. Kelly, *A commentary on the Epistles of Peter and of Jude* (London: A. & C. Black, 1969) 362.

[42] *Apocalypse of Abraham* 28–30: the text is partly corrupt and in ch. 29 has suffered Christian interpolation, so that it is difficult to be sure of the chronological reckonings. It seems that the whole of this 'age of ungodliness' is reckoned as one day of twelve hours (perhaps on the basis on Gen. 15:11), and perhaps each hour lasts 400 years (as in ch. 32) rather than 100 years (as the present text of ch. 28 seems to indicate). In any case, the general approach to Gen. 15 is similar to that in *Pirqe de R. Eliezer* 28, and it is relevant that L. Hartman, 'The Functions of Some So-Called Apocalyptic Timetables', *NTS* 22 (1975–6) 10, considers that the message of the 'timetable' in the *Apocalypse of Abraham* 'is not a calculation of the end, but rather an attempt to solve the moral and religious problem posed by the situation of the faithful'.

it in this context. From the text of Genesis 15 it is deduced that the period during which Abraham (according to 15:11) drove away the birds of prey from the sacrificial carcasses was a day, from sunrise to sunset. The birds of prey are taken to represent the Gentile oppressors of Israel during the period of the four kingdoms. Therefore, R. Eleazar says, 'From this incident thou mayest learn that the rule of these four kingdoms will only last one day according to the day of the Holy One, blessed be he'.[43] The reference to 'the day of the Holy One' must be to the maxim 'A day of the Lord is a thousand years'.

The relevance of this text is that, unlike the other rabbinic texts already mentioned, it does relate to the delay of the End, for in Jewish apocalyptic the period of the four kingdoms is precisely the period of delay. Moreover, I doubt whether the exegesis is primarily intended as a chronological calculation,[44] again unlike the other texts. The point is that the rule of the four kingdoms 'will only last one day', i. e. that although for oppressed Israel the time seems very long, from God's eternal perspective it is a very brief period. This reflection therefore has the function of consolation for Israel, in that it relativizes the importance of the period of Gentile domination. It thus provides a parallel to the thought of 2 Peter 3:8, which is surely that those who complain of the delay have got it out of perspective: in the perspective of eternity it is only a short time.

With the second parallel we are on chronologically safer ground, for it comes from the *Apocalypse of Baruch*. In a passage clearly inspired by Psalm 90, Baruch reflects on the contrast between the transience of man and the eternity of God:

For in a little time are we born,
and in a little time do we return.
But with thee the hours are as the ages,
and the days are as the generations (2 *Baruch* 48:12 f).[45]

---

[43] *Pirqe de R. Eliezer* 28: translation from G. Friedlander, *Pirkê de Rabbi Eliezer* (New York: Hermon Press, 1965²) 200. I owe my knowledge of this text to P. Bogaert, *op. cit.* II 88, who quotes from the same tradition in *Yalquṭ Shim'oni* 76.

[44] If the text were interpreted chronologically, then perhaps it would be plausible to suggest a date of origin for the tradition when the end of a period of one thousand years from 586 BC was approaching. But even in the case of texts which appear to be more interested in chronology, such calculations of date cannot be trusted: if *4 Ezra* 10:45 f; 14:11 f were taken literally and according to modern chronology, the End would have been far distant in the future when the book was written; similarly Ps-Philo, *Lib. Ant. Bib.* 19:15 (accepting the very plausible emendation proposed by M. Wadsworth, 'The Death of Moses and the Riddle of the End of Time in Pseudo-Philo,' *JJS* 28 (1977) 14 f).

[45] As R.H. Charles, *The Apocalypse of Baruch* (London: A. & C. Black, 1896) 75, *ad loc.*, notes, we should have expected 'the ages are as the hours and the generations are as the days'; perhaps this should caution us against seeing too much detailed significance in the two halves of the saying in 2 Pet. 3:8.

At least this text proves that it was possible for a contemporary of the author of 2 Peter to read Psalm 90:4 in its original sense of a contrast between God's endless existence and man's brief span of life. In its immediate context in *2 Baruch* it is not directly related to the problem of delay, but it is an instance of Baruch's frequent theme of God's sovereignty over the times, which, as we have seen, is one of the themes which serves to balance the theme of eschatological imminence.

These two parallels seem to me to illuminate the meaning of 2 Peter 3:8. This verse is not, as Käsemann complains, 'a philosophical speculation about the being of God, to which a different conception of time is made to apply from that which applies to us'.[46] It does not mean that God's perception of time is so utterly unrelated to ours that the very idea of delay becomes quite meaningless and nothing can any longer be said about the time until the *parousia*. Rather the verse contrasts man man's transience with God's everlastingness, the limited perspective of man whose expectations tend to be bounded by his own brief lifetime with the perspective of the eternal God who surveys the whole of history. The reason why the imminent expectation of the apocalyptist tends to mean to him the expectation of the End within his own lifetime is, partly at least, this human limitation: he is impatient to see the redemption *himself*. The eternal God is free from that particular impatience.[47] The implication is not that the believer should discard the imminent expectation,[48] but that he must set against it the consideration that the delay which seems so lengthy to him may not be so significant within that total perspective on the total course of history which God commands.

In 2 Peter 3:9 the author offers his positive understanding of the delay: 'The Lord is not slow about his promise, as some count slowness, but is forbearing toward you, not wishing that any should perish, but that all should reach repentance.' I hope that adequate comment on this verse has already been provided by the whole of our study of the Jewish apocalyptic material. The problem of delay is here met in a way which had become standard in the Jewish thinking of the time:[49] in fact this verse is a succinct statement

---

[46] *Op. cit.* 194.

[47] *Cf.* Augustine's saying, quoted by C. Bigg, *A Critical and Exegetical Commentary on the Epistles of St Peter and St Jude* (Edinburgh: T. & T. Clark, 1901) 295, and repeated by M. Green, *The Second Epistle General of Peter and the General Epistle of Jude* (London: IVP, 1968) 134, that God is *patiens quia eternus*.

[48] T. Fornberg, *An Early Church in a Pluralistic Society* (Coniectanea Biblica: NT Series 9. Lund: Gleerup, 1977) 68, thinks that '2 Pet. 3:8 is the earliest example of the *explicit* abandonment by an orthodox Christian writer of the expectation of a *speedy* Parousia'.

[49] Fornberg, *ibid.* 71, who wishes to stress the Hellenistic and non-Jewish character of 2 Peter, neglects the Jewish parallels to 3:9 in favour of the parallel in Plutarch, *De sera numinis vindicata*. But the whole context makes the Jewish parallels the relevant ones.

of the ideas about the delay which we have traced in Jewish apocalyptic. There is first of all the appeal to God's sovereignty: he is not *late* in fulfilling his promise (this point is made by means of the standard reference to Hab. 2:3);[50] the delay belongs to his purpose. Then the positive meaning of the delay is explained as R. Eliezer and the *Apocalypse of Baruch* explained it. God restrains his anger in order to give his people (now Christians rather than Jews) opportunity to repent.[51]

The author of 2 Peter, then, met the problem of delay as posed by the 'scoffers' from the resources of the Jewish apocalyptic tradition. His arguments were not novel arguments hastily contrived to meet the unexpected crisis of delay. They were arguments familiar in contemporary Jewish circles where the problem of delay was part and parcel of the apocalyptic tradition. Like the author of the *Apocalypse of Baruch*, the author of 2 Peter recognized that alongside the theological factors which make for imminence must be set theological factors which account for delay. Against the apocalyptists' longing for eschatological righteousness, which this writer clearly shared (3:13), must be set the patience of God who characteristically holds back from condemning the sinner while he may still repent. The believer must hold the two sides of the matter in tension. Only God from the perspective of eternity knows the temporal point at which they meet, where the tension will be resolved in the event of the End. The problem of delay is thus contained within the expectation, as it always had been in the Jewish tradition.

(d) The Apocalypse of John

Finally, we turn to the Apocalypse of John, which, rooted as it is in the apocalyptic tradition, employs the traditional Jewish approaches to the problem of delay, but also, being a deeply Christian apocalypse, employs them with far more creative Christian reinterpretation than we have found in 2 Peter.

---

[50] Cf. Ecclus. 35:18, but there is the emphasis is very different.

[51] The πάντας must mean, initially at least, all the readers. The Christian mission is not here in view: *contra* A.L. Moore, *The Parousia in the New Testament* (Supplements to Novum Testamentum 13. Leiden: E.J. Brill, 1966) 154.

The further comment, in 3:12, that Christians by living holy lives may 'hasten' the coming of the End is the observe of 3:9. The reference to Is. 60:12 was traditional (see n. 13 above), though it is usually God who is said to hasten the time of the End. There are, however, rabbinic parallels, such as the saying of R. Judah, 'Great is charity, for it brings redemption nearer' (*b Baba Batra* 10a), and the saying of R. Jose the Galilean, 'Great is repentance, for it brings redemption nearer' (*b Yoma* 86b).

As we have already noticed in the case of R. Eliezer and the *Apocalypse of Baruch*, this idea need not contradict the view that God has appointed the time of the End; it only means that God's sovereign determination takes human affairs into account.

By now it should come as no surprise to learn that the imminent expectation and the delay of the *parousia* both feature in Revelation. The note of imminence is more obvious, owing to the emphasis it receives in the opening and closing sections of the book (1:1,3; 22:6,7,10,12,20). The motif of delay is somewhat less evident to us, but would have been clear enough to John's readers: it can be found principally in the section chapters 6–11.

We should notice first how the imminent expectation receives a thoroughly Christian character: if is the *parousia* of Jesus Christ which is expected. Not simply the End, but Jesus, is coming soon (2:16; 3:11; 22:7,12,20; *cf.* 1:7; 3:3; 16:15). Moreover, this Jesus has already won the eschatological victory over evil (3:21; 5:5; 12:7–11); as the passover Lamb he has already accomplished the new Exodus of the End-time (5:6–10; *cf.* 15:3); he already holds the keys of death, and rules the world from his Father's throne (1:18; 3:21; 1:5).

It has frequently been said that, by comparison with Jewish apocalyptic, the problem of eschatological delay was less acute for the early church because of the element of realized eschatology in Christian thinking. No longer was the future expectation paramount, because in the death and resurrection of Jesus in the *past* God had already accomplished the decisive eschatological act.[52] There is truth in this argument – and, as we shall see, it is this past act of God in Christ which gives the present time of delay its positive meaning in Revelation – but it should also be noticed that the tension of 'already' ands 'not yet' in early Christianity also functioned to heighten the sense of eschatological imminence. For if the victory over evil has already been won, it seems even more necessary that the actual eradication of evil from the world should follow very soon. The powers of evil at work in the world loom large in the imagery of Revelation: the problems of theodicy which they pose are, in one sense, not not alleviated but intensified by the faith that Christ has already conquered them. Thus the characteristic tension of imminence and delay in Jewish apocalyptic seems to be, if anything, sharpened by the 'already' of Christian faith, since it contributes to *both* sides of the tension.

The message of Revelation is conveyed as much by literary impact as by conventional theological statement, and this is true of the motif of delay in chapters 6–11. In those chapters John portrays the movement from Christ's victory on the cross towards the fulfilment of that victory at the *parousia,* and he structures that movement in the series of sevens: the seven seals, the seven trumpets, and the further series of seven bowls which follows in chapter 16. In chapter 5 the reader has heard of the victory of the Lamb, who is declared worthy to open the scroll, *i. e.* to release into the world God's

---

[52] *Cf.* Cullmann, *Christ and Time,* 86–90, though Cullmann does acknowledge that the 'already' of primitive Christianity did intensify the eschatological expectation.

purpose of establishing his Kingdom. The Lamb's victory on the cross is the fundamental achievement of that purpose; all that remains is its outworking in world history. So John's original readers would move into chapter 6 full of expectancy: a rapid series of apocalyptic judgments would quickly crush all opposition and inaugurate the Kingdom. This expectancy, however, is deliberately frustrated throughout chapters 6–11. The impressive quartet of horsemen who are released into history when the Lamb opens the first four seals turn out (6:8) to be disappointingly moderate judgments, affecting only a quarter of the earth. The readers' sense of disappointment will correspond to the cry of the martyrs, 'How long?', at the opening of the fifth seal (6:10). With the sixth seal, however, expectation will mount again: the familiar apocalyptic imagery heralds the actual arrival of the day of judgment. But again John holds his readers in suspense, inserting a long parenthesis (ch. 7) before the final, seventh seal.

The series of trumpets follow a similar pattern. The judgments are now intensified, but they are still limited, this time affecting a third of the earth and its inhabitants. Instead of accomplishing a swift annihilation of the enemies of God, it becomes clear that these judgments are preliminary warning judgments, designed, in the patience of God, to give men the opportunity of repentance. Following the sixth trumpet, however, we are told that these judgments have not brought men to repentance; they remain as impenitent as ever (9:20f). Once again, therefore, the readers' expectation will rise: God's patience must now be exhausted; surely the final judgment of the seventh trumpet will now follow. Once again, however, John frustrates this expectation, inserting a long passage between the sixth and seventh trumpets, just as he had done between the sixth and seventh seals. Only when we reach the seven bowls (ch. 16), with which 'the wrath of God is ended' (15:1), do we find an uninterrupted series of total judgments moving rapidly to the final extinction of the evil powers.

In this way John has incorporated the motif of delay into the structure of his book, especially in the form of the parentheses which precede the final seal and the final trumpet. John's understanding of the meaning of the delay we shall expect to find in the content of these parentheses, and also in the episode of the fifth seal (6:9–11), which is his first explicit treatment of the issue of delay.

The martyrs' cry 'How long?' (6:10) is the traditional apocalyptic question about the delay (Dn. 12:6; Hab. 1:2; Zc. 1:12; *2 Baruch* 21:25; *4 Ezra* 4:33,35), and the problem from which it arises – the problem of justice and vindication for the martyrs – dates at least from the time of the Maccabean martyrs. The answer to the question is also traditional. The delay will last 'a little while longer' (*cf.* Is. 26:20; Hg. 2:6; Heb. 10:37; the same motif in Rev. 12:12; 17:10) until the predetermined quota of martyrs is complete. This idea is clearly akin to *2 Baruch* 23:2–5 (discussed above) and even closer to *1 Enoch* 47 and *4 Ezra* 4:35–37: the last passage may suggest that John has taken over even the depiction of the scene from tradition.

John has therefore taken over this tradition about the meaning of delay without modification, *except that* he has placed it in the context of the significance of martyrdom according to his work as a whole.[53] For John, Christian martyrdom belongs to the Christian's discipleship of Jesus and the Christian's participation in Jesus' own witness and victory through the cross. In that context the meaning of the delay in this passage goes deeper than the idea of an arbitrarily decreed quota of martyrdoms. In advance of his final victory over evil by power, God has already won the victory of sacrificial suffering, the victory of the slain Lamb. He has done so because he prefers to come to sinners in grace, rather than in merely destructive wrath. But the Lamb's mission and victory must be continued in the followers of the Lamb. Therefore the vindication of the martyrs must wait until all have sealed their witness in blood and God's purposes of grace for the world have been fulfilled through them. The logic of delay here is the logic of the cross. This is the significance which 6:9–11 will gain as the rest of Revelation unfolds the significance of the martyrs.

John does not, in so many words, attribute the delay to the longsuffering of God, but characteristically he pictures this motif. Chapter 7, the parenthesis between the sixth and seventh seals, opens with the picture of the four angels holding back the four winds of the earth, to prevent them from harming the earth: a picture of what Baruch called 'the restraint of wrath' (*2 Baruch* 59:6). God holds back the release of his final judgment on the world until the angels 'have sealed the servants of God on their foreheads' (7:3): in other words, the delay is the period in which men become Christians and are therefore protected from the coming wrath of God. (Paradoxically, this protection makes them potential martyrs: 7:14.)

Thus, from the treatment of delay within the seven seals section, we learn that God delays the End for the sake of the church, so that the Lamb may be the leader of a vast new people of God drawn from every nation and sharing his victory through suffering.

The treatment of delay in the seven trumpets section is less easy to follow, because the parenthesis between the sixth and seventh trumpets (10:1–11:13) is probably the most obscure passage in Revelation, as the wide variety of suggested interpretations shows. It will be easier to begin with the latter part of it: the story of the two witnesses (11:3–13). With many commentators, I

---

[53] *Cf.* G. B. Caird, *The Revelation of St John the Divine* (London: A. & C. Black, 1966) 87; J. Sweet. *Revelation* (London: SCM, 1979) 142.

take this as a parable of the church's mission to the world.[54] The witnesses are two because of the Deuteronomic requirement of two witnesses. They prophesy for three and half years (11:3) because this is the symbolic figure (taken over from Daniel) which John uses to designate the 'little while' of the delay. Along with many Old Testament allusions in the passage, the fact that the witnesses' career is modelled on that of Jesus is noteworthy: their dead bodies lie in the street of the city 'where their Lord was crucified' (11:8), and after three and a half days they are raised and ascend to heaven. In all probability the final words of the section, 'the rest were terrified and gave glory to the God of heaven' (11:13), are intended to indicate sincere repentance.[55] In other words, the men who after the judgments of the six trumpet-blasts remained impenitent (9:20f) are now brought to repentance through the suffering witness of the church.

Thus the question with which the original readers may well have concluded chapter 9 – 'Surely God will no longer be patient?' – is answered in chapter 11. Yes, he will be patient because he has another strategy to reach the impenitent, a strategy which began with the sacrifice of the Lamb and continues in the suffering witness of his followers. This is John's further answer to the meaning of delay: not only is the delay for the sake of the church itself (ch. 7), it is for the sake of the church's witness to the world. God's desire that sinners should repent does not stop at simply giving them time, or even at inflicting warning judgments on them; more than that, God actively seeks them in the mission of his Son and his church. The delay of the *parousia* is filled with the mission of the church.

We turn to the problematic chapter 10. The episode of the seven thunders (10:3f) has puzzled the commentators. Probably the seven thunders represent a further series of warning judgments, like the seals and the trumpets.[56] The command to 'seal up what the seven thunders have said' (10:3) is odd,

---

[54] I have discussed this passage briefly in 'The Role of the Spirit in the Apocalypse', *EQ* 52 (1980) 66–83. Commentators who take a similar view include H.B. Swete, *The Apocalypse of St John* (London: Macmillan, [2]1907) 134–41; M. Kiddle, *The Revelation of St John* (London: Hodder and Stoughton, 1940) 176–206; Caird, *op. cit.* 133–40; G.R. Beasley-Murray, *The Book of Revelation* (London: Oliphants, 1974) 176–87; R.H. Mounce, *The Book of Revelation* (Grand Rapids: Eerdmans, 1977) 222–9; Sweet, *op. cit.* 181–9.

[55] So Swete, *op. cit.* 141; R.H. Charles, *A Critical and Exegetical Commentary on the Revelation of St John* (Edinburgh: T. & T. Clark, 1920) I, 291f; Caird, *op. cit.* 139f; L. Morris, *The Revelation of St John* (London: Tyndale Press, 1969) 152; G.E. Ladd, *A Commentary on the Revelation of John* (Grand Rapids: Eerdmans, 1972) 139f; Beasley-Murray, *op. cit.* 187; Sweet, *op. cit.* 189.

[56] J. Day, 'Echoes of Baal's seven thunders and lightnings in Psalm xxix and Habakkuk iii 9 and the identity of the seraphim in Isaiah vi,' *VT* 29 (1979) 143–51, finds a Ugaritic reference to the seven thunders of Baal, which are reflected in Ps. 29. Probably, therefore, John's reference to 'the seven thunders' (10:3) is to a standard apocalyptic image which derives ultimately, like much apocalyptic imagery, from Canaanite mythology.

since John has not written what they said, and he is told not to write it: there is no document to seal up. Some have suggested that the content of the seven thunders is to be kept secret: John is not to reveal it as he has revealed the content of the seven trumpets.[57] In that case, there are to be further warning judgments, but John's readers are not permitted to know about them. This explanation has the disadvantage of seeming to contradict verse 6, where the angel swears that there will be no more delay. The alternative suggestion is that the seven thunders represent a further series of warning judgments which are *revoked*.[58] They are sealed up because they are not do occur. Here 'seal up' is being used as the antithesis of 'open the seal' in chapter 6: if to 'open the seal' means to release the contents of the document into history, then to 'seal up' would mean to prevent the seven thunders being released into history. On this view, verse 6 follows logically: God has cut short the series of warning judgments, and so there will be no more delay before the final judgment of the seventh trumpet.

However, when we turn to the angel's statement in verses 6 f, there are further problems. These verses are dependent on Daniel 12:6 f, where in reply to Daniel's question 'How long?,' the angel swears that it will be 'for a time, two times, and half a time; and that when the shattering of the power of the holy people comes to an end all these things would be accomplished'. John's angel appears to contradict Daniel's: instead of three and a half times (years) of delay, there will be no more delay.[59] But if John means to indicate that the words of Daniel's angel are inappropriate at this stage of history because there is now to be no more delay, it is strange that, almost immediately (in 11:2 f), he goes on to use Daniel's period of three and a half years as his own symbol of the period of delay before the End, during which the power of the new holy people, the church, is being shattered in martyrdom. On grounds of structure[60] I would reject the suggestion[61] that in chapter 10 John stands at the end of the three and a half years and then in chapter 11 recapitulates the three and a half years.

[57] So Swete, *op. cit.* 128; W. Hendriksen, *More than Conquerors* (London: Inter-Varsity Press, 1962) 124; Morris, *op. cit.* 139; Ladd, *op. cit.* 143.

[58] So A. M. Farrer, *The Revelation of St John the Divine* (Oxford: Clarendon Press, 1964) 125; Caird, *op. cit.* 126 f; Mounce, *op. cit.* 209 f.

[59] All commentators now agree that χρόνος οὐκέτι ἔσται (10:6), should be translated 'there shall be no more delay'. The words probably echo Hab. 2:3.

[60] The whole section 10:1–11:13 is a unit closely associated with the sixth trumpet (9:13–21) by means of 9:12 and 11:24. It is clear from 10:8 that 10:8–11 *succeeds* the episode of the seven thunders: John is forbidden to reveal the content of the thunders but instead is given a new commission to prophesy (10:11). This commission is fulfilled initially in 11:1–13, more expansively in chs. 12–14.

[61] Hendrikson, *op. cit.* 125; Morris, *op. cit.* 140.

We seem, then, to be faced with a straight contradiction. In 10:1–7 we are told that there are to be no more warning judgments and *no more delay* before the final trumpet-blast which is about to sound.[62] In 11:1–13 (to which 10:8–11 is introductory) we find *a delay* which is filled with the church's mission: if God has revoked further warning judgments it is not because his patience is ended, but because he purposes to reach men through the church's witness.

I tentatively suggest that John intended this contradiction. The days of the sixth trumpet in which he placed himself are the days in which 'the time is near' (1:3; 22:10), when the final 'woe' is coming 'soon' (11:24), when there is to be no more delay (10:7). And yet, *while* God *does* still delay, the church is called to bear her faithful witness in prophecy and martyrdom (11:1–13). The tension of imminence and delay is here starkly set out, and John makes no attempt to resolve it: he only knows that the church must live in this tension.

To conclude: Revelation maintains the typical apocalyptic tension of imminence and delay, now sharpened and characterized in a peculiarly Christian manner. The imminent expectation focuses on the *parousia* of the already victorious Christ: and the book ends with the promise, 'I am coming soon', and the church's urgent response, 'Amen. Come, Lord Jesus!' (22:20). But the manner of the victory which Christ has already won – a sacrificial offering to ransom sinners from every nation (5:9) – gives fresh meaning to the delay, which now becomes the time of the church's universal mission, characterized by suffering witness in discipleship to the crucified Christ. In this way, it should be noticed, the apocalyptic theodicy problem of innocent suffering gains a fresh perspective. Innocent suffering still cries out for eschatological righteousness (6:10; *cf.* 18:1–19:3). But on the other hand, God delays the *parousia* not simply in spite of his people's sufferings, but actually so that his people may suffer that positive, creative suffering which comes to the followers of the cross of Christ.

---

[62] Some have sought to evade the difficulty by arguing either (1) that 10:6 f means only that there will be no more delay *before the period of three and a half years* (so Charles, *op. cit.* I, 263, 265 f; Caird, *op. cit.* 127 f; Mounce, op. cit. 211; Sweet, *op. cit.* 127 f), or (2) that 10:6 f means only that *when the seventh trumpet sounds* there will be no more delay (so Swete, *op. cit.* 129). But these are evasions which miss the point of the passage.

6. A Note on a Problem
in the Greek Version of 1 Enoch 1. 9*

In Codex Panopolitanus (C) the opening clause of 1 Enoch i. 9 reads: ὅτι[1] ἔρχεται σὺν ταῖς[2] μυριάσιν αὐτοῦ καὶ τοῖς ἁγίοις αὐτοῦ... The quotation of this verse in Jude 14 differs considerably: ἰδοὺ ἦλθεν Κύριος ἐν ἁγίαις μυριάσιν αὐτοῦ... Cf. Ethiopic: 'And behold! he comes with ten thousand holy ones...'[3]; Pseudo-Cyprian: 'ecce venit cum multis milibus nuntiorum suorum...'[4]

Although it is widely agreed that Jude has inserted Κύριος,[5] at three other points where his version differs from C it is likely that he is closer to the original Aramaic: (a) ἰδού: Jude agrees with the Ethiopic and Pseudo-Cyprian against C;[6] (b) ἦλθεν: Jude's 'prophetic perfect'[7] is found also in Pseudo-Cyprian; (c) ἐν ἁγίαις μυριάσιν αὐτοῦ:[8] Jude agrees with the Ethiopic and, more importantly, with the Qumran Aramaic fragment (4Q

---

* First publication: *Journal of Theological Studies* 32 (1981) 136–138.

[1] MS. οτει.

[2] MS τοις.

[3] M. A. Knibb, *The Ethiopic Book of Enoch* (Oxford, 1978), vol. ii, pp. 59 f.

[4] *Ad Novatianum*, xvi; text in R. H. Charles, *The Book of Enoch* (2 nd edn., Oxford, 1912), p. 275.

[5] Presumably as a Christological interpretation, but perhaps also by analogy with other theophany texts (Isa. xl. 10, lxvi. 15; Zech. xiv. 5) which were also applied to the parousia in primitive Christianity.

[6] In favour of the originality of Jude's version here are Charles, op. cit., p. 8; M. Black, 'The Maranatha Invocation and Jude 14, 15 (I Enoch 1: 9)', in *Christ and Spirit in the New Testament; in honour of C. F. D. Moule*, ed. B. Lindars and S. S. Smalley (Cambridge, 1973), p. 195 ('It is a definite possibility that ἰδού should be restored in the Aramaic text'); C. D. Osburn, 'The Christological Use of I Enoch i. 9 in Jude 14, 15', *N. T. S.* xxiii (1976–7), pp. 335 f.; cf. J. vander Kam, 'The Theophany of Enoch I 3 b–7, 9', *V. T.* xxiii (1973), pp. 147 f. J. T. Milik, *The Books of Enoch: Aramaic Fragments of Qumrân Cave 4* (Oxford, 1976), p. 186, unaccountably prefers οτει in C, corrected to ὅτε, as rendering Aramaic כדי.

[7] Jude's aorist is widely regarded as equivalent to a prophetic perfect: e. g. J. B. Mayor, *The Epistle of St. Jude and the Second Epistle of St. Peter* (London, 1907), p. 45; J. Chaine, *Les épîtres catholiques* (2 nd edn., Paris, 1939), p. 322; W. Grundmann, *Der Brief des Judas und der zweite Brief des Petrus* (Berlin, 1974), p. 42.

[8] The best attested reading in Jude (cf. discussion in Osburn, art. cit., pp. 337 f.); on the variants, including P[72], which add ἀγγέλων, see below.

En^c 1 i. 15): [ברבו[את קדיש[הי].^{9} The readings of C in the first two of these cases have been explained: *(a)* both ἰδού and ὅτι may derive from an original ארי, as Knibb suggests,^{10} or possibly from an original ארי הא, the phrase with which the Targum renders כי הנה in Mic. i. 3 (a theophany text on which 1 Enoch i. 4–6 depends), where the Septuagint has διότι ἰδού;^{11} *(b)* ἔρχεται, like the Ethiopic's 'he comes', is a more idiomatic rendering of an Aramaic prophetic perfect, while ἦλθεν is the more literal translation.^{12} It is more difficult, however, to explain the reading of C at *(c)*.

A possible solution to this difficulty may be found by considering the early Christian treatment of a very similar eschatological theophany passage: Zech. xiv. 5 b, which the Septuagint renders: καὶ ἥξει Κύριος ὁ θεός μου, καὶ πάντες οἱ ἅγιοι μετ' αὐτοῦ. Like many other Old Testament theophany texts, this was from an early stage in primitive Christianity interpreted Christologically of the parousia of the Lord Jesus. It is explicitly quoted in Didache xvi. 7, but probably also lies behind many other early Christian texts: Matt. xvi. 27, xxv. 31; Mark viii. 38; Luke ix. 26; 1 Thess. iii. 13; 2 Thess. i. 7; Rev. xix. 14; Apocalypse of Peter i (Ethiopic); Ascension of Isaiah iv. 14; Sibylline Oracles ii. 242, viii. 221. It was the main source (though compare also Deut. xxxiii. 2; Ps. lxviii. 18) of the expectation that the Lord at his parousia would be accompanied by a retinue of angels.

The early church usually (and correctly) understood οἱ ἅγιοι in Zech. xiv. 5 to be the angels, the divine Warrior's heavenly army. It is given this sense in Matt. xvi. 27, xxv. 31; Mark viii. 37; Luke ix. 26; 2 Thess. i. 7; Apocalypse of Peter i (Ethiopic); Sibylline Oracle ii. 242; and probably in 1 Thess. iii. 13. But although 'the holy ones' was commonly used to mean angels in Judaism (and especially in the Qumran texts),^{13} in the ordinary usage of the early church οἱ ἅγιοι usually meant Christians, not angels. Probably the only New Testament texts in which οἱ ἅγιοι are angels are 1 Thess. iii. 13 (echoing Zech. xiv. 5); Jude 14 (quoting 1 Enoch i. 9); Eph. i. 18; Col. i. 12 (both, if they do refer to angels, echoing an established phrase).^{14} Most of

---

^{9} Milik, op. cit., p. 184 and Plate IX.

^{10} Op. cit. ii, p. 59. For ארי = 'for', see J. A. Fitzmyer, *The Genesis Apocryphon of Qumran Cave I: A Commentary* (2nd edn. Rome, 1971), p. 96; and especially 1Q GenApoc xxi 14.

^{11} vander Kam, art. cit., pp. 147f.

^{12} Ibid., p. 148; Osburn, art. cit., p. 337. The prophetic perfect is rare in Aramaic, but does exist: M. Black, art. cit., p. 196; idem, 'The Christological Use of the old Testament in the New Testament', *N. T. S.* xviii (1971–2), p. 10n.

^{13} S. F. Noll, *Angelology in the Qumran Texts* (unpublished Ph.D. thesis, University of Manchester, 1979), pp. 220–2, lists fifty-four examples of קדיש and קדוש meaning angels in the Qumran texts.

^{14} Cf. E. Lohse, *Colossians and Philemon* (Philadelphia, 1971), pp. 35f.; cf. QS xi. 7; Wisd. v. 5. 2 Thess. i. 10 echoes Ps. lxxxviii. 7 LXX, but probably with reference to Christians, not angels.

the passages which reflect an interpretation of Zech. xiv. 5 as referring to angels do so by introducing the *word* ἄγγελοι (Matt. xvi. 27, xxv. 31; Mark viii. 38; Luke ix. 26; 2 Thess. i. 7; Apocalypse of Peter i (Ethiopic); Sibylline Oracle ii. 242). The variant readings at Jude 14 (beginning with P⁷²), which introduce ἀγγέλων, also attest that ἅγιοι was not easily understood to mean angels, but needed an explanatory gloss.[15]

It is therefore not surprising that some early Christian texts provide evidence of an alternative interpretation of Zech. xiv. 5 in which οἱ ἅγιοι (especially in the light of the teaching of 1 Thess. iv. 14, 16 f.) were taken to be Christians. In Rev. xix. 15 it seems (cf. xvii. 14) that the heavenly army is composed of the Christian martyrs. Didache xvi. 7 quotes Zech. xiv. 5 with explicit reference to the Christians who will rise from the dead and accompany the Lord at his parousia. Finally, in Ascension of Isa. iv. 14 the two traditions of interpretation are combined: 'the Lord will come with his angels and with the hosts of the holy ones' (and compare 16, which makes clear that 'the holy ones' are the Christian dead).

It is this *combination* of the two early Christian interpretations of Zech. xiv. 5 which is reflected in the Greek version of 1 Enoch i. 9.[16] Early Christian readers would immediately understand ταῖς μυριάσιν αὐτοῦ as a reference to the angels (cf. Deut. xxxiii. 2; Ps. lxviii. 18; Dan. vii. 10; Matt. xxvi. 53; Heb. xii. 22; 1 Clem. xxxiv. 6) and τοῖς ἁγίοις αὐτοῦ as a reference to Christians. The reading of C must therefore be explained either as a Christian interpretative gloss on a Greek text which originally rendered the Aramaic more accurately, or possibly (though this, of course, would need to be supported by other evidence) as an indication that C represents an originally Christian translation of 1 Enoch.[17]

---

[15] The use of the term 'the holy angels' was a way of preserving the traditional epithet but removing the ambiguity: Mark viii. 38; Luke ix. 26; Acts x. 22; Rev. xiv. 10; Hermas, *Vis.* II. ii. 7; III, iv. 1 f.

[16] Note that Ascension of Isaiah derives from those Christian apocalyptic circles which must especially have valued the Enoch literature.

[17] J. Barr, 'Aramaic-Greek notes on the Book of Enoch (II)', *J.S.S.* xxiv (1979), p. 191, concludes tentatively: 'It seems at first sight probable that the translation of Enoch into Greek belonged to the same general stage and stratum of translation as the LXX translation of Daniel.'

7. The Son of Man:
'A Man in my Position' or 'Someone'?[*]

A critique of Barnabas Lindars's proposal

Professor Barnabas Lindar's new book, *Jesus Son of Man*,[1] is a work of major importance for the 'Son of Man' debate, and deserves the closest consideration. Its importance lies as much in its discussion of the extension and development of Son of Man sayings in Q and the four Gospels as in its novel proposal on the meaning of Jesus' use of the phrase, but my comments here are largely concerned with the latter. Lindars stands within the general trend of Son of Man scholarship pioneered (in its recent phase) by Geza Vermes and pursued also by Maurice Casey, which takes as the clue to Jesus' usage the examples of *bar nash* and *bar nasha* as a form of self-reference in later Jewish Aramaic. But, like Casey, he rejects Vermes's claim that there are examples in which *bar nasha* is an idiomatic form of exclusive self-reference (a periphrasis for 'I'), and agrees with Casey that all the examples in which *bar nasha* functions as a self-reference are examples of the generic use, in which self-reference is possible because the speaker is included among those to whom *bar nasha* refers. But whereas Casey recognized only a properly generic use (*bar nasha* = 'mankind', 'each and every man'), Lindars claims that there are examples of 'the idiomatic use of the generic article, in which the speaker refers to a class of persons, with whom he identifies himself' (*bar nasha* = 'a man in my position'). 'It is this idiom... which provides the best guidance to the use of Son of Man in the sayings of Jesus'.[2] He proceeds to use this idiom as a criterion of dominical authenticity: only Son of Man sayings which use the phrase as this kind of self-reference can be considered authentic. On this basis, Lindars identifies (in chapter 3) six Son of Man sayings from Mark and Q as authentic, and (in chapter 4) adds three passion predictions: a total of nine authentic Son of Man sayings which can be plausibly interpreted according to the 'idiomatic generic' use of *bar nasha*.

---

[*] First publication: *Journal for the Study of the New Testament* 23 (1985) 23–33.
[1] London, 1983
[2] B. Lindars, *Jesus Son of Man*, p. 24.

This brilliantly argued case unfortunately, it seems to me, fails at two points: in the use of rabbinic examples to establish the idiom, and in the application of the idiom to sayings of Jesus. On the first point, it should first be noticed that Lindars discusses only four passages in which *bar nash(a)* is a self-reference, and considers two of these examples of the alleged 'idiomatic generic' use. These four passages are the four adduced in Vermes's abbreviated discussion in *Jesus the Jew*.[3] Lindars does not discuss the other five passages included in Vermes's more extended, original discussion.[4] This is unfortunate. The known cases of *bar nash(a)* as a self-reference are so few that any attempt to determine their exact nuance should take all of them into consideration. It is especially unfortunate for Lindars's own case, since two or three of the passages he does not discuss would fit the idiom he is attempting to establish as well as or even better than the two passages which are his actual evidence for it.

His discussion of these two passages (jBer. 3 b; jSheb. 38 d, with parallels) does not convince me that they are not examples of the properly generic use (*bar nasha* = 'mankind'). In the first, Simeon ben Yohai is, of course, only *interested* in requesting two mouths for those who are going to use one to recite the Torah, and really only interested in requesting two mouths for himself, since it is he who wants to do this, but possession of one or two mouths is a feature of *human nature* and so his prayer has to be that God would create mankind, human nature as such, with two mouths. Lindar's argument, that *bar nasha* refers to a class of men of which Simeon is in fact the only member, though in principle there might be others, seems rather contrived. Any statement about one person which *could* in principle also be true of other similar people, if there were such people, would by this argument become 'generic'.

In the second example (jSheb. 38 d) I see even less reason to prefer Lindars's interpretation to the properly generic one. To understand the sense of Simeon's conclusion as simply, 'No man perishes without the will of heaven', seems both obvious and wholly appropriate to the context. More to the point would have been a passage not discussed by Lindars (jBer. 5 b: 'The disciple of *bar nasha* is as dear to him as his son'[5]), where one has to concede that the generic sense of *bar nasha* is a qualified generic sense. It applies not to every man, but to every man who has a disciple (i. e. every rabbi). But this is a natural way of using a noun generically, because the qualification is obviously provided by the context (just as it is 'A man who...' or 'A

---

[3] G. Vermes, *Jesus the Jew* (London, [2]1976), pp. 164–67.

[4] G. Vermes, 'The Use of BAR NASH / BAR NASHA in Jewish Aramaic', in *Post-Biblical Jewish Studies* (Leiden, 1975), pp. 147–65 (reprinted from M. Black, *An Aramaic Approach to the Gospels and Acts* [Oxford, [3]1967], pp. 310–28).

[5] Quoted, *ibid.*, p. 160.

good man…'). It does not justify postulating an idiom in which *bar nasha* refers to a limited class of men ('a man in my position') where the limitation is *not* obviously provided by the context.

Even if Lindar's 'idiomatic use of the generic article' were established from the later Jewish evidence, it has to be stretched considerably to accommodate most of the six allegedly authentic sayings discussed in chapter 3. The saying which it fits most easily is the first (Mt. 8.20 = Lk 9.58), where *bar enasha* could in that case be rendered 'everyone in my position' (this is what the idiomatic generic use ought to mean). But it certainly cannot be said that 'the generic usage is *essential* to the purpose of the saying', as Lindars claims.[6] If the Son of Man were an exclusive self-reference (and Lindars must admit that this is how the Evangelists understood it), it would still be a perfectly adequate reply to the disciple's words in Mt. 8.19 = Lk. 9.57.

In saying 3 (Mt. 12.32 = Lk. 12.10) the case for a generic sense is a good one, but here it is the proper generic sense ('mankind'), and Lindars makes no attempt to argue for the special idiomatic generic sense in which the reference is restricted to a class of men. It should also be noticed that a simple indefinite sense ('a man') would also be an appropriate interpretation, since in this kind of generalizing context ('Everyone who speaks a word against a man') there is no real difference between the generic and indefinite senses.

A good test of whether the alleged idiomatic generic sense can really be detected in the sayings examined in chapter 3 is to try the translation, 'everyone in my position', since the idiom means that what is said of *bar enasha* is said of every man in the class to which the speaker belongs. This translation appears possible in saying 5 (Mt. 9.6 = Mk 2.10–11 = Lk. 5.24), but impossible in sayings 2,4 and 6, because in these sayings what is said of *bar enasha* actually applies to one man only, even if there *could* in principle be other people to whom it *could* be applied. Thus in saying 2 (Mt. 11.19 = Lk. 7.34) Jesus is not suggesting that his hearers are saying, 'Behold, a glutton and a drunkard…' about a whole class of non-ascetic evangelists. It will not do to claim that 'the generic *bar enasha* raises the matter to the level of a principle',[7] because the statement about *bar enasha* is not made in the *form* of a principle, but in the form of a statement of a specific fact about one man, precisely parallel to the preceding statement about John the Baptist. *Bar enasha* could be made generic only by changing the grammatic structure of the sentence and spoiling the parallelism with the statement about the Baptist. Of course, the statement does not exclude the possibility that there *could* be other people in a similar position (non-ascetic evangelists) who

---

[6] Lindars, *op. cit.*, p. 30.
[7] *Ibid.*, p. 33.

would incur the same treatment;[8] but it does not refer to them. As a matter of fact, the translation of *bar enasha* which Lindars himself offers for this saying is not, 'everyone in my position' (or something of that kind), but 'someone else'.[9] This translation makes good sense, but 'someone else' is indefinite, not generic.

The suspicion that 'generic' and 'indefinite' are being misleadingly equated is confirmed in the discussion of saying 4 (Lk. 11.30): 'It is another case of the generic usage... Just as Jonah was a sign to the Ninevites... so there is a man who will be a sign to the present generation'.[10] But this is not a generic usage. 'A man' here is neither 'each and every man' nor 'each and every member of a class of men', but just one man. *Bar enasha*, in that case, would be indefinite ('a man', 'someone'), not generic ('each and every man'). The role of being a sign to the present generation might be one which a number of men *could*, in principle, fulfil, but the saying is a statement about only the one man who does (or will) fulfil it. Again, only a grammatical change (which Lindars suggests, but does not insist on, as the meaning of the postulated Aramaic original[11]) could make *bar enasha* generic here: 'so a man *may be* to this generation'.[12] Is it not easier to explain *bar enash(a)* as indefinite?

Lindars makes the same move in the discussion of saying 5, where he offers the translation, 'But that you may know that *a man may have authority...*',[13] but in the case of saying 6 no such suggestion is made. Lindars's exegesis of saying 6 (Mt. 10.32–33 = Lk 12.8–9) is attractive and plausible, but it involves no real attempt to make *bar enasha* generic, as distinct from indefinite. Lindars's paraphrase of the first half of the saying is: 'All those who confess me before men will have a man to speak for them (i.e. an advocate) before the judgment seat of God...' The point is intended to be that Jesus stresses that there will be an advocate, rather than that he himself will be the advocate (though this is implied). But then *bar enasha* means 'someone' (indefinite), not 'each and every man' (generic) or 'each and every member of the class of men that includes me' (idiomatic generic). In this saying, any appeal to the special idiom seems to have become quite redundant. According to Lindars's own exegesis, Jesus is not identifying himself with some class of people (advocates at the last judgment) but referring to himself obliquely as 'someone'. Reconsideration of sayings 2, 4 and 5 suggests that this is also likely to be the idiom there.

---

8 Cf. *ibid.*, p. 33.
9 *Ibid.*, pp. 33, 174.
10 *Ibid.*, p. 41.
11 *Ibid.*, p. 42.
12 Cf. *ibid.*, p. 172.
13 *Ibid.*, p. 45; his italics.

Besides the six Son of Man sayings discussed in chapter 3, Lindars believes that three passion predictions, discussed in chapter 4, are authentic because they use the alleged idiomatic generic idiom. The argument of this chapter (too intricate to be discussed here) involves reconstruction and interpretation of the sayings which can really only be justified if the alleged idiom has already been established as characteristic of Jesus' usage. The argument of chapter 4 requires that of chapter 3 for its premise; it cannot come to its aid.

I conclude that this highly ingenious attempt to make Jesus' usage conform to an otherwise attested idiomatic use of *bar nasha* is a failure, though an heroic one. The idiom is not convincingly attested elsewhere, and it cannot explain all of even the small number of sayings of Jesus which Lindars judges authentic. However, as will become apparent, I do not consider Lindar's exegetical work to be wasted.

Where do we go from here?

Recent study of the available Jewish evidence seems to me to lead to the following two conclusions, which must be taken as premises for further discussion of 'Son of Man' in the Gospels: (1) 'Son of Man' was not a recognized title for an apocalyptic figure, and cannot therefore by itself constitute an allusion to Daniel 7.[14] Only Son of Man sayings which otherwise allude to Daniel 7 could have been understood as allusions to the figure in Dan. 7.13 on the lips of Jesus. (2) The later Jewish evidence for the use of *bar nash(a)* as a self-reference seems to be evidence only for the properly generic use, where what is said of *bar nash(a)* is true of all men (unless the context provides an obvious qualification of 'all') and therefore also of the speaker. There is no real support for *bar nash(a)* as an exclusive self-reference equivalent to *hahu gabra* (Vermes),[15] or for Lindars's idiomatic generic use.

These conclusions imply that, if Jesus' use of 'Son of Man' conformed to an accepted usage for which we have evidence, there would seem to be only two possible types of authentic sayings: (1) Authentic Son of Man sayings are those in which allusion to Daniel 7 is explicit apart from the phrase 'Son

---

[14] For the growing acceptance of this point in recent scholarship, see G. Vermes, 'The Present State of the "Son of Man" Debate', *JJS* 29 (1978), pp. 130–32.

[15] J. A. Fitzmyer, 'Another View of the "Son of Man" Debate', *JSNT* 4 (1979), p. 58, seems to admit that Vermes's interpretation applies in one case: the Cairo geniza fragment of the Palestinian Targum to Gen. 4.14 (see Vermes, 'The Use of BAR NASH', p. 159). Clearly *bar nash* is here a substitute for 'I', but it may be a substitute introduced precisely in order to give an additional, generic nuance: no *man* (such as Cain) can hide from *God*.

of Man' itself.[16] (2) Authentic Son of Man sayings are those which conform to the properly generic use (Casey). However, neither of these possibilities is at all satisfactory. The major problem in each case is that such a body of authentic sayings makes it very difficult to account for the later proliferation of Son of Man sayings in the Gospel traditions, particularly in the light of Lindars's very valuable study of the use of 'Son of Man' in Q and the four Gospels. Lindars shows that there was never a Son of Man Christology in the early church: the use of 'Son of Man' was purely a feature of the literary editing of the sayings of Jesus. But in that case there has to have been a sufficient body of authentic Son of Man sayings to establish 'Son of Man' as a characteristic self-designation of Jesus, which could then be extended to other sayings. Lindars also demonstrates that, although in the Gospels 'Son of Man' becomes at least quasi-titular, it is not understood as a true messianic title but as a self-designation of Jesus, which not even the Evangelists (except perhaps Mark) regard as everywhere carrying an allusion to Dan. 7.13. This makes it difficult to regard 'Son of Man' as a title for Jesus which originates purely from exegesis of Dan. 7.13. To account for Son of Man sayings which have nothing to do with Dan. 7.13, it seems there must have been some authentic sayings of this type.

Thus the possibility that the original Son of Man sayings (whether authentic or not) were only sayings which allude to Dan. 7.13 is ruled out. But Casey's view, that the only authentic sayings are those in which *bar enash(a)* can carry the properly generic sense, is also problematic. Very few sayings can plausibly be given this sense without becoming incredible (e.g. Mt. 8.20 = Lk. 9.58) or rather banal, and it could be argued that Casey, like Lindars, has extended his list of authentic sayings by including cases where the meaning he accepts is really indefinite, not generic.[17] But the fewer the authentic Son of Man sayings and the more restricted the types of Son of Man sayings which are regarded as authentic, the more difficult it is to account for the existence of inauthentic Son of Man sayings. Three or four authentic sayings in which *bar enash(a)* means 'mankind' are not likely to have given the impression that the term was a characteristic self-designation of Jesus or to have suggested a connection with Dan. 7.13.

---

[16] Against the thesis of A.J.B. Higgins, *The Son of Man in the Teaching of Jesus* (SNTSMS, 39; Cambridge, 1980), it is important to emphasize that, of the future Son of Man sayings, it is those in which the allusion to Dan. 7.13 is most explicit which have the best chance of authenticity, since the phrase 'Son of Man' *itself* cannot convey the idea of an eschatological judge.

[17] E.g. Mt. 11.19 = Lk. 7.34, which M. Casey, *Son of Man: The Interpretation and Influence of Daniel 7* (London, 1979), p. 229, calls a 'general statement', on the authority (*ibid.*, p. 240 n. 13) of Colpe and Jeremias, but in fact both these scholars are quite explicit in interpreting it as indefinite, not generic: C. Colpe, *TDNT*, VIII, pp. 431–32 (especially n. 241), and J. Jeremias, *New Testament Theology*, I (E. Tr.; London, 1971), pp. 261–62.

A further possibility, however, should be explored: that Jesus used *bar enash* (probably, rather than *bar enasha*) in the indefinite sense ('a man', 'someone'), which is itself a very common usage,[18] but used it as a form of deliberately oblique or ambiguous self-reference. This possibility has been suggested by my criticism of Lindars above, and would in fact preserve as correct a good deal of Lindars's exegesis of the sayings he accepts as authentic.[19] It should be noticed that although this use of *bar enash* is *grammatically* indefinite, meaning 'someone', in practice it can easily and naturally (like 'someone' in English) refer to a definite, though unidentified, person.[20] (Vermes gives an example from jYeb. 13 a: 'I am sending you *bar nash* like myself'.[21]) Thus it could be used as an oblique self-reference, in which the self-reference would normally be exclusive but implicit. Jesus would be referring to an unidentified 'someone', but those who fully understood his meaning would infer that the 'someone' was himself. Since the indefinite use (like 'a man' in English) can have a generic sense in certain contexts (e. g. jBer. 5 c; jKet. 35 a[22]), there will be no need to exclude the generic sense with self-reference in the few cases where it works (notably Mt. 12.32 = Lk 12.10), but in a much larger number of sayings the plausible meaning is indefinite, referring not to 'everyone' but to 'someone' (Mk 2.10 = Mt. 9.6 = Lk. 5.24; Mk. 2.28 = Mt. 12.8 = Lk 6.5; Mk. 8.31 = Lk. 9.22; Mk. 9.12; Mk. 9.31 = Mt. 17.22 = Lk 9.44; Mk. 10.33 = Mt. 22.18 = Lk. 18.31; Mk. 14.21 = Mt. 26.24 = Lk. 22.22; Mk. 14.41 = Mt. 26.45; Mt. 8.20 = Lk. 9.58; Mt. 11.19 = Lk. 7.34; Mt. 12.40 = Lk. 11.30; Mt. 26.2; Lk. 12.8–9 [cf. Mk. 8.38 = Lk. 9.26]; Lk. 22.48; Jn 1.51).

This proposal permits the authenticity of a similar range of sayings to those accepted by Casey and Lindars (to determine precisely which sayings are, by this criterion, authentic, would of course require detailed discussion), while allowing them, in some cases, a more natural exegesis, in other cases, a very similar exegesis. It also has other advantages. It would not, in the first place, necessarily exclude the authenticity of some Son of Man sayings which allude to Daniel 7. (The most obvious candidate for authenticity here would be Mk. 14.62.) In such sayings, the use of the indefinite 'a man' (*bar enash*) would be neither a title nor unambiguously a self-reference, but a literal echo of Dan. 7.13 *(ke-bar enash)*. There seems no reason why Jesus

---

[18] Cf. Vermes, 'The use of BAR NASH', pp. 155–56.

[19] The suggestion has been made with reference to a few sayings (J. Y. Campbell, 'The Origin and Meaning of the Term Son of Man', *JTS* 48 (1947), p. 152, of Mt. 11.19; Colpe, *TDNT,* VIII, pp. 430–33; Jeremias, *op. cit.,* pp. 261–62, both of Mk 2.10; Mt. 11.19; Mt. 8.20), but I know of no attempt to see it as Jesus' characteristic usage in a substantial number of sayings.

[20] So Campbell, *art. cit.,* pp. 151–52.

[21] Vermes, 'The Use of BAR NASH', p. 156.

[22] Quoted in *ibid.,* pp. 158–160.

could not have exploited the coincidence between his accustomed form of oblique self-reference and the language of Dan. 7.13, so that *bar enash* in a saying alluding to Dan. 7.13 becomes the same kind of veiled hint of his own status as other authentic son of Man sayings convey. This would not at all imply that *bar enash* has any connection with Dan. 7.13 in sayings which do not themselves allude to Daniel 7.

The indefinite use therefore permits the authenticity of a wide range of types of Son of Man sayings, including some future Son of Man sayings which allude to Daniel 7. This makes the process by which 'Son of Man', understood in Greek translation as quasi-titular,[23] was extended to other sayings, whether freshly created sayings or sayings in which 'Son of Man' was not original, quite readily intelligible. Once 'Son of Man' was understood as quasi-titular, this extension was simply an extension of the same kind of usage as was known in the authentic sayings.

It might appear a disadvantage of the proposal that it cannot appeal to parallels in later Jewish Aramaic.[24] But if Jesus' use of *bar enash* was a form of deliberately ambiguous self-reference, then *ex hypothesi* there do not need to be parallels to it. If Jesus had used a well established form of indirect self-reference, such as *hahu gabra*, the self-reference would have been explicit and easily recognized in most contexts.[25] But if Jesus wished to refer to himself in a way which was not necessarily immediately obvious, so that his hearers had to infer or guess the self-reference, then it is understandable that he should adopt a way of speaking which was not so well recognized an idiom. For such a purpose the use of the indefinite 'a man' or 'someone' is well suited. It is in fact a relatively straightforward development of the natural use of 'a man' with reference to the speaker in contexts which make the reference entirely obvious (e. g. Jn 8.40).[26]

The ambiguity of the self-reference will vary from saying to saying, from cases where the self-reference is obvious in the context (Lk. 22.48), through cases where the self-reference is deliberately unstressed (Mt. 10.32–33 = Lk. 12.8–9, following Lindars's exegesis), to cases where the saying has a somewhat enigmatic or riddling[27] character (Lk. 11.30; the passion predic-

---

[23] The translation of *bar enash* by the definite ὁ υἱὸς τοῦ ἀνθρώπου is sufficiently explained by the translator's wish to avoid the ambiguity of Jesus' own idiom: in his mind ὁ υἱὸς τοῦ ἀνθρώπου was a definite person, Jesus (cf. Casey, *op. cit.*, p. 230).

[24] But cf. Paul's use of ἄνθρωπον (as a modest form of self-reference) in 2 Cor. 12.2.

[25] Of course, in particular contexts *hahu gabra* may be ambiguous, as Vermes ('The Present State', p. 126) shows; but it remains true that an established idiom has less scope for ambiguity than an innovatory idiom.

[26] Note how easily the omission of με in Jn 8.40 would produce an oblique self-reference quite comparable with Mt. 11.19 = Lk. 7.34.

[27] Cf. e. g., indirect and riddling references to himself and his mission in Mt. 11.4–5 = Lk. 7.22; Mt. 12.41–42 = Lk. 11.32–33; Mk 3.27. For an interpretation of Son of Man say-

tions[28]), and cases where some hearers might easily assume Jesus' reference to be to a figure other than himself (sayings alluding to Daniel 7). This does not make the proposed usage inconsistent, but rather reveals an habitual form of oblique self-reference which in all cases expresses Jesus' accustomed reticence about his status and authority, for which there is abundant evidence. The point is not that Jesus did not wish his God-given role and authority to be recognized, but that he wanted people to recognize them for themselves. Claims are easy to make and as easily dismissed. By his oblique self-reference Jesus avoided claims, but invited people to think for themselves about the implications of the undeniable facts of his ministry. Then, in the paradoxical situation of the suffering and rejected prophet, he made the only kind of claim which is appropriate to that situation: a reference to future vindication, in which the obliqueness of the self-reference serves to leave the vindication to God who alone can vindicate him.

For the present, three brief illustrations must suffice:

(1) Mk. 2.10–11. The reference to 'a man' follows naturally as a response to v. 7, but the point is not that Jesus' healing of the paralytic demonstrates the general principle that men have authority to forgive sins. Jesus neither denies nor asserts that others have such authority, but points to his healing as evidence that at any rate one man, himself, does have it. Thus he claims no more than his deed demonstrates, and the obliqueness of the self-reference serves to make his authority not so much a claim as an inference which his hearers may draw for themselves from what they see.

(2) Lk. 11.30. Here the self-reference is less obvious, more enigmatic, but the implication is similar. To those who see the significance of Jesus and his ministry, he *is* a sign. To those who do not, who cannot recognize the evidence which is before their eyes, there is no point in *claiming* to be a sign. All that can be said is that there is someone who is a sign.

(3) Mt. 26.64 = Mk. 14.62 = Lk. 22.67–68. Jesus avoids a direct claim to messiahship which, if his accusers cannot believe it from the evidence they already have (cf. Lk. 22.67), he cannot prove. Although, in the context, the allusion to Dan. 7.13 must amount to a self-reference, the obliqueness makes his status one which he leaves it to God to vindicate. The allusion to Dan. 7.13 is made not because Jesus prefers the 'title' Son of Man to those offered by the high priest, but because (along with Ps. 110.1) it is appropriate to the thought of eschatological vindication and allows an indefinite third person reference.

---

ings as riddling self-references, see also G. Lindeskog, 'Das Rätsel des Menschensohnes', *Studia theologica* 22 (1968), pp. 149–75, though he takes Son of Man to be an apocalyptic title.

[28] Following Jeremias's interpretation of these as riddles (*op. cit.*, pp. 281–82).

8. The Apocalypses in the New Pseudepigrapha*

The publication of *The Old Testament Pseudepigrapha* (henceforth *OTP*), edited by J. H. Charlesworth,[1] is a major event for the current renaissance of pseudepigrapha studies and for biblical studies generally. The purpose of this article is to offer some assessment of the treatment of apocalyptic literature in vol. 1 of *OTP*,[2] with the interests of NT students and scholars especially in mind.

OTP is the first collected edition of the pseudepigrapha in English translation since 1913, when *The Apocrypha and Pseudepigrapha of the Old Testament* (henceforth *APOT*), edited by R. H. Charles, was published. Its most obvious difference from *APOT* is the very much larger number of works which are included. *APOT* contained only six apocalyptic works (4 Ezra, 2 Baruch, 3 Baruch, 1 Enoch, 2 Enoch and *Sib. Or.* 3–5). *OTP* includes these six, three of them in longer forms (4 Ezra with the additional chs. 1–2, 15–16; 2 Enoch with the final chs. 69–73; and the complete collection of *Sib. Or.* 1–14), and in addition thirteen other works in its section 'Apocalyptic Literature and Related Works'. None of these thirteen appear in *APOT*. In fact there are also two more works which really belong in this section of *OTP*, since they are unambiguously apocalypses *(Ladder of Jacob* and *Ascension of Isaiah)*, but which have been assigned to vol. 2.[3] *OTP*'s selection of apocalypses is also larger than that projected for the series *Jüdische Schriften aus hellenistisch-römischer Zeit* (henceforth *JSHRZ*) or included in *The Apocryphal Old Testament*, edited by H. F. D. Sparks.[4]

---

* First publication: *Journal for the Study of the New Testament* 26 (1986) 97–117; reprinted in: Evans / Porter ed., *New Testament Backgrounds: A Sheffield Reader* (Biblical Seminar 43; Sheffield: Sheffield Academic Press, 1997) 67–88.

[1] Vol. 1: *Apocalyptic Literature and Testaments* (New York: Doubleday; London: Darton, Longman & Todd, 1983).

[2] In order to keep this article within reasonable bounds, I shall not discuss the testaments, which are also in vol. 1, even though some of them include apocalyptic material.

[3] Since this article was written before the publication of vol. 2, I cannot discuss these two works. Presumably they are included in vol. 2 because they are regarded as legendary expansions of the OT, but they are no more so than *1 Enoch* or the *Apocalypse of Abraham*, both of which include narrative material as well as apocalyptic visions.

[4] This volume, from Oxford University Press, was not yet published when this article was written. I owe the information about its contents and those of *JSHRZ* to J. H. Char-

Of course, biblical scholars have never depended solely on *APOT* for their knowledge of the pseudepigrapha, but it has tended to influence their sence of the range of pseuepigraphical works which are really relevant as 'background' to the NT. Certainly, the common views of the character of ancient Jewish apocalyptic have been largely based on *APOT*'s selection of apocalypses, and illuminating parallels to the NT have usually been sought in these. The standard studies of apocalyptic are based on these apocalypses, usually with the addition of the *Apocalypse of Abraham*. As *OTP* becomes the standard work of reference, this may or may not change. Much depends on whether *OTP*'s additional apocalypses can really be treated as in any way reliable evidence for the Judaism of the NT period, a question which requires careful assessment in each case. In what follows I shall offer comments on *OTP*'s treatment of each apocalyptic work, with the exception of the two calendrical works *(Treatise of Shem* and *Revelation of Ezra)*, which belong in a distinct category of their own. These comments will, I hope, be of use to those who will be using *OTP* as a work of reference. I shall then offer some more general comments on the range of apocalypses which have been selected for inclusion in *OTP*.

(1) 1 Enoch (E. Isaac) is probably the most important non-canonical apocalypse for students of the NT, though its *direct* influence on the NT has often been vastly exaggerated (as here: p. 10). It has also been the object of a great deal of important recent research, rather little of which is reflected in Isaac's introduction and notes.

Essentially Isaac gives us an introduction to and translation of the Ethiopic version of *1 Enoch*. Controversy is likely to surround his use of the Ethiopic manuscripts, in particular his judgment that one manuscript (Lake Tana 9) is not only the oldest but very much the best, so that its readings are usually to be preferred.[5] His translation is of this manuscript, correcting only its obvious errors, though many variants in other manuscripts are given in the apparatus. As far as a reader who is not an Ethiopic scholar can judge, a fair number of this manuscript's unique or unusual readings are preferable, sometimes because they agree with the Greek version against other Ethiopic manuscripts (e.g. at 1,9; 24.5), but its readings cannot be preferable in every instance. This translation may supplement, but cannot replace, that of Knibb (whose edition of Ethiopic Enoch[6] appeared after Isaac's work was completed).

---

lesworth, *The Pseudepigrapha and Modern Research with a Supplement* (SBLSCS, 7S; Chico: Scholars Press, 1981), pp. 29–30.

[5] This judgment is maintained in greater detail in E. Isaac, 'New Light Upon the Book of Enoch from Newly-Found Ethiopic MSS', *JOAS* 103 (1983), pp. 399–411.

[6] M. A. Knibb, *The Ethiopic Book of Enoch*, 2 vols. (Oxford: Clarendon Press, 1978).

The Greek versions of *1 Enoch* are cited quite often in the apparatus, the Qumram Aramaic fragments only rarely. But the latter, though very fragmentary, are evidence of *1 Enoch* in its (probably) original language, while the Greek versions cover about forty chapters of the book. In view of the special importance of *1 Enoch* among the pseudepigrapha, should we not have been given translations of all versions, Greek, Ethiopic, and Aramaic, in parallel columns?

(2) 2 Enoch (F. I. Andersen). Of all the apocalypses in *APOT, 2 Enoch* has always been the most puzzling and controversal. Some have insisted that it is Christian and of relatively late date, and the problems of provenance and date have scarcely been helped by disagreements over the relative priority of the two recensions, longer and shorter. Andersen's principal achievement is to provide us with a translation (of the two recensions in parallel) based on more and better manuscripts than previous translations, though he is the first to insist on its provisionality. More work on the text still needs to be done before we have an entirely secure basis for answering other questions. Andersen rightly argues that the question of priority between the two recensions should not be hastily answered: the evidence is too complicated to allow the assumption that either the shortest or the longest text is always the original.

Andersen inclines to regard *2 Enoch* as an ancient work from some group (perhaps of God-fearers) on the fringes of Judaism, but he is more frankly cautious about his conclusions than many contributors to this volume: 'In every respect 2 Enoch remains an enigma. So long as the date and location remain unknown, no use can be made of it for historical purposes' (p. 97). Rereading *2 Enoch* in Andersen's translation, I found myself constantly deciding that the material must be ancient. But a great deal of patient study of all the available parallels to *2 Enoch*'s contents will be necessary before NT scholars are able to base anything on quotations from *2 Enoch*.

(3) 3 Enoch (P. Alexander) is the one Merkabah text already quite well known to NT scholars, through Odeberg's edition and translation. Alexander's improved translation is based on a corrected text, and is accompanied by abundant, very informative notes. The introduction is in fact a masterly brief introduction to Merkabah mysticism in general, including its relationship to ancient Jewish apocalyptic and specifically to some of the texts in *OTP*. The links between aspects of apocalyptic texts of the first and second centuries AD and the Merkabah texts are becoming increasingly apparent, and make an acquaintance with the latter essential for scholars interested in the former. Perhaps this justifies the inclusion of at least one Merkabah text in *OTP*, but not necessarily the inclusion of this text, which, despite its dependence on some very old traditions, is in Alexander's view to be dated in the fifth or sixth century AD, i.e. it is probably not, as Odeberg thought,

one of the earliest, but one of the later, Merkabah texts. Reliable translations of the other major texts are an urgent need.

(4) Sibylline Oracles (J.J. Collins). Although the *Sibylline Oracles* are part Jewish, part Christian, and were written over a long period (book 14 is probably seventh-century), they form a continuous tradition of writing, and it is extremely useful to have for the first time an accessible translation of the whole collection, with excellent introductions and notes.

Particularly neglected but important are the Jewish parts of books 1–2, which were left out of *APOT*, and also out of Hennecke's *New Testament Apocrypha*, in which translations of only the Christian parts of books 1–2 were given.[7] However, Collins overestimates the possible extent of Jewish material in book 2 (p. 330), because he has taken no account of M.R. James's demonstration that 2.196–338 is dependent on the *Apocalypse of Peter*[8] (in fact, it is largely a poetic paraphrase of *Apoc. Pet.* 4–14). Since the passages in book 2 which are paralleled in book 8 (p. 332) are precisely the parts of this section which are not borrowed from the *Apocalypse of Peter*, the priority of book 8 to book 2 can also be demonstrated, with implications for the date of both books.

(5) Apocryphon of Ezekiel (J.R. Mueller and S.E. Robinson). The *Apocryphon of Ezekiel* survives only in a few fragments: the five which can be fairly securely identified are translated here (though the two longest are not, despite the claim in the section heading, *new* translations). Clement of Alexandria in fact gives a little more of fragment 5 than is translated here (while the Chester Beatty papyrus gives a good deal more, but in a highly fragmentary, untranslatable state). It would have been useful to have had some reference to other possible fragments (such as the quotation in Tertullian, *De res.* 22).

That the work dates from the late first century BC or early first century AD is well established. Its parable of the resurrection (the longest fragment) is well known, but has probably not been given the attention it deserves as evidence of Jewish ideas about resurrection in NT times. It also has some relevance to the study of Gospel parables (cf. Matt. 22.2; Mark 12.9), as may the expansion of Ezekiel's image of the shepherd in fragment 5.

(6) Apocalypse of Zephaniah (O.S. Wintermute). Of the apocalypses which *OTP* adds to *APOT*'s selection, this is the only one which has a real chance of being a pre-Christian Jewish work (apart from the fragmentary *Apocryphon of Ezekiel*). It has also been extraordinarily neglected by schol-

---

[7] E. Hennecke, *New Testament Apocrypha,* ed. W. Schneemelcher and R. McL. Wilson (London: Lutterworth, 1963, 1965), II, pp. 709–19.

[8] M.R. James, 'A New Text of the Apocalypse of Peter', *JTS* 12 (1911), pp. 39–44, 51–52. The material is all ultimately Jewish in origin, but reached the *Sibylline Oracle* via the *Apocalypse of Peter*.

ars.[9] Its inclusion in *OTP* is therefore fully justified, and any discussion which served to bring it to general scholarly attention would be welcome. While Wintermute's treatment is not wholly satisfactory, it is a significant start. His notes to the text are gratifyingly extensive. It is unfortunate that he apparently wrote before Martha Himmelfarb's dissertation became available:[10] her discussion of the *Apocalypse of Zephaniah* (which she continues to call 'the Anonymous Apocalypse') within the broad context of tours of hell in Jewish and Christian apocalyptic is one of the most important contributions so far to the study of this apocalypse. It has the general effect of vindicating a fairly early date. Wintermute has also missed Scholem's discussion of the passage quoted by Clement of Alexandria:[11] both Scholem and Himmelfarb would have alerted him to the contacts between these texts and the Merkabah literature.

The texts in question are three: a short quotation in Clement of Alexandria, a brief manuscript fragment in Sahidic, and a long manuscript fragment in Akhmimic. The two Coptic fragments are from manuscripts which also contained the Coptic *Apocalypse of Elijah.* Clement's quotation is explicitly said to be from the *Apocalypse of Zephaniah;* the Sahidic fragment contains the words, 'I, Zephaniah, saw these things in my vision'; but the Akhmimic fragments contains no indication of the identity of the seer (and has therefore sometimes been called the Anonymous Apocalypse). Two problems arise: (a) Are Clement's quotation and the Sahidic fragment from the same *Apocalypse of Zephaniah?* (b) Are the Sahidic and Akhmimic fragments from the same work? Wintermute answers both questions affirmatively, but probably with too much assurance. It is true that the two Coptic fragments are closely related in style and content, but we could be dealing with two distinct apocalypses, either by the same author or one based on the other. My hesitation about identifying the Akhmimic text as the *Apocalypse of Zephaniah* arises from 6.10, in which the seer refers to events of the Babylonian exile as past historical events. This could be a slip on the author's part, but ancient pseudepigraphal writers, including apocalyptists, were usually careful to avoid such blatant anachronisms. (In the apocalypses in this volume, I think the only other examples are *Greek Apocalypse of Ezra*

---

[9] Surprisingly it is not mentioned in G. W. E. Nickelsburg, *Jewish Literature Between the Bible and the Mishnah* (London: SCM Press, 1981) or in C. Rowland, *The Open Heaven: A Study of Apocalpytic in Judaism and Early Christianity* (London: SPCK, 1982).

[10] M. Himmelfarb, *Tours of Hell: The Development and Transmission of an Apocalyptic Form in Jewish and Christian Literature* (diss.; University of Pennsylvania, 1981; University Microfilms 8117791). I have not yet seen this work in its published form (Philadelphia, 1983).

[11] G. G. Scholem, *Jewish Gnosticism, Merkabah Mysticism, and Talmudic Tradition* (New York: Jewish Theological Seminary of America, ²1965), pp. 18–19.

1.19; 2.1; 4.11; 5.22; *Vision of Ezra* 38; *Apocalypse of Sedrach* 15.2–5 – an indication that the authors or redactors of these late Christian apocalypses had lost any real sense of the historical identity of the pseudonym.) If the seer is therefore a post-exilic OT figure,[12] not many candidates are available. I wonder whether the text might be the *Apocalypse of Zechariah*,[13] which in the Stichometry of Nicephorus is listed after the *Apocalypses of Elijah and Zephaniah*.[14] Some support for this suggestion, which can only be conjecture, may come from the fact that the visions are partly modelled on those of Zech. 1–6 (though this is also true of the Sahidic fragment).[15] At any rate, the relationship between the Sahidic and Akhmimic texts cannot be regarded as settled. Just as problematic is the relationship between these texts and the quotation in Clement: the difficulties in supposing that the latter is from the same work as even the Sahidic fragment alone seem to me greater than Wintermute allows (p. 500).

I agree with Wintermute that there is no reason to regard the Coptic texts as (a) Christian work(s), though I am more inclined than he is to see 10.9 as a minor Christian embellishment. On the other hand, 8.9 ('my sons…') does not have to be a 'homiletical aside', indicating that the text was meant to be read in a religious assembly. It could be that the seer is represented as recounting his visions to his sons (cf. Isaiah's apostrophes to 'Hezekiah and Jasub my son', which punctuate his account of his vision in *Ascension of Isaiah* 4.1; 8.24; 9.22; 11.16), perhaps in a testamentary context (cf. Enoch's account of his visions, mixed with homiletical comments to his sons, in *2 Enoch* 40–47).

The extraordinary incoherence of the Akhmimic text (which not even the *Greek Apocalypse of Ezra* equals) must, it seems to me, result from abbreviation. We know from other cases where more than one recension survives that scribes not infrequently tried to abbreviate apocalypses (cf. *2 Enoch, 3 Baruch, Ascension of Isaiah, Apocalypse of Peter*), sometimes resulting in the kind of non sequiturs and abrupt transitions which the Akhmimic text here shows. But in that case we cannot rely on the length

---

[12] A NT pseudonym seems ruled out by the purely OT context of the account: cf. 3.4; 6.10; 7.7; 9.4; 11.4.

[13] The quotation which Origen (comment on Eph. 4.27, in J. A. F. Gregg (ed.), 'The Commentary of Origen upon the Epistle to the Ephesians: Part III', *JTS* 3 [1902], p. 554) ascribes to Zechariah the father of John (cf. next note) would not be out of place in the work of which the Akhmimic text is part.

[14] It is there called, 'Of Zechariah the father of John', but this may be a mistaken Christian identification of the seer. The ancient lists of apocryphal books nevertheless include this work among the OT apocrypha in the chronological position of Zechariah the prophet.

[15] This dependence on Zech. 1–6 needs to be studied in connection with Himmelfarb's study of the 'demonstrative explanations' in tours of hell: *Tours of Hell*, ch. 3.

given for the *Apocalypse of Zephaniah* (or for the *Apocalypse of Zechariah*) in the Stichometry of Nicephorus for calculations related to our fragment (cf. *OTP*, pp. 497–98). The manuscript which contained our Akhmimic fragment could have included abbreviated versions of two apocalypses (*Apocalypse of Zephaniah* and *Apocalypse of Zechariah?*) as well as the *Apocalypse of Elijah*.

Probably the most important aspect of the Coptic texts is that they may well be, along with a fragment of the *Apocalypse of Elijah*,[16] the earliest examples, in the apocalyptic tradition, of detailed visions of the punishments of the damned in hell. The tradition of such visions is very old (cf. *1 Enoch* 22; 27), and from brief references to such visions in apocalypses which do not actually describe them (*2 Apoc. Bar.* 59.10–11; *Apocalypse of Abraham* 21.3; *Ascension of Isaiah* 1.3;[17] 4 *Ezra* 7.84; *3 Apoc. Bar.* 16.4 S; *2 Enoch* 40–41; cf. *Bib. Ant.* 23.6), we can be sure that they were to be found in apocalypses of the NT period. Scholars have tended to think of the genre of the apocalyptic tour of the punishments of hell as belonging to a later period, from the second century AD onwards,[18] but in fact the evidence is good that it flourished already in the first century AD.[19] These Coptic '*Apocalypse of Zephaniah*' texts may well be among the early sources of the whole tradition. At least in the present abbreviated texts, they refer only in a perfunctory way (9.4) to the parallel tradition of visions of the bliss of the righteous in paradise.

These rather extended comments may serve to welcome one of the more important 'newcomers' to the pseudepigrapha, and also to indicate that much work needs to be done on it.

(7) 4 Ezra (B.M. Metzger). Here the words 'a new translation' included in the title of this, as of other sections of the volume, are quite misleading: the translation is that of the RSV Apocrypha (prepared by Metzger), first

---

[16] This is the fragment quoted in the apocryphal *Epistle of Titus*. It is published, with related material, in M.E. Stone and J. Strugnell, *The Books of Elijah: Parts 1–2* (SBLTT, 18; Missoula, Montana: Scholars Press, 1979), pp. 14–26.

[17] In my opinion this is not meant to be a reference to any of the contents of the present *Ascension of Isaiah*, but refers to a lost *Testament of Hezekiah*, which must have been a work of the first century AD or earlier, in which Hezekiah described his descent to Hades (the idea no doubt developed from Isa. 38).

[18] The classic treatments are the Christian apocalypses of Peter, Paul and the Virgin; cf. also, in *OTP*, the *Greek Apocalypse of Ezra* and the *Vision of Ezra*. In both Jewish and early Christian apocalyptic the genre flourished right through the medieval period.

[19] The account of the punishments in hell in the early second century *Apocalypse of Peter* must be based on a Jewish apocalypse, perhaps that of Elijah: cf. my discussion in 'The Apocalypse of Peter: An Account of Research', in *Aufstieg und Niedergang der römischen Welt* (ed. H. Temporini und W. Haase; Berlin, New York: de Gruyter), 2.25.6, pp. 4712–4750; and Himmelfarb, *Tours of Hell*, ch. 5.

published in 1957, and only slightly amended here.[20] Notes to the text are purely textual, and the marginal references do not even include the important parallels in *2 Baruch*. The study of 4 Ezra is not advanced by this contribution, but probably we should not expect it to be, since 4 Ezra is one of the few non-canonical apocalypses on which much of the basic scholarly work has already been done.

Much more disappointing is the treatment of the additions to the original apocalypse: chs. 1–2 *(5 Ezra)* and 15–16 *(6 Ezra)*, which were not included in *APOT*, though they have always been well known from their inclusion in the Protestant Apocrypha, as well as the appendix to the Vulgate. *OTP* includes them as part of the translation of 4 Ezra, bur readers are given practically no guidance on what to make of them. Metzger's introduction to 4 Ezra scarcely mentions them, except to inform us (with unjustified dogmatism) that 'Near the middle or in the second half of the third century four chapters were added... by one or more Christian writers' (p. 520). In fact, *5 Ezra* has been most commonly and most plausibly dated in the second century, as most recently by Daniélou[21] and by Stanton.[22] It is scarcely conceivable that both 5 and 6 *Ezra* come from the same author.

5 Ezra is a patently Jewish Christian work. In the case of *6 Ezra*, which lacks any overtly Christian characteristics, the Jewish or Christian origin of the text is certainly open to debate, Against the usual, but not very well-founded, belief in its Christian origin, Schrage[23] and Harnisch[24] have argued that it is a purely Jewish apocalyptic work, to be dated perhaps earlier than 4 Ezra. Such arguments should have been discussed and assessed in *OTP*, which may thus have missed an important opportunity of rehabilitating a neglected Jewish apocalypse. Even if 5 and 6 *Ezra* are both Christian, they bear the same kind of relationship to underlying Jewish apocalyptic traditions as do several other Christian works included in *OTP*, and are also probably earlier in date than the other Ezra apocalypses (apart from 4 Ezra) which *OTP* includes. They therefore merit the same kind of extended treatment as pseudepigraphal works in their own right.

Furthermore, the same principles which have led to the inclusion of 5 and 6 *Ezra* and the later apocrypha in *OTP* should also have led to the inclu-

---

[20] Metzger points this out: *OTP*, p. 518.

[21] J. Daniélou, *The Origins of Latin Christianity* (ET, ed. J.A. Baker; London: Darton, Longman & Todd; Philadelphia: Westminster Press, 1977), p. 18.

[22] G.N. Stanton, '5 Ezra and Matthean Christianity in the Second Century', *JTS* 28 (1977), pp. 67–83.

[23] W. Schrage, 'Die Stellung zur Welt bei Paulus, Epiktet und in der Apokalyptik. Ein Beitrag zu 1 Kor 7,29–31', *ZTK* 61 (1964), pp. 139–54.

[24] W. Harnisch, *Eschatologische Existenz* (FRLANT, 110; Göttingen: Vandenhoeck & Ruprecht, 1973), pp. 72–74.

sion of a translation of the Armenian version of 4 Ezra.[25] This is, in effect, a rather thoroughly revised version of 4 Ezra, including substantial additions to the text. Stone argues that these did not originate in Armenian, but derive from the Greek text behind the Armenian version and date from the fourth century at the latest. Though they constitute a Christian version of 4 Ezra, they may depend on early Jewish sources.[26] The inclusion of these additions to 4 Ezra in *OTP* would have been particularly useful because they belong to the same category of material inspired by 4 Ezra as do the *Greek Apocalypse of Ezra,* the *Vision of Ezra* and the *Apocalypse of Sedrach.* With their inclusion, *OTP* could have given us a fairly complete collection of apocalyptic works inspired by 4 Ezra.[27] Another missed opportunity!

(8) Greek Apocalypse of Ezra (M. E. Stone). The translation of this work was made from one manuscript (that used by Tischendorf) and was completed before the publication of Wahl's edition of the text,[28] which is based on two manuscripts, but in fact the latter would have made practically no difference to the translation. The introduction and notes are thorough and learned, and constitute the fullest study of this work so far produced (fuller than Müller's in *JSHRZ*).[29]

It is important to realize that this work's OT pseudonym, which is one of the criteria for its inclusion in *OTP*, probably results simply from the fact that its author took 4 Ezra as a model for the kind of work he wished to write (a debate with God about his righteousness and mercy in judging sinners). It is no necessary indication of the Jewish (as opposed to Christian) character of its contents, and there is no real reason to regard this work (which is unquestionably Christian in its present form) as a Christian edition of an earlier Jewish apocalypse. (The same comments apply to other Ezra apocrypha: *Vision of Ezra* and *Questions of Ezra.*). As Stone recognizes, the work itself is Christian, but, as both the jumbled nature of its contents and the parellels with other works indicate, it is closely reliant on several sources, probably Jewish as well as Christian. That there is ancient Jewish apocalyptic material here is very probable. Its reliable identification

---

[25] M. E. Stone, *The Armenian Version of IV Ezra* (University of Pennsylvania Armenian Texts and Studies 1; Missoula, Montana: Scholars Press, 1979).

[26] Stone, *Armenian Version,* p. ix; cf. also M. E. Stone, 'Jewish Apocryphal Literature in the Armenian Church', *Le Muséon* 95 (1982), p. 292. Stone promises to give detailed evidence for this in his forthcoming *Textual Commentary on the Armenian Version of 4 Ezra.*

[27] The Syriac *Apocalypse of Ezra* and the Falasha *Apocalypse of Ezra* are also inspired by 4 Ezra.

[28] O. Wahl (ed.), *Apocalypsis Esdrae, Apocalypsis Sedrach, Visio Beati Esdrae* (PVTG, 4; Leiden: E. J. Brill, 1977).

[29] Once again, it is a pity that it was written too soon to take account of Himmelfarb, *Tours of Hell.*

must await further study especially in conjunction with paralled material in other Jewish and Christian apocalypses.

In view of the nature of the work and the state of scholarship on it, Stone wisely draws almost no conclusions about date or provenance: 'a date sometime between AD 150 and 850 is probable. Its provenance cannot be discerned' (p. 563).

(9) Vision of Ezra (J. R. Mueller and G. A. Robbins). This work is quite closely related to the *Greek Apocalypse of Ezra,* but the relationship is not one of simple dependence in either direction. I would be inclined to date it later than the *Greek Apocalypse,* partly because the role of Ezra is further removed from his role in 4 Ezra, which provided the original inspiration for this cycle of Ezra apocalypses. However, even the date which Mueller and Robbins suggest (between 350 and 600 AD) is, on present evidence, too precise: it might even be earlier, it could certainly be later.

As Mueller and Robbins recognize, this work's closest relationships (apart from with other works in the Ezra cycle) are with the apocalypses of Peter, Paul and the Virgin, and the apocryphal *Apocalypse of John.* This raises an important issue about the criteria for inclusion in a collection of OT pseudepigrapha. All these apocalypses, whether they bear OT or NT pseudonyms, are Christian works which draw on Jewish apocalyptic sources and traditions. In fact, the *Apocalypses of Peter* and *Paul* are probably closer to ancient Jewish apocalyptic sources than are the *Greek Apocalypse of Ezra* and the *Vision of Ezra.* To distinguish here between OT pseudepigrapha, which bear an OT pseudonym, and NT apocrypha, which bear a NT pseudonym, is to draw a quite artificial distinction among works which are closely related to each other and are equally useful, but also equally problematic, means of access to Jewish apocalyptic traditions.

(10) Questions of Ezra (M. E. Stone), of which Recension B is here published in translation for the first time, is an intriguing work, much of whose content must surely go back to ancient Jewish sources. But not even Stone can decide whether it originated in Armenian or not. This is an extreme case of the tantalizing character of so many of the ostensibly late pseudepigrapha, which seem to preserve early material but offer no clues to their time of origin.

(11) Apocalypse of Sedrach (S. Agourides). It is annoying to find that this work has been given verse numbers which do not correspond to those in Wahl's edition (1977).[30] Although Agourides's work was completed without knowledge of Wahl's edition, the verse numbers could easily have been brought into line with what is likely to remain the standard edition of the Greek text.

---

[30] See n. 28 above.

This work is related to the apocalypses of the Ezra cycle, but presses further the theme of the seer's debate with God in relation to his compassion for sinners. Agourides's arguments for seeing it as a Jewish work which has been only superficially Christianized should be considered carefully, but do not carry complete conviction. The claim that much of its doctrinal content is 'atypical of medieval Christianity' (p. 606) is too broad a generalization to be useful. In the many centuries of Christian history during which the *Apocalypse of Sedrach* could, on present evidence, have originated, there is plenty of evidence of minority Christian viewpoints not dissimilar to those of the apocalypse. Its general doctrinal tendency is consistent, for example, with the views of some of the 'merciful' Christians *(misericordes)* reported by Augustine *(De civ. Dei* 21,17–27). Views less extreme but tending in the same direction are found in the *Apocalypse of Paul* and the *Apocalypse of the Virgin,* and even though their ideas about mercy for the damned probably derive from Jewish sources, the popularity of these apocalypses shows that there were Christian circles in which such ideas were welcomed and propagated.[31] Moreover, the apocalyptic genre of the seer's debate with God was attractive precisely to writers, whether Jewish or Christian, who wanted a vehicle for some degree of protest against the official theology.

The attribution of the apocalypse to Sedrach is not easy to explain if it is Christian, but not much easier to explain if it is Jewish. The problem disappears if we accept the suggestion[32] that the name is a corruption of Ezra.

This is not to deny that Jewish sources have undoubtedly been used (e.g. the substitution of Christ for Michael in ch. 9 is transparent), but the identification of Jewish material requires caution.

The intriguing possibility that 6.4–6 preserves a pre-Christian parable of the prodigal son, which Jesus deliberately adapted to make a different point, should not be dismissed without further consideration, but it is also possible that the author has deliberately used only the beginning of Jesus' parable (as he understood it), leaving open the possibility of the prodigal's repentance, which forms the theme of the later part of his work.

(12) 2 Baruch (A. F. J. Klijn). Klijn's introduction is largely a translation of his German introduction in *JSHRZ.* It is a commendably thorough treatment within its scope.

(13) 3 Baruch (H. E. Gaylord, Jr) is the most neglected of the apocalypses which were included in *APOT,* no doubt partly because it seems to have little relevance to NT studies. But this neglect is mistaken, arising as it does

---

[31] On the place of the teaching of these apocalypses, as well as the *Apocalypses of Sedrach* and *Ezra,* in the early Christian tradition, see now E. Lupieri, 'Poena aeterna nelle più antiche apocalissi cristiane apocrife non gnostiche', *Augustinianum* 2 (1983), pp. 361–72.

[32] M. E. Stone, 'The Metamorphosis of Ezra', *JTS* 33 (1982), p. 6.

from the tendency to restrict relevance to the mere search for parallels. A proper understanding of early Christianity requires a rounded picture of the religious context in which it originated and grew, and in this sense it is as important for the student of the NT to understand aspects of contemporary Judaism which bear little resemblance to anything in the NT as it is for him to study those which influenced early Christianity. If early Christians did not share the concerns of *3 Baruch,* it is at least worth asking why they did not. Precisely because the NT scholar is unlikely to find *3 Baruch* very interesting, he should make the effort to study it! It is a post-70 AD Jewish apocalypse which reacts very differently to the catastrophe from the way in which the authors of *4 Ezra* and *2 Baruch* reacted. Baruch's attention is turned away from the fate of the earthly Jerusalem and the problems of history and eschatology, and towards the mysteries of the heavenly realms. But this interest (which includes meteorological and astronomical topics as well as more obviously religious subjects) had always been a feature of the Jewish apocalypses, as we have recently been becoming more aware.

3 Baruch survives both in Greek and in a Slavonic version. As in *APOT,* the translations of the two versions are here printed in parallel, since the differences between the two are such that any other treatment of them would be very misleading. By far the most important advance on *APOT* is in the textual basis for the translation of the Slavonic and in the resulting estimation of the value of the Slavonic for access to the original apocalypse. The translation is based on Gaylord's forthcoming edition of the Slavonic text, for which he has examined all known manuscripts of the Slavonic (though, unfortunately, in one respect the translation here is not as definitive as that in his forthcoming edition will be: see p. 655). From this it now becomes clear that where the Slavonic and the Greek diverge, it is the Slavonic that is frequently more original and represents a less Christianized version of the apocalypse than the extant Greek manuscripts do. Thus Gaylord's work on the Slavonic not only takes us closer to the original apocalypse; it also increases our confidence that *3 Baruch* is an originally Jewish work. (Gaylord himself is unwilling to assert this last conclusion, because he thinks that too sharp a distinction between Jewish and Christian works in the first two centuries AD may be artificial. He has a point.) Gaylord's work on *3 Baruch* is thus a striking instance of the great importance of work on the Slavonic versions of the pseudepigrapha.

Gaylord seems to me too cautious about identifying *3 Baruch* with the Baruch apocryphon known to Origen, especially since he concludes for other reasons that *3 Baruch* was written before Origen. The problem is that there were seven heavens in the work known to Origen, whereas in both our versions of *3 Baruch* Baruch gets no further than the fourth heaven. However, precisely Gaylord's vindication of the greater originality of the

Slavonic indicates that both our versions of *3 Baruch* are abbreviated. 16.4–8 in the Slavonic must be an abbreviation of an originally longer ending in which Baruch travelled to higher heavens in order to view the punishments of the damned and the resting-place of the righteous. An early abbreviation of *3 Baruch* by Christian copyists is easily explained, in that material on hell and paradise was readily available in well-known early Christian apocalypses such as those of Peter and Paul (the latter perhaps drew some of its material on these subjects from *3 Baruch*), whereas *3 Baruch* would have been copied and read for the sake of its more unusual material on the contents of the lower heavens.

(14) Apocalypse of Abraham (R. Rubinkiewicz and H. G. Lunt). There can be no real doubt about the *Apocalypse of Abraham*'s place among the ancient Jewish apocalypses: it should be the least controversial of *OTP*'s additions to the apocalypses in *APOT*. But since it has been preserved only in Slavonic, there is room for doubt about the originality of everything in the Slavonic version. Rubinkiewicz's suggestions of Bogomil interpolations (p. 684)[33] probably go too far (23.5–11 seems to me the passage most likely to have been adapted under Bogomil influence), but in a Slavonic apocryphon they are always possible. Nor can we tell what might have been omitted as objectionable in Bogomil eyes (e.g. reference to bodily resurrection). However, most of the contents of the apocalypse have sufficient parallels in other early Jewish documents to give us confidence in their originality.

The translation offers few really major differences from that of Box and Landsman,[34] but it has a better textual basis, and it stays closer to the original, with the result that, so far from clearing up obscurities in Box and Landsman's translation, it extends obscurity to passages Box and Landsman had made relatively clear. It is as well that the English reader thereby gains a sense of the real difficulty of the Slavonic text. The French translation in the new edition by Philonenko-Sayor and Philonenko[35] (which appeared too late to be noticed here) quite often makes plausible sense of passages which Rubinkiewicz and Hunt deliberately leave obscure.[36] The scholar who cannot read Slavonic will probably have the best access he can have to the text by using these two new translations together.

---

[33] He discussed these at greater length in R. Rubinkiewicz, 'La vision de l'histoire dans l'Apocalypse d'Abraham', in *Aufstieg und Niedergang der römischen Welt* (ed. H. Temporini and W. Haase; Berlin, New York: de Gruyter, 1979), 2.19.1.

[34] G. H. Box and J. I. Landsman, *The Apocalypse of Abraham* (London: SPCK, 1918).

[35] B. Philonenko-Sayor and M. Philonenko, *L'Apocalypse d'Abraham: Introduction, texte slave, traduction et notes* (= *Sem* 31 [1981]).

[36] E.g. their paraphrase of 10.12 (10.11 in *OTP*'s numbering) is clearly, in the light of the following verse, the correct interpretation.

The notes are purely textual. For help in understanding the text the reader must go to Box (whose notes are still very useful) and to Philonenko. The introduction is also disappointing: the work's relation to other Abraham traditions, its close affinity with the *Ladder of Jacob*, its important relationship to Merkabah mysticism, all go unmentioned. Its particular response to the fall of Jerusalem is hardly adequately characterized.

(15) Apocalypse of Adam (G. MacRae) is the only Gnostic apocalypse included in *OTP*, chosen because of its arguably pre-Christian character.

(16) Apocalypse of Elijah (O. S. Wintermute). There was an ancient Jewish *Apocalypse of Elijah*, probably existing as early as the first century AD, but this is not it. The ancient apocalypse survives probably in three reliably attributed quotations, the rather complex evidence for which has been collected in the edition by Stone and Strugnell.[37] These are more reliable evidence for the contents of the original apocalypse than anything in the Coptic *Apoclaypse of Elijah*, which is translated here, and should certainly have been included in *OTP* (they are nearly as extensive as the fragments of the *Apocryphon of Ezekiel*). It seems that out of the original Jewish *Apocalypse of Elijah* developed two later works, whose precise relationship to it can only be guessed: the Coptic *Apocalypse of Elijah*, translated here, which in its present form is a Christian work of perhaps the forth century, and the *Hebrew Apocalypse of Elijah*, which, although in its present form is later, is as likely as the Coptic *Apocalypse* to preserve material from the original apocalypse. It could well have been included in *OTP*, both for this reason and as a representative of the large body of medieval Hebrew apocalypses, in the same way as *3 Enoch* is included as a representative of the Hekalot literature.

The Coptic *Apocalypse* itself is an interesting work, for which Wintermute provides a thorough introduction and useful notes. He is wisely cautious about the identification of a Jewish stratum (though he is sure it exists) until much more work on this and related documents is one. It is not clear to me how his suggestion (plausible in itself) that the title *Apocalypse of Elijah* is only a secondary identification resulting from the Christian account of Elijah's martyrdom (p. 722), is consistent with his acceptance of the view that a common ancestor lies behind this and the *Hebrew Apocalypse of Elijah* (p. 729). He has not noticed the Coptic *Apocalypse's* dependence on the *Apocalypse of Peter* (at 3.1–4; 5.26–29).

(17) Apocalypse of Daniel (G. T. Zervos). Again it is an unnecessary inconvenience to have the text divided into chapters and verses different from those in Berger's edition,[38] which is bound to remain the standard edition of

---

[37] Stone and Strugnell, *Books of Elijah.*
[38] K. Berger, *Die griechische Daniel-Diegese* (SPB, 27; Leiden; E. J. Brill, 1976).

the text (despite some deficiencies: *OTP*, p. 756) and the fullest commentary on the work.

Zervos folllows Berger in dating the work to the early ninth century, on the basis of an alleged reference to the coronation of Charlemagne in 7.14. Even if this reference is not quite certain, the date is approximately correct. This is therefore one of the very large number of Byzantine apocalypses from the early medieval period, which include a confusingly large number of other Daniel apocalypses, the Armenian Vision of Enoch, and the several versions of Pseudo-Methodius. The fact that this text is attributed in one manuscript to Daniel and in another to Methodius is an indication of the fact that in the Byzantine period these were regarded as the two most appropriate pseudonyms for historical-eschatological apocalypses. Whether there is any particular justification for choosing this rather than other Byzantine apoclypses for inclusion in *OTP* I am not sure,[39] but it is an extremely interesting work, which illustrates rather well the way in which such late apocalypses do preserve early material. But Berger's commentary on this work (invaluable as an introduction to the whole field of later Christian apocalyptic) is an education in the vast complexity of the task of understanding how early traditions passed to an through such later apocalypses.

General comments

It is likely that *OTP* will be criticized for including works which are too late and / or too Christian to be evidence for the Judaism of the period before 200 AD. There probably are some works which should not have been included. On the other hand, provided readers of *OTP* are fully aware of the character of the late works and of the problems of detecting early Jewish material in such works, inclusiveness can well be regarded as a virtue. Widening horizons is always better than restricting them. Many of the apocalyptic 'newcomers' in *OTP* merit at least further study, which may or may not vindicate their relevance to the study of the NT and early Judaism. While the question remains open, it is better to have them brought into the limelight for a time rather than left in the shadows where they have been until now.

The real problem is whether *OTP*, in selecting apocalyptic works other than those which because of their undoubtedly early date and Jewish

---

[39] An equally well qualified candidate for inclusion might be the Tiburtine Sybil, on which see P. J. Alexander, *The Oracle of Baalbek: The Tiburtine Sibyl in Greek Dress* (Dumbarton Oaks Studies, 19; Washington, D. C.: Dumbarton Oaks Centre for Byzantine Studies, 1967); D. Flusser, 'An early Jewish-Christian Document in the Tiburtine Sibyl', in *Paganisme, Judaïsme, Christianisme: Mélanges offerts à Marcel Simon* (ed. A. Benoit, M. Philonenko, C. Vogel; Paris: E. de Boccard, 1978), pp. 153–83.

character must be included, has not made a quite arbitrary selection. I have already pointed out several examples of works which are excluded, but whose claim to inclusion is at least as good as that of some works which have been included. The point should not be pressed too far, lest we be in danger of regarding the limits of the pseudepigrapha as another 'canon' to be fixed. Rather than discussing what the limits should be, it would be more profitable to establish that the pseudepigrapha must remain an open and fluid collection, not to be closed and fixed by *OTP* any more than it should have been by *APOT*. Once the limits of the OT pseudepigrapha have been opened to include works which are not even probably Jewish works of the period before 200 AD, then the limits can never be closed again, because the range of such works which may to some degree depend on early Jewish sources or preserve early Jewish traditions is very large indeed, and scholarly judgments about them will always vary.

However, there is one issue which may make the very concept of a collection of OT pseudepigrapha, as *OTP* has conceived it, less than useful. A collection of 'OT pseudepigrapha' can hardly include the *Apocalypse of Peter*, the *Apocalypse of Paul*, the apocryphal *Apocalypse of John*, or a host of other Christian apocalypses bearing NT pseudonyms. Yet, as I have already pointed out above, such apocalypses are closely related to the Christian apocalypses which bear OT pseudonyms, some of which are included in *OTP*. The distinction, which the concept of the 'OT pseudepigrapha' forces, is quite foreign to the nature of the literature itself. Charlesworth's claim that the NT apocrypha 'only infrequently were shaped by early Jewish tradition' (*OTP*, p. xxvii) may be more true of other categories of NT apocrypha, but it is quite untrue of apocalypses. The impression (which *OTP* is bound to propagate) that a Christian apocalypse written under the name of Ezra or Daniel is, in some undefined sense, more 'Jewish' than one written under the name of Thomas or the Virgin Mary, is wholly misleading. Both classes of apocalypse are equally likely to preserve early Jewish apocalyptic material. Moreover, the two classes can only be adequately studied together, as one class, as well as in relation to older apocalyptic writings. It is a further danger of the concept of 'OT pseudepigrapha' that it tends to encourage the study of relatively late works primarily by means of their affinities with earlier works, whereas they also need to be very thoroughly related to the historical and literary context to which, in their present form, they belong. It will not advance our understanding of the Christian apocalypses with bear OT pseudonyms if, by their inclusion in the OT pseudepigrapha, they are artifically extracted from their place in the broader tradition of Christian apocalyptic literature.[40]

---

[40] I do not mean here to exclude their possible relationship also to later Jewish apoca-

I would suggest that the student of ancient Jewish apocalyptic, especially in the NT period, really needs to be acquainted with four bodies of literature, which for practical purposes can be distinguished as follows:

(1) Apocalypses which were written or probably written before 200 AD, and which have suffered no more than minor editing at a later date. This category will include both Jewish works (*1 Enoch, 2 Enoch?, Sib. Or. 3–5, 11, Apocryphon of Ezekiel, Apocalypse of Eliajah* fragments, 'Apocalypse of Zephaniah', 4 Ezra, 2 Baruch, 3 Baruch, Apocalypse of Abraham, Ladder of Jacob*) and Christian works (NT *Apocalypse of John, Shepherd* of Hermas, *Ascension of Isaiah, Apocalypse of Peter, Sib. Or. 1–2, 7–8, 5 Ezra*), since in this period at least Christian apocalyptic was still in very close contact with Jewish apocalyptic. (With the exception of *Sib. Or.* 12–14, it is probable that no Jewish apocalypses from after 200 AD have been preserved outside categories (3) and (4) below.)

(2) Christian apocalypses, whether bearing OT or NT pseudonyms or others (e.g. Methodius), written during the period from 200 AD to at least 1000 AD. This is a very large body of literature.

(3) The Hebrew Merkabah texts written from c. 300 AD onwards (see Alexander's list in *OTP*, pp. 250–51).

(4) The Hebrew apocalypses, such as the *Hebrew Apocalypse of Elijah,* the *Book of Zerubbabel,* the *Secrets of Rabbi Simon ben Yoḥai.*[41]

The apocalyptic tradition should be envisaged as essentially a continuous stream, which after c. 200 AD divided into the three streams (2), (3) and (4), which from then on produced distinct bodies of literature (though they were not without influence on each other).[42] But because the tradition was essentially continuous and also notably conservative, preserving and at the same time constantly reusing and adapting earlier material, all three later branches of the tradition are capable of illuminating ancient apocalyptic. They may throw light on the meaning of ancient material, they may preserve ancient traditions and reflect the contents of ancient apocalypses which as such are no longer extant, they may even contain as yet unidentified ancient documents. Because the apocalyptic literature we have from the period before 200 AD has almost exclusively been passed down to us via

---

lyptic. Later Christian and later Jewish apocalyptic probably developed with more cross-fertilization than is often recognized.

[41] A convenient, if not wholly satisfactory, collection of translations is in G. W. Buchanan, *Revelation and Redemption* (Dillsboro, North Carolina: Western North Carolina Press, 1978). See also the listing and description of some of the works in categories (3) and (4) in A. J. Saldarini, 'Apocalypses and "Apocalyptic" in Rabbinic Literature and Mysticism', *Semeia* 14 (1979), pp. 187–205.

[42] Of course, further divisions occur within (2): Ethiopia, for example, has its own apocalyptic tradition.

stream (2), the Christian stream, we have tended to look especially to this stream for further light on ancient apocalyptic. Recently, the light which stream (3) can throw on ancient apocalyptic has begun to be appreciated. The contribution of stream (4) has as yet been scarcely at all explored. It should be stressed that all three later streams can only contribute reliably to the study of ancient apocalyptic if they are first of all understood in their own right, as literature of their own period. If they are simply plundered for parallels or scoured for ancient-looking material, serious mistakes are likely to be made.

In relation to this classification of apocalyptic literature, it can be seen that *OTP* tends to distort the picture: it does not even include all of (1); it includes a fairly arbitrary selection of (2), one example, not the earliest, of (3), and no examples of (4). Even this, however, is probably better than a very narrowly defined collection of ancient Jewish apocalypses. For the student of ancient apocalyptic must be encouraged to acquaint himself with the later phases of the tradition. Otherwise he will not be able to perform even such necessary tasks as assessing arguments for a late date for *2 Enoch* or for the Parables of Enoch, or assessing the extent of Christian editing in a work such as *3 Baruch*. He will therefore have to venture into many unfamiliar areas, such as Byzantine history or Merkabah mysticism or Bogomil religion or Ethiopian Christianity, and will have to rely heavily on specialists in such areas. But this simply highlights once again the necessarily cooperative and interdisciplinary nature of peudepigraphal studies.

Finally, it is worth pointing out that serious attention to the collection of apocalypses in *OTP*, for all its deficiencies, ought to change our common impressions of Jewish apocalyptic and its relationship to the NT. Used with proper discrimination for the light they can shed on Jewish apocalyptic in NT times, these documents bring to light a concern with a very wide range of apocalyptic revelations: tours of the seven heavens with their various meterological, astronomical and angelological secrets; tours of hell and paradise; revelations of the secrets of the creation and the primeval history; visions of the glory of God and his worship in heaven; anguished demands for answers to problems of theodicy; as well as interpretation of history and the events of the last days. Most of these themes go back in some form as far as the early parts of *1 Enoch*, and scholars such as Stone[43] and Rowland[44] have pointed out how mistaken it is to see eschatology as the only or even in every case the central concern of Jewish apocalyptic. But the prominence of some of these topics in some of the later apocalypses helps to focus our attention more carefully on their presence in the earlier literature too. What

---

[43] M. E. Stone, *Scriptures, Sects and Visions* (Oxford: Blackwell, 1982).
[44] Rowland, *Open Heaven*.

we have still to take full account of is the fact that most of the concerns of Jewish apocalyptic in NT times do not appear in the NT writings. Heavily influenced by apocalyptic as primitive Christianity undoubtedly was, it was also highly selective in the aspects of apocalyptic which it took over. This is a fact about the NT which can only be appreciated by diligent study of pseudepigraphal works which do not look at all relevant to the NT!

9. Pseudo-Apostolic Letters[*]

New Testament scholars are now nearly unanimous in the opinion that at least one NT letter, 2 Peter, is pseudepigraphal,[1] but opinions are still to a greater or lesser extent divided over the authenticity of a considerable number of other NT letters which have been alleged to be pseudepigraphal. It seems unlikely that further progress will be made without the use of some fresh criteria for distinguishing pseudepigraphal from authentic letters. This article aims to derive such criteria from the study of undoubtedly pseudepigraphal letters among the Jewish pseudepigrapha and the NT apocrypha.[2]

The problem of pseudepigraphy in the NT has often been set within the very large context of the general phenomenon of pseudepigraphy in the ancient world, without sufficient appreciation of the fact that the pseudepigraphal *letter* is a genre with some special features of its own. In the first section of this article we shall explain these specific features of the pseudepigraphal letter by setting it within the context of a comprehensive classification of types of letters in antiquity. The pseudepigraphal letter itself will be subdivided into a series of types, which for the sake of clarity will in this first section be simply explained without reference to actual examples from ancient Jewish and Christian literature. Then, in sections II and III, comprehensive accounts of ancient Jewish pseudepigraphal letters and of pseudoapostolic letters among the NT apocrypha will demonstrate that all such letters do in fact conform to the types of pseudepigraphal letters explained in section I. This will establish the presumption that any pseudepigraphal letter in the NT ought also to conform to one of these types, and

---

[*] First publication: *Journal of Biblical Literature* 107 (1988) 469–494.

[1] For the history of the debate about the authenticity of 2 Peter and the growth of the current consensus, see my article "2 Peter: An Account of Research", in *ANRW* 2.25.5 (1988) 3719–3724.

[2] The most useful previous attempts to do something of this kind are those of D. Guthrie: *New Testament Introduction* (3 d ed.; London: InterVarsity, 1970) 672–77; and "Acts and Epistles in Apocryphal Writings," in *Apostolic History and the Gospel: Biblical and Historical Essays presented to F. F. Bruce on his 60 th Birthday* (ed. W. Ward Gasque and R. P. Martin; Exeter: Paternoster, 1970) 328–425. But Guthrie missed the most important Jewish examples and failed to see the importance of the issue of the addressees of a pseudepigraphal letter.

therefore in the last two sections of the article conformity to the types of pseudepigraphal letter known from ancient Jewish and Christian literature outside the NT will be used as a criterion to test the pseudepigraphy or authenticity of NT letters.

I. Types of Pseudepigraphal Letters

Types of letters

Authentic Letters	Pseudepigraphal Letters

A. *Real letter*
content: specific
general
	AP. *Real letter*
	content: specific
	   1. imaginative
	   2. historiographical
	   3. unchanged situation
	   4. typological situation
	   5. testamentary
	     6. general

Aa. *Real letter* *not in letter form* content: specific general	AaP. *Real letter* *not in letter form* content: 1–6 (as above)
B. *Letter-essay* content: general	BP. *Letter-essay*
C. *Literary letter* (only formally a letter) content: usually general	
D. *Work not in letter form,* *wrongly called a letter*	DP. *Work not in letter form* *wrongly called letter*
	EP. *Misattributed work*

The diagram is an attempt at a rough classification of types of letters in the ancient world, made primarily with a view to understanding the types of pseudepigraphal letters which will be studied in this article.[3] For the purposes of this article and the diagram, authentic letters are defined as those whose professed author is in some sense the real author, and include letters which may have been written, partly or even wholly, by a secretary or colleague of the professed author,[4] so long as the professed author authorized the letter;

---

[3] Because the purpose is different, this classification differs from that of W. G. Doty, "The Classification of Epistolary Literature," *CBQ* 31 (1969) 195–98; idem, *Letters in Primitive Christianity* (Philadelphia: Fortress, 1973) 4–8. His category of "non-real" letters fails to indicate that in most cases these are fictional versions of the other types.

[4] For the role of secretaries in ancient letter-writing, see G. J. Bahr, "Paul and Letter Writing in the First Century", *CBQ* 28 (1966) 465–77.

that is, it was sent out in the author's name with the author's consent. For the purposes of this article, a pseudepigraphal letter is defined as one whose real author attributed it to a figure of the past. This definition excludes letters falsely attributed to someone during his own lifetime. Such letters were written in antiquity[5] and could quite properly be called pseudepigraphal letters, but since it is very unlikely that any NT letter belongs in this category they will not be considered in this article. Nor is this article concerned with letters whose real authors did not intend them to be pseudepigraphal, but which later came to be mistakenly attributed to other authors. A good deal of ancient literature is pseudepigraphal in this sense of mistaken attribution;[6] and this type of pseudepigraphal letter is included in the diagram as type EP, but letters in this category will be mentioned only in order to be left out of the discussion. Some NT letters may well belong in this category (Hebrews almost certainly does), but this article will not help to identify them.

Originally and properly the letter is a literary genre that enables a writer to address a specific person or persons directly. It is a literary substitute for speaking to someone in person, used when for some reason (most commonly, geographical distance) the contents of the letter cannot be communicated orally. Thus, what makes a letter a letter is not so much the nature of its contents, which can vary enormously,[7] but the fact that the content is directly addressed by one person to another (or, of course, more than one person in either case[8]). Hence the really essential feature of the literary form of the letter is the parties formula in which the sender(s) and the recipient(s) are named or specified in some other way. In order to write a letter, an author must name himself and must name or otherwise specify his adressees.[9] (An anonymous letter is a defective letter, a deliberate abuse of the form, as the recipient's reaction to its anonymity shows.) In special cases, the addressees may be an extremely large group: Nebuchadnezzar in Daniel 4 addresses a letter to "all peoples, nations, and languages that dwell in all the earth" (a conventional hyperbole for all his subjects). But even so, the addressees must be specified and directly addressed.

Type A, the authentic real letter, is the original type of letter, and the model of which types AP, B, BP, and C are imitations. Type A is the letter

---

[5] Jerome (*Apol.* 3.25) complains of a forged letter put about under his name, and if 2 Thessalonians is authentic, 2:2 seems to mean that forged letters attributed to Paul circulated during his own lifetime.

[6] See B.M. Metzger, "Pseudepigraphy in the Israelite Literary Tradition", in *Pseudepigrapha I: Pseudopythagorica – Lettres de Platon – Littérature pseudépigraphique juive* (ed. K. von Fritz; Entretiens sur l'antiquité classique 17; Geneva: Vandoeuvres, 1971) 194–98.

[7] Doty, *Letters*, 15–16.

[8] For coauthorship, see Cicero *Ad. Att.* 11.5.1.

[9] For these features of the definition of a letter, see Doty, *Letters*, 193.

whose real author writes in his own name with the intention of addressing
the recipient(s) named or otherwise specified in the parties formula. In every
such letter the contents are intended for the recipient(s), but the nature of
the contents can vary from material which bears very specifically on the recipient's situation or relationship with the author and which would make no
sense addressed to anyone else, to material of a very general character (say,
an account of the author's philosophical views) which *could* be addressed
to any interested reader. Many letters, of course, contain a mixture of relatively specific and relatively general contents, but a letter that is largely or
even exclusively general in content is still a real letter (type A) so long as it
is genuinely meant for its specified addressee(s).[10] Even though the special
value of the letter genre for most letter writers is that it makes it possible to
communicate relatively specific material, there is nothing to prevent a letter
writer who wishes to communicate very general material to the recipient(s)
from doing so.[11]

However, the fact that a real letter can contain general material that
would be of interest to readers other than the specified addressee(s) makes
possible the extension of the use of the letter genre to types B and C. For
type B, I rely on M. L. Stirewalt's study of the "Greek letter-essay," but I
would define it a little less restrictively than he does.[12] This is a letter which,
while formally and really addressed to a named recipient, is also explicitly
intended to be read by a much wider readership, to whom its main content
will be equally relevant.[13] For example, Epicurus, addressing an account of

---

[10] Of course, it is possible for a letter to be really meant for its specified addressees,
but for the writer also to have in mind the possibility of future publication for a wider
readership; see Doty, *Letters,* 2–3. For simplicity, and because it is scarcely relevant to
psdeudepigraphal letters, this possibility is not included in the diagram.

[11] NT scholars sometimes argue that a letter whose content is of general applicability
must be a "literary letter" (my type C), not a real letter; see, on James, S. Laws, *A Commentary on The Epistle of James* (Black's NT Commentarie; London: A. & C. Black, 1980)
6. But from this point of view there is no reason why James should not be a real letter,
written and delivered to actual Jewish Christian communities.

[12] M. L. Stirewalt, Jr., "The Form and Function of the Greek Letter-Essay", in *The
Romans Debate* (ed. K. P. Donfried; Minneapolis: Augsburg, 1977) 175–206. I do not
consider it essential that a type B letter should be "supplementary in some way to another
writing" (Stirewalt, "Form," 176).

[13] "The letter-setting behind the letter is triangular, I-thou-they" (Stirewalt, "Form,"
204). Col 4:16 probably does not put Colossians in this category, since the letter is presumably written for the Colossians and has their own situation in view. That the Laodiceans may
also find it valuable is quite secondary to its purpose. To the extent that Paul envisaged the
wider circulation of his letters to specific churches, his letters are type A verging somewhat
toward type B. I am not convinced by the argument of K. P. Donfried ("False Presuppositions in the Study of Romans," *CBQ* 36 [1974] 332–55 [reprinted in *The Romans Debate,*
120–48]) to the effect that Romans actually belongs to type B. The later church (cf. the
Muratorian Canon) came to think of Paul's letters as implicity type B letters; that is, while
addressing specific churches Paul was implicitly addressing all churches.

his philosophy to Pythocles, says that "many others besides you will find these reasonings useful" (*ap.* Diogenes Laertius 10.85). Such a letter may often be a response to an actual request from the recipient and is therefore a real letter, but it is also written for the benefit of others to whom the recipient is expected to pass it on. The specified recipient is thus, as it were, a stage on the way to the general publication of the work for an indefinite readership. Type B letters are therefore very similar in function to dedicated treatises and are readily distinguishable only by their use of the letter form, consisting of at least a formal letter opening.[14]

Type C letters are those which, while retaining the form of a real letter, naming and addressing a specific recipient, are actually letters only in form. The named addressee is (though he may be a real person) only fictionally the addressee, for the work is in fact intended for a general readership. Since type C letters do not differ in form, but only in intention, from type A letters (which can, of course, be published later for a general readership), it will not be easy to identify them with certainty,[15] but some ancient letters, such as those of Seneca, are normally considered examples of type C. It should be noted that the element of fiction which type C letters introduce into the use of the letter form creates a distinction between the supposed addressee(s) and the real readers. This is a distinction that (as we shall see) characterizes most pseudepigraphal letters.

The only really essential formal feature of a letter was the letter opening, consisting of at least the parties formula, normally also a greeting. There were, of course, in the ancient world more extensive letter forms, which have been usefully studied, but they were not *essential* to the letter and do not affect the argument of this article. The fact that only a letter opening is required to make a letter a letter means that a letter could easily be written that *also* belonged to *another* literary genre. A speech or a sermon that would have been delivered orally had the author been able to visit the addressees becomes a letter when instead he writes it down for them and adds an epistolary opening and perhaps also an epistolary conclusion. Genres that are written forms of oral address (speeches and sermons) are the most obvious genres to be combined with that of the letter,[16] but in principle almost any genre could also be a letter. The papyri offer examples of legal documents in letter form. The book of Revelation is an apocalypse put into

---

[14] The dedicated treatise is more likely to confine direct address to the dedicatee to the preface and conclusion, but this is not an absolute distinction.

[15] Doty therefore rejects the use of intention as a criterion for distinguishing types of letters ("Classification," 194–95). I agree that it cannot be a basis for distinguishing letter *forms,* but it is nevertheless a real distinction.

[16] See J. L. White, "Saint Paul and the Apostolic Letter Tradition," *CBQ* 45 (1983) 435–56.

the form of a circular letter to the seven churches of Asia and containing a specific address to each church.[17]

There are examples of letters that lack every trace of specifically epistolary form, even the parties formula.[18] In some cases this may be because the literary context in which the letter has been preserved (or, in the case of some pseudepigraphal letters, composed) provides the information that the parties formula would give (e. g., 2 Chr 21:12?; Jer 29:4?; Bar 1:10; Ep Jer 2). In other cases the letter opening may have been thought inapplicable when the letter was copied for a wider readership (Hebrews?. 1 John?, *Barnabas?*). It may also be that there were occasions when a speech or sermon was written and sent as a letter, but it was left to the messenger to supply the information that an epistolary opening would normally provide.[19] All such cases of documents that functioned as letters but now lack epistolary form are included in type Aa (pseudepigraphal examples in type AaP).

However, a written speech or sermon that lacks any element of epistolary form may often be indistinguishable from one written either for the author to read aloud to the hearers or in order to preserve it for the hearers' benefit after they have first heard it delivered orally. Some works may therefore have been misclassified as letters in antiquity (type D). A good example is *2 Clement* (first called a letter in Eusebius *Hist. eccl.* 3.38.4), whose text makes it clear that it is a sermon read aloud by the speaker in the actual presence of the congregation (15:2; 17:3; and especially 19:1).[20] There is some evidence to suggest that ancient scribes, working on the principle that a letter is a literary substitute for oral address to specific persons, tended to classify works written in the form of direct address as letters.[21] Such misclassified works must be ruled out of our discussion.

---

[17] See E. Schüssler Fiorenza, "Composition and Structure of the Revelation of John," *CBQ* 39 (1977) 367–81; White, "Saint Paul," 444.

[18] A special category here is documents that lack the parties formula but display some other epistolary features. Hebrews lacks any epistolary opening, but has a conclusion that must be epistolary (13:22–25). F. O. Francis argues for epistolary features in 1 John, which lacks a parties formula ("The Form and Function of the Opening and Closing Paragraphs of James and 1 John," *ZNW* 61 [1970] 110–26), but against the view that 1 John is in any sense a letter, see R. E. Brown, *The Epistles of John* (AB30; Garden City, NY: Doubleday, 1983) 86–92.

[19] For the importance of the messenger in the ancient epistolary situation, see Doty, "Classification," 193–94; *Letters,* 2, 30.

[20] On the genre of *2 Clement,* which Donfried classifies as a "hortatory address", see K. P. Donfried, *The setting of Second Clement in early Christianity* (NovTSup 38; Leiden: Brill, 1974) 19–48. But, even in the case of *2 Clement,* we cannot rule out the possibility that this hortatory address was later sent as a letter to other churches (Donfried, *Second Clement,* 47–48).

[21] Thus, in the longer version of the *Apocalypse of Thomas,* the second part of the work, which is a discourse of Christ addressed to Thomas, is introduced: *incipit epistula domini*

Pseudepigraphal letters are not, of course, distinguishable in form from authentic letters, of which they are fictional imitations. The diagram does not include type CP, which could in theory exist, but would be a rather sophisticated fiction, involving two levels of fiction, and is therefore unlikely. In fact, as will become clear, type AP6 could well be regarded in another sense as the pseudepigraphal equivalent of type C.

All letters, including pseudepigraphal letters, must specify both sender(s) and recipient(s). In the case of pseudepigraphal letters the supposed author, named in the parties formula, is not the real author. But it is important to notice also, since the point is sometimes neglected, that the supposed addressee(s), specified in the parties formula, cannot be the real readers for whom the real author is writing. The supposed addressee(s) must (except in some special cases to be considered later) be a contemporary or contemporaries of the supposed author. Not only does the "I" in a pseudepigraphal letter not refer to the real author, but "you" does not refer to the real readers. The readers of a pseudepigraphal letter cannot read it as though they were being directly addressed either by the supposed author or by the real author (except in the special cases to be noted later); they must read it as a letter written to *other* people, in the past.

Thus, the pseudepigraphal letter, by its very nature, requires a distinction between the supposed addressee(s) and the real readers. We shall discover a few cases of pseudepigraphal letters that contrive by special devices to include the real readers in the supposed addressees. But in no indubitably pseudepigraphal letter known to me are the supposed addressees and the real readers identical. This means that a pseudepigraphal letter cannot, as scholars sometimes too readily assume, perform the same function as an authentic real letter. The authentic real letter (type A) is a form of direct address to specific addressee(s). The pseudepigraphal letter, it seems, can be this only fictionally. The real author of a pseudepigraphal letter can only address real readers indirectly, under cover of direct address to *other* people. This is what distinguishes the pseudepigraphal letter from most other types of pseudepigraphal literature, which do not need to have addressees at all.

For the writers of the vast majority of ancient pseudepigraphal letters this was no problem. The typical ancient pseudepigraphal letter is a letter from a famous figure of the past to one of his contemporaries, and is intended to be of interest to its real readers for the same kinds of reasons as an authentic letter preserved from the past might be. Most ancient pseudepigraphal letters can be classified as either imaginative literature (type AP1) or as historiography (type AP2). The point of letters of type AP1 was simply to entertain

---

ad Thomam. See E. Hennecke, *New Testament Apocrypha* (ed. W. Schneemelcher and R. McL. Wilson; London: Lutterworth, 1963, 1965) 2. 799 n. 1.

or to instruct in the ways in which fiction can entertain and instruct. Letters of famous men were often written as exercises in the rhetorical schools, and pseudepigraphal letters of this kind, often in the form of collections, became in the early centuries of the Common Era one of the most popular forms of light reading. Classics of this type were the letters of Alciphron, some attributed to invented characters, some to real historical characters, such as the nineteen letters of famous courtesans. Some pseudepigraphal letter collections are really historical novels in the form of letters. The so-called *Socratic Epistles* (thirty-seven letters to and from philosophers and their friends in the circle of Socrates) are full of historical details in which fiction is liberally mingled with fact.

The line between historical romance and serious historiography is not always easy to draw, but we should probably distinguish letters (type AP2) that serve a more properly historiographical purpose, whether as forgeries to provide documentation for alleged historical facts not otherwise documented or as historical illustration written on the Thucydidean principle of historical speeches.

Thus, types AP1 and AP2, which cover the vast majority of ancient pseudepigraphal letters, are types in which no problem is caused for the author by the fact that the supposed addressees of the letter cannot be the real readers. The author is not writing the type of literature in which he needs to address real readers directly. In other words, he does not want his fictional letter to perform *for him and his readers* the function which an authentic real letter would perform, that of making possible direct address to specific addressee(s). Both for him and for his readers, it is *someone else's* letter to *other* people. But suppose an author wished to write, under a pseudonym, a letter with the kind of content characteristic of NT letters: religious teaching and ethical exhortation. How could the genre, which necessitates direct address to supposed readers in the past, accommodate didactic material applicable to the real readers? The problem for the author in this case is that he wants his pseudepigraphal letter to perform for him and his readers something like the function which an authentic real letter from him to his readers would perform. He wants, under cover of his pseudonym, to *address* his real readers, but his genre allows his letter to be addressed only to supposed addressees contemporary with the supposed author. Thus, he needs to find some way in which material that is ostensibly addressed to supposed addressees in the past can be taken by his real readers as actually or also addressed to them,. The various ways in which this can be and was done define the remaining types of pseudepigraphal letters, and they will also become our criteria for testing the alleged pseudepigraphy of NT letters. For any pseudepigraphal letter which has the didactic aims of NT letters must find some such way of bridging the gap between the supposed addressee(s) and the real readers, which the pseudepigraphal letter as a genre seems necessarily to create.

The solution to the problem was not especially difficult if the intended real readers were a very general readership which the author is content to address in very general terms. In this case he could write a letter of type AP6; that is, he could represent his pseudonym as addressing to the supposed addressee(s) material so general that it *could* equally well be addressed to anyone (or, at any rate, to anyone of the author's religion). By this means the author could do with a pseudepigraphal letter much the same as an author writing in his own name could do with a letter of type C. Even more suitable to the pseudepigraphal writer's purpose would be a letter of type BP, in which he can explicitly say that the material addressed to the supposed recipient is also relevant to others, among whom the real readers will understand themselves to be included. In a letter of this type, the supposed recipient can even be asked or instructed to pass the material on to others, thus creating a fictional channel by which the letter written initially for the supposed addressee in the past can be supposed to have been handed down to the real readers in the present.

However, in themselves these two expedients (AP6 and BP) only enable the pseudepigraphal writer to address a general readership in general terms. They do not enable him to do what Paul did in his authentic letters, that is, to write material of specific relevance to specific churches in specific situations. There seem to have been only three ways which writers of pseudepigraphal letters found to move beyond general didactic material to material of more specific application to their real readers (types AP3, AP4, AP5), though they never reached the degree of specificity found in most Pauline letters. Two of these possibilities bridge the gap between the supposed addressees and the real readers by placing the supposed addressees in a historical situation in the past that was similar to the situation of the intended real readers in the present, so that remarks relevant to the situation of the supposed addressees will be relevant also to the situation of the real readers. One way to do this was to address supposed addressees who were ancestors or predecessors of the real readers in a situation supposed not to have changed, in relevant respects, up to the present, so that the real readers are still in the same situation as the supposed addressees once were (type AP3). A second possibility was to depict the historical situation of the supposed addressees as a kind of type of the similar present situation of the real readers, so that what is said to the supposed addressees applies typologically to the real readers (type AP4). In both these cases the situation of the supposed addressees has to be described sufficiently for the real readers to identify it as analogous to their own.

The final possibility (type AP5) was to write a testament or farewell speech in the form of a letter. The farewell speech was a well-established genre of Jewish literature, in which a biblical figure, shortly before his death, could be represented as addressing not only his immediate hearers but also future generations to whom his words will be transmitted, and with prophetic insight as foreseeing the situation of future generations, especially the generation of the end-time. The writing of such a farewell speech in letter form makes possible a pseudepigraphal letter explicitly addressed to readers living after the death of the supposed author. Thus, in some ways at least, the testamentary letter appears to be the ideal solution to the problem of writing a pseudepigraphal letter with didactic intentions.

By these three means a few pseudepigraphal letter writers, as we shall see in the following sections, managed to say something *relatively* specific to their contemporaries. What must be emphasized, in conclusion, is that without an explicit literary device such as the testament, no pseudepigraphal letter could be addressed by a figure of the past to addressees living in the real author's present. This would have been a blatant transgression of the logic of the genre, and therefore it is not found in any indubitably pseudepigraphal letter from antiquity. If a pseudepigraphal writer wished to address his own contemporaries under cover of the supposed addressees of a pseudepigraphal letter, then *either* he had to keep his content very general (types AP6, BP) *or* he had to make clear that the situation of the supposed addressees was comparable to that of the real readers (types AP3, AP4). Only in a very special kind of pseudepigraphal letter (type AP5), in which the supposed author actually expresses his intention of addressing readers living after his death and foresees their situation, can the real readers of a pseudepigraphal letter be explicitly addressed.

This case still needs to be established from the study of indubitably pseudepigraphal letters outside the NT. The next two sections of this article will survey Jewish pseudepigraphal letters and those attributed to apostles in the NT apocrypha, on the assumption that these categories are likely to include some of the most relevant material for comparison with the NT letters.

II. Jewish Pseudepigraphal Letters[22]

For the sake of completeness, we shall first mention works which were misclassified as letters in antiquity, in order to rule them out of our discussion and letters of the imaginative and historiographical types, before

---

[22] For brief comments on such letters, see M. Smith, "Pseudepigraphy," 212–13, 215: he sees them as largely due to Greek influence on Jewish literature, and thus to be distinguished from the indigenous Israelite tradition of pseudepigraphy. A very valuable survey of ancient Jewish letters, both authentic and pseudepigraphal, is P. S. Alexander,

considering in detail the four didactic letters, which bear some comparison with NT letters:

(1) *Misclassified* (type DP), The so-called *Letter of Aristeas*, which is not described as a letter by the earliest writers who refer to it,[23] should probably be classified as a dedicated treatise. If a letter, it is type AaP2. The book of Esther is called a letter in Add Esth 11:1, probably because the author of this colophon to the Greek Esther identified the book as Mordecai's letter to which Esth 9:20–23 refers; but plainly the author of Esther did not intend it to be a letter.

(2) *Imaginative and historiographical types* (AP1, AaP1, AP2, AaP2). These include the majority of Jewish pseudepigraphal letters, and for our purposes the two types need not be distinguished. Omitting examples of seriously disputed authenticity, we may list: 2 Chr 21:12–15; Dan 4:1–37; 6:25–28; Add Esth 13:1–7; 16:1–24; *Ep. Arist.* 35–40; 41–46; 3 Macc 3:12–29; 7:1–19; Eupolemus, *ap.* Eusebius, *Praep. evang.* 9.31–34.3; Josephus, *Ant.* 8.2.6–7 §50–54; Philo, *De leg.* 276–329; *Par. Jer. (4 Bar.)* 6:19–25; 7:24–34. These letters call for no special discussion here.

(3) *Didactic letters.* There are only four examples (*1 Enoch* 92–105; Epistle of Jeremiah; 1 Baruch; *2 Bar.* 78–87), but all four are of considerable significance for our purpose.

The Epistle of Enoch (Ἐπιστολὴ Ἐνώχ) is the title given to the section (chaps. 91[92]–105) of *1 Enoch* in the Chester Beatty Michigan papyrus of the Greek version of these chapters.[24] The work also refers to itself as τῆς ἐπιστολῆς ταύτης in 100:6, where the Ethiopic versions has "this book." No Aramaic fragment from Qumran survives for 100:6. It may therefore be that the work was not unambiguously called a letter in the Aramaic original, but that the Greek translator introduced the term. The work is in fact Enoch's farewell speech before his assumption to heaven. But whereas most farewell speeches in Jewish and Christian literature are represented as delivered orally and then reported as speeches in narrative works written by others, Enoch is said to have written his testament and then to have read it aloud to his sons (92:1; 93:1,3). That this written testament should have been regarded as a letter is analogous to the practice already noted of describing written sermons as letters. It may be significant that in Jewish and Christian literature only three other testaments are supposed to have been put in writ-

"Epistolary Literature," in *Jewish Writings of the Second Temple Period* (ed. M. E. Stone; CRINT 2.2; Assen: Van Gorcum; Philadelphia: Fortress, 1984) 579–96.

[23] Josephus, *Ant.* 12.100; Epiphanius, *De mensuris et ponderibus* 9 a; Eusebius, *Praep. evang.* 9.38. See A. Pelletier, *Lettre d'Aristée à Philocrate* (SC 89; Paris: Cerf, 1962) 47; Alexander, "Epistolary Literature," 580.

[24] The title is a subscription after chap. 107, but chaps. 106–7 cannot have been originally part of the work. Only 97:6–107 survives in the papyrus.

ten form by the testator himself, and all three are in letter form (*2 Bar.* 78–87; 2 Timothy; 2 Peter). The opening of Enoch's testament in fact reads more or less like the parties formula of a letter, in which the writer names himself and specifies his addressees: "Written by Enoch the scribe... for all my sons who dwell upon the earth and for the last generations who will practise uprightness and peace" (92:1).[25] The term "letter" may be inappropriate for Enoch's testament as read aloud to his sons, but it is intelligibly applicable to Enoch's testament as bequeathed to future generations. We may therefore regard the Epistle of Enoch as a pseudepigraphal letter of type AP5.

The description of the addressees in 92:1 is remarkable: not only Enoch's contemporaries, his sons, but also the righteous of the last generations – which, of course, means a group of the real author's contemporaries, the religious group to which he belonged. As an apocalyptic seer, Enoch can foresee the circumstances of this group and prophesy their future, but because he is writing a testament he can not only foresee them but also directly address them, as he does throughout the work, in direct exhortations and promises (he also turns aside to address woes to their enemies). It is clear that Enoch's sons, to whom he reads the testament, are (as in many testaments) merely a channel through which it can be passed down to the elect of the last days, who are his real addressees. As we can see clearly from this example, the written testament is a letter with the almost unique capacity of allowing a supposed writer in one age explicitly to address readers in a later age.

The three other didactic letters to be discussed are all associated with Baruch or Jeremiah. This is no accident. The reason is not just that Jeremiah's letter to the exiles in Jeremiah 29 provided a model for such letters, though this is one factor. A further important factor is that the years immediately before and after the fall of Jerusalem, in which these three pseudepigraphal letters are set, provided a situation *analogous* to that of the Jews in the periods when these works were written, that is, a situation where Jews lived not only in the land of Israel but also in the Diaspora. Writers who wished to address either Jews in the situation of Diaspora or Jews in both situations (the land of Israel and the Diaspora), and who wished to do so under an OT pseudonym, rather naturally went back to the historical origin of this state of affairs, a period when (as Jeremiah 29 shows) letters were exchanged between Jews in Jerusalem and Jews in exile in Babylon. This historical situation could be treated either as a situation which had not changed up to the present, making possible a type AP3 letter, or as a type of the similar situation in which the real readers lived, making possible a type AP4 letter.

---

[25] Ethiopic, trans. in M.A. Knibb, *The Ethiopic Book of Enoch* (Oxford: Clarendon, 1978) 2.222. The Greek is not extant. 4QEn^g 1.2.22–24 (J.T. Milik, *The Books of Enoch* [Oxford: Clarendon, 1976] 261) is very fragmentary: it confirms something similar to, but not exactly; the text rendered by the Ethiopic.

The Epistle of Jeremiah seems to reflect a tradition, also found in *Tg. Ps.-J.* Jer 10:11,[26] that Jer 10:11 (which is in Aramaic) is an extract from a letter of Jeremiah. Certainly it is based on Jer 10:11 and surrounding verses, and the rather surprising fact that it is addressed to Jews who are soon to go into exile, rather than to Jews already in exile, must result from the place of Jer 10:11 in the book of Jeremiah. This is interesting evidence for a pseudepigraphal letter writer's careful attention to the supposed historical setting of his letter. The work is entirely devoted to warning the addressees how to react to the pagan idolatry they will encounter in Babylon. Obviously this message could still apply to Jews in the Babylonian exile when the work was written (probably late fourth century B.C.)[27] because the situation was unchanged (and the letter therefore belongs to type AaP3). But it is noteworthy that the writer does not simply take this for granted, but very carefully makes the continued applicability of the letter explicit. In Jeremiah's authentic letter (Jeremiah 29) the prophet predicted seventy years of exile; the Epistle of Jeremiah (3) reinterprets this period as seven generations: "when you come to Babylon you will remain there for many years, for a long time, up to seven generations; after that I will bring you away from there in peace." In this way, at the outset of his work, the author establishes that his "you" means not only Jeremiah's contemporaries, but also their descendants, up to seven generations. Because Jeremiah the prophet can foresee that the situation will not have changed by the real author's time, he can address not only his own contemporaries, but also succeeding generations up to and including the real author's contemporaries. This is the only example known to me of a pseudepigraphal letter, other than testamentary letters, in which the real readers are explicitly addressed along with supposed addressees in the past. This is possible in this case, as in testamentary letters, only by means of a clear and deliberate literary device, according to which the supposed author foresees the future.

1 Baruch (called βιβλίον in 1:1, following Jer 36:1 LXX) is, apart from the introduction (1:1–9), in the form of a work (1:15–5:9) sent with a covering letter (1:10–14) from the Jewish exiles in Babylon to the Jews in Jerusalem.[28]

---

[26] It is possible that the targum here reflects the existence of the Epistle of Jeremiah.

[27] See C. A. Moore, *Daniel, Esther, and Jeremiah: The Additions* (AB 44; Garden City; NY: Doubleday, 1977) 328; G. W. E. Nickelsburg, *Jewish Literature between the Bible and the Mishnah* (London: SCM, 1981) 38. This approximate date is securely based on v 3, but cannot be made too precise because we do not know how accurately the author reckoned the period from the fall of Jerusalem to his own time.

[28] This work is called the *Epistle of Baruch* in Armenian, and the *Second Epistle of Baruch* in Syriac (the *First* is *2 Apoc. Bar.* 78–86). We need not be concerned here with the possible previous existence of parts of the work, since it can be only in its present form that 1 Baruch is a letter.

It is supposed to have been written by Baruch[29] in Babylon five years after
the fall of Jerusalem and is said to have been read by Baruch to the exiles
(1:3–4) and then sent to the Jews still in Jerusalem, who are to recite the
prayers contained in it on the site of the Temple.[30] Thus, the real author
contrives to write both for Jews in the Diaspora in his own day and for Jews
in Jerusalem. Whether the situation of the book is simply one that remains
unchanged in the author's day (type AaP3) or whether it is typological
(type AaP4) depends on whether the book should be dated in the aftermath
of an event analogous to the fall of Jerusalem in 586: that is, Antiochus's sack
of Jerusalem in 169 B.C.[31] or the fall of Jerusalem in A.D. 70.[32]

In *2 Baruch* there is no doubt that the situation is typological: Baruch's
reflections on the fall of Jerusalem in 586 are really the author's reflections
on the fall of Jerusalem in A.D. 70.[33] The testament device is rather extensively used in *2 Baruch:*[34] Baruch delivers two farewell speeches before his
assumption to heaven, one (chaps. 44–46) to the leaders of the people in
Jerusalem (where Baruch has remained after the destruction of the city) and
another (77:1–10) to all the people. But the people then ask him if, before
leaving him, he would also write his message, "a letter of doctrine and a roll
of hope" (77:12),[35] to the exiles. So Baruch writes two letters: one to the two
and a half tribes in Babylon and one to the nine and a half tribes in exile since
the fall of the northern kingdom.

Rather surprisingly, the former is not recorded,[36] but the latter occupies
chaps. 78–86 of the book.[37] Why does the author choose to record this let-

---

[29] P. M. Bogaert shows that 1 Baruch was widely known as part of Jeremiah, rather than
as a separate book of Baruch, and consequently it was often quoted under the name of
Jeremiah ("La nom de Baruch dans la littérature pseudépigraphique: l'apocalypse syriaque
et le livre deutérocanonique," in *Quelques problèmes* [ed. W. C. van Unnik; RechBib 9,
Leiden: Brill, 1974] 56–72). But it is difficult to believe that it was *intended* by its author to
be a Jeremiah pseudepigraphon. If Bar 1:1 means that Baruch wrote at Jeremiah's dictation,
it is surprising that Jeremiah is not mentioned (cf. Jer 36:4, 32; 45:1).

[30] In fact 1:14 has, "in the house of the Lord," perhaps betraying that in the real author's
day there was a temple in Jerusalem.

[31] Nicklesburg, *Jewish Literature,* 113.

[32] O. C. Whitehouse in *The Apocrypha and Pseudepigrapha of the Old Testament*
(ed. R. H. Charles; Oxford: Clarendon, 1912–13) 569; J. J. Kneucker, *Das Buch Baruch*
(Leipzig: Brockhaus, 1879).

[33] Bogaert, "La nom," 57–58; idem, *Apocalypse de Baruch* (SC 144–45; Paris: Cerf,
1969) 1. 453–54.

[34] Ibid., 1. 121–26.

[35] Trans. A. F. J. Klijn in *The Old Testament Pseudepigrapha* (ed. J. H. Charlesworth;
2 vols.; London: Darton, Longman & Todd, 1983, 1985) 1. 647.

[36] For suggestions as to the identity of this (lost?) letter; see Bogaert, *Apocalypse,* 1.
78–80.

[37] Bogaert shows that the letter is an integral part of *2 Baruch,* and its circulation as an
independent work in Syriac is a secondary phenomenon (*Apocalypse,* 1. 67–68). Cf. the
relationship between *3 Corinthians* and the *Acts of Paul,* discussed below.

ter, when his real readers would have associated themselves more readily with the two and a half tribes in exile?[38] The answer is to be found in the logic of the typological situation. In this letter the author wants to address the Diaspora Jews of his own day, Jews who have lived in the Diaspora for generations and have no immediate connection with the fall of Jerusalem in A.D. 70. Those who were in an analogous situation after 586 were not the exiles of Judah but the exiles of the northern kingdom. Baruch's account of the religious significance of 586 for the exiles of the northern tribes is *typologically* an account of the religious significance of A.D. 70 for Diaspora Jews.

Although Baruch does ask that the recipients of his letter pass it on to their descendants (84:9), the author does not really exploit the potential of a testamentary letter to address future generations explicitly. He did not need to do so because instead he has made Baruch's contemporaries types of some of his real readers (those in the Diaspora). *2 Baruch* 78–86 is a clear case of type AP4, and its applicability to its real readers depends on their recognition of its typological character.

III. Noncanonical Pseudo-Apostolic Letters

Again we shall list all apocryphal letters attributed to apostles, but the first two categories need not detain us long:

(1) *Misattributed* (type EP). The *Epistle of Barnabas*, which lacks an introductory parties formula, probably only later came to be attributed to Barnabas, as Hebrews did to Paul. The *Epistle of Titus* is identifiable as such only from its title: it is probably an anonymous homily, misclassified as a letter (type DP) and misattributed to Titus (type EP). If either of these works was in fact written as a pseudepigraphal letter, it would be type A(a) P6.

(2) *Imaginative and historiographical* (types AP1, AP2). These are represented only by the correspondence of Paul and Seneca, and the letter which opens the Nag Hammadi tractate called *Letter of Peter to Philip* (CG VIII, 2).[39]

---

[38] At the time of writing of *2 Baruch,* the nine and a half (ten) tribes were believed to be in a remote, inaccessible land (4 Ezra 13:40–46). The problem is not alleviated if we follow Bogaert (*Apocalypse,* 1. chap. 11) in taking the two and a half tribes to represent the western Diaspora and the nine and a half tribes the eastern Diaspora. On the contrary, this makes the problem of the missing letter to the two and a half tribes even more acute.

[39] Presumably the title was originally that of the letter itself (132:10–133:8) but was later appropriated as the title of the tractate. On the title, see M. W. Meyer, *The Letter of Peter to Philip* (SBLDS 53; Chico, CA: Scholars Press, 1981) 91–93, and on the letter itself, ibid., 93–101.

(3) Letters with mainly Gospel content. Two letters can be classed together here: the *Apocryphon of James* (CG I, 2) and the *Epistle of the Apostles.* Though their content is more comparable with that of the NT Gospels than with that of the NT letters, they are letters in form and the means by which they bridge the gap between the supposed addressee(s) and the real readers are instructive for our purpose.

The *Apocryphon of James* belongs to the very popular second- and third-century genre of postresurrection dialogues between Christ and the disciples. But it is also a letter, with an epistolary opening and a first paragraph addressed to the recipient. Unfortunately, the recipient's name, given in the parties formula (1:2), has been lost in the manuscript except for the last syllable *(-thos);* a very plausible suggestion is Cerinthus.[40] The point of this letter form is to authenticate one of the chains of secret tradition by which Gnostic teaching was held to have passed down from the risen Christ to later Gnostics. The *Apocryphon of James* is a "secret book," revealed by Christ only to James and Peter (1:11–12, 23–24, 35; 2:34–37) and communicated to the recipient, "a minister of the salvation of the saints" (1:19–20), so that he may pass it on to others but not to "many" (1:21–22). The work can therefore be classified as a special form of type BP:[41] the content is explicitly intended for a readership wider than the recipient himself and he is to pass it on to others, but the Gnostic concern for a secret message for the few means that the wider readership is not a very wide readership, but a deliberately restricted one.

The *Epistle of the Apostles,* which is anti-Gnostic, also contains largely Gospel material. The eleven apostles narrate the whole Gospel history in outline (chaps. 3–5, 9–12) and a long conversation with the risen Christ (chaps. 12–51). Nevertheless, it is a letter in form, addressed by the eleven apostles to "the churches of the east and west, towards north and south" (chap. 2).[42] This letter form enabled the apostles to address Christians directly in a short passage of exhortation (chaps. 6–7), which is mainly concerned with urging Christians to remain in the true faith and to avoid

---

[40] J. Helderman, "Anapausis in the Epistula Jacobi Apocrypha," in *Nag Hammadi and Gnosis* (ed. R. McL. Wilson; NHS 14; Leiden: Brill, 1978) 37, following H.-M. Schenke.

[41] The *Apocryphon of James* fits Stirewalt's criteria for the "letter-essay" remarkably well: it is a response to the recipient's request (1:8–10) and is supplementary to another "secret book" previously sent (1:29–31). See Stirewalt, "Form," 186, 195, 197–99.

[42] Translation from the Ethiopic in Hennecke, *New Testament Apocrypha* 1. 192. According to the introduction (chap. 1) this means "the whole world," but this may be a later misunderstanding (chaps. 1–6 are extant only in the Ethiopic), since chap. 30 suggests that originally the churches in all parts of the land of Israel may have been intended. The letter would then be represented as having been written before the Gentile mission. But the survival of the work only in the Coptic and Ethiopic versions makes it impossible to be sure of this.

the false teaching of Simon and Cerinthus, who are travelling around the churches (chap. 7). Thus, the addressees are imagined as first-century Christians, troubled by the first-century heretics Simon and Cerinthus, whom second-century Christians believed to have sown the seeds of later Gnostic heresy. It is therefore set within a first-century situation which is regarded either as unchanged (type AP3) or as typological (type AP4) from the point of view of the real readers threatened by mid-second-century Gnosticism.

(4) *Didactic letters:* the *Epistle of Peter to James, Laodiceans, 3 Corinthians.* The *Epistle of Peter to James,* prefaced to the *Pseudo-Clementine Homilies,* can be included under this heading when it is regarded as a covering letter for "the books of my (Peter's) preachings" which accompanied it, since these were of general didactic content.[43] The letter functions very similarly to the *Apocryphon of James,* since Peter instructs James to pass on his preachings not to Gentile Christians or to any Jewish Christian (1:2) but to seventy carefully selected brethren (1:2), who in turn are to use them to instruct teachers (2:1). This is therefore an example of type BP. But there is a further feature of the letter which introduces a small element of specificity into the situation envisaged. Peter explains the need for his teaching to be carefully preserved by trustworthy teachers in the way he describes, by referring to false teachers who misrepresent him (2:3–4). From the beginnings of this danger in his lifetime, Peter concludes (by common sense, not prophecy, 2:2) that it is likely to increase in the future: "if they falsely assert such a thing whilst I am still alive, how much more after my death will those who come later venture to do so?" (2:7).[44] Thus, the real author contrives to let Peter foresee the situation of those to whom his "preachings" will be passed in the future, that is, the real readers. Once again we see an explicit attempt to bridge the gap which the pseudepigraphal letter genre requires between the supposed addressee and the real readers.

None of the pseudo-apostolic letters so far discussed are comparable to the major Pauline letters in being addressed to a specific church. Three noncanonical pseudo-Pauline letters of this type are known to have existed, though only two of these have survived. The lost *Letter to the Alexandrians* is known only from the Muratorian Canon, which describes it as a Marcionite forgery.[45] The two surviving letters, *Laodiceans* and *3 Corinthians,*

---

[43] It is thought to have originally introduced the *Kerygmata Petrou,* which formed a source for the later *Clementine Homilies;* see G. Strecker in Hennecke, *New Testament Apocrypha* 2. 103–6.

[44] Trans. in Hennecke, *New Testament Apocrypha* 2. 112. This reference is not sufficient to make the letter a testamentary letter.

[45] The Muratorian Canon also mentions "many other" *(alia plura)* pseudo-Pauline letters, which is probably an exaggeration. We have no other information about them. For other possible traces of lost pseudo-apostolic letters, see W. Schneemelcher in Hennecke, *New Testament Apocrypha* 2, 91–92: it is unlikely that they existed.

may both be attempts to fill gaps in the existing Pauline corpus of letters. Laodiceans is certainly supposed to be the missing letter to which Col 4:16 refers, and 3 Corinthians may well be intended as the "severe letter" written between 1 and 2 Corinthians (2 Cor 2:4; cf. *3 Cor.* 2:5).[46] The practice of filling gaps in an existing correspondence is one that is attested also in Hellenistic pseudepigraphal letter writing, but can scarcely have been operative in the writing of NT letters, unless Ephesians really was originally meant to be *Laodiceans,* as Marcion believed.

Laodiceans (which can be classified as type AP6) is a remarkably incompetent attempt to fill the gap. It is nothing but a patchwork of Pauline sentences and phrases from other letters, mainly Philippians. The result is a series of highly generalized exhortations which address no particular situation and reveal no intention by the author to communicate any clear message.[47] It seems as though he may really have been motivated only by the desire to produce something that would look as though Paul could have written it, and so it *might* be better to regard *Laodiceans* as a type AP1 or AP2 letter, rather than a type AP6 letter in which the author actually intends a didactic message for his readers.

3 Corinthians is more interesting, and is the only extracanonical apostolic letter that bears any real comparison with the major NT letters; that is, it addresses itself to the particular situation of a particular church. It is part of the late second-century *Acts of Paul.* Some have argued that it was originally independent and only subsequently incorporated in the *Acts of Paul,*[48] but their arguments are not convincing.[49] All the indications are that it was composed for its context in the *Acts of Paul* and only later circulated separately as an extract.[50]

---

[46] See Guthrie, "Acts," 339–40.

[47] This makes it very unlikely that *Laodiceans* is a Marcionite work, as argued by A. Harnack and G. Quispel (see Schneemelcher in Hennecke, *New Testament Apocrypha* 2. 130–31). The theory is based on the Muratorian Canon's reference to a letter to the Laodiceans as a Marcionite forgery along with *Alexandrians (finctae ad heresem Marcionis).* This reference may be based on a confusion, since Marcion himself thought that Ephesians was the letter to Laodicea (Tertullian, *Adv. Marc.* 5.11.17). Otherwise the Marcionite letter to the Laodiceans must be another work, now lost.

[48] A. F. J. Klijn, "The Apocryphal Correspondence between Paul and the Corinthians," *VC* 17 (1963) 10–16; M. Testuz, "La correspondance apocryphe de saint Paul et des Corinthiens," in *Littérature et Théologie Pauliniennes* (ed. A. Descamps et al.; RechBib 5; Louvain: Desclée de Brouwer, 1960) 221–22.

[49] So W. Schneemelcher in Hennecke, *New Testament Apocrypha* 2. 341–42; Guthrie, "Acts," 339. The fact that material has undoubtedly been lost at the beginning and end of the Philippi episode of the *Acts of Paul* makes some of Klijn's arguments weak. *3 Cor.* 1:8, 2:2 clearly require previous narrative material for their explanation.

[50] When it did circulate independently, the Corinthians' letter to Paul always accompanied Paul's reply, and frequently the narrative connecting them was retained.

Paul's letter is set within a narrative that relates the arrival of the false teachers Simon and Cleobius in Corinth, explains their teaching and the Corinthians' decision to write to Paul about it, includes a copy of the Corinthians' letter to Paul, relates its delivery to Paul in Philippi and the circumstances in which Paul wrote his reply. Probably (though the subsequent section of the *Acts of Paul* is lost) the reception of Paul's letter in Corinth was then described. Thus, Paul's letter is firmly anchored in a carefully described first-century situation. His addressees are unmistakably first-century Corinthian Christians, troubled by the first-century false teachers Simon (Magus) and Cleobius.[51]

The false teaching is quite carefully described and, although it comes quite close to Marcionite views, is probably not meant as a precise account of the teaching of any particular second-century Gnostic group. The description is of Gnostic beliefs with quite wide currency in the second century, and Paul's response to them consists of typical second-century anti-Gnostic argument. However, two points should be noticed about the setting of these teachings in first-century Corinth. First, the author may well have thought that Simon and Cleobius really taught these doctrines: Christians in his time commonly traced such views back to the first-century precursors of Gnosticism. Second, he has found for them their most plausible setting within Paul's ministry, since he knew that Paul's authentic correspondence with Corinth had to deal with denials of the resurrection. Doubtless the author intended *3 Corinthians* to be relevant to the Gnostic controversies of his own time, but he went so some lengths to give it a pseudo-historical setting which he probably thought entirely plausible.

It should also be noticed that, although in its supposed first-century setting *3 Corinthians* resembles a genuine Pauline letter in addressing the situation in a specific church, as far as its relevance to the late second century goes that particularity vanishes. It is not aimed at the late second-century church in Corinth – or anywhere else in particular – but only at the widespread problem of Gnostic teaching.

Since in the lost section of the *Acts of Paul* which followed *3 Corinthians* the author probably described the success of Paul's letter in extirpating the false teaching in Corinth,[52] we should probably regard the situation of *3 Corinthians* as typological (AP4) rather than unchanged.

Finally, it is worth observing the rarity of apocryphal apostolic letters, by comparison with other genres of Christians apocryphal literature (Gospels, Acts, Apocalypses). The authentic letter remained a vigorous literary genre

---

[51] For Cleobius, see Hegesippus, ap. Eusebius, *Hist. eccl.* 4.22.5. The mention of Simon and Cleobius in *Apost. Const.* (6.8.1; 6.10.1) may be dependent on *3 Corinthians*.

[52] Cf. *Acts of Paul* 9 (Hamburg Papyrus, p. 6). He may even have described the conversion of Cleobius to the truth.

in second- and third-century Christianity, when many Christian leaders wrote letters to churches in their own names, but pseudepigraphal letters from that period are rare. Whatever other reasons there may be for this,[53] one reason may well have been the sheer difficulty of using a pseudepigraphal letter to perform the same functions as an authentic letter.

IV. General Conclusions on Epistolary Pseudepigraphy in the New Testament

The evidence examined in sections II and III establishes and illustrates the conclusion to section I. In all examples studied, pseudepigraphal letters are addressed to supposed addressees living in the past, contemporaries of the supposed author, except in the case of the testamentary letter (Epistle of Enoch) and in a special case of type AP3 (Epistle of Jeremiah), where the supposed authors are able, by prophetic foresight, explicitly to address readers living after their deaths. In one other case (*Epistle of Peter to James*) the supposed author is credited with natural foresight of the situation after his death, so that he can refer explicitly to an aspect of the situation of the ultimate recipients of this type BP letter (or rather, strictly speaking, of the material for which this type BP letter is the covering letter). In other cases, where the supposed author is not credited with foresight of the situation after his death, relevance to the real readers is achieved either by making the content so generalized as not to presuppose a specific situation at all (type AP6: *Laodiceans;* type BP: *Apocryphon of James*), or by describing the situation of the supposed addresses in such terms as to make it analogous to that of the real readers (types AP3, AP4: 1 Baruch, *2 Baruch* 78–86, *Epistle of the Apostles, 3 Corinthians*).

It should be noted that among the letters surveyed there is no really good example of a pseudepigraphal letter that achieves didactic relevance by the generality of its contents (types AP6 and BP). *Laodiceans* is only a poor example. The *Apocryphon of James* is a letter whose contents actually belong to another genre, the postresurrection dialogue. It seems that not many pseudepigraphal writers wished to produce generalized didactic works, and those who did preferred other genres, such as wisdom literature (cf. Wisdom of Solomon, *Teachings of Silvanus*).

On the other hand, the seven pseudepigraphal letters in which there is a serious attempt to address relatively specific situations (Epistle of Enoch, Epistle of Jeremiah, 1 Baruch, *2 Baruch* 78–86, *Epistle of the Apostles, Epistle*

---

[53] For suggestions, see M. R. James, *The Apocryphal New Testament* (2 d ed.; Oxford: Clarendon, 1953) 476; Guthrie, "Acts," 338, 344–45.

of Peter to James, 3 Corinthians) achieve only *relatively* specific relevance to the real readers. Only one of them, the Epistle of Enoch, is likely to have been intended for one specific community or small group of communities. The others were meant for a wide Jewish or Christian readership. The three pseudo-apostolic letters are specific only in the sense of envisaging heretical teaching that was widespread in the author's time. None of these letters achieves anything like the particularity of the major Pauline letters, or even of such allegedly pseudepigraphal letters as Colossians and Jude.

We must now enquire whether the actual types of pseudepigraphal letters which we have discussed are applicable to any NT letters.

(1) *Type AP6.* Are there NT letters whose content is so general that it could equally well be addressed not only to the supposed recipients but also to any Christians at any time? Only Ephesians and James seem serious candidates for this category.[54] If their contents can rightly be regarded as generalized in this way, then, as far as our criteria go, they *could* be pseudepigraphal. Of course, they could also be authentic, since authentic real letters (type A) and authentic literary letters (type C) can also have very general content. But it is important to notice that in the case of these two letters, since they conform to no other type of pseudepigraphal letter, the *possibility* of their being pseudepigraphal *depends* upon the generality of their content. The more exegesis tends toward envisaging a specific situation as addressed in these letters, the less likely pseudepigraphy becomes.

(2) *Type BP.* A useful means of bridging the gap between the supposed addressee(s) and the real readers of a pseudepigraphal letter was the letter whose contents are explicitly meant to be passed on to others by the named addressee. Again, of course, the presence of such a feature raises only the *possibility* of pseudepigraphy, since it is found also in authentic letters (type B) of which type BP letters are fictional imitations. Among NT letters, this feature is found only in the Pastorals, which frequently instruct Timothy and Titus to pass on their teaching to others (1 Tim 4:6, 11; 6:2; 2 Tim

---

[54] Opinions differ on how far James addresses a specific situation; see the most recent assessment in P.H. Davids, *The Epistle of James* (NIGTC; Exeter: Paternoster, 1982) 28–34. Davids seems to hold that the contents of James address a Palestinian situation, but that the letter was sent to Jewish Christian communities outside Palestine, probably in Syria and Asia Minor (ibid., 64). The generality of the address (Jas 1:1) is not an infallible indication that the letter was meant for all Jewish Christians indiscriminately or for all Jewish Christians outside Palestine. Specific addresses were sometimes eliminated when letters were copied for circulation beyond the churches originally addressed: see N.A. Dahl, "The particularity of the Pauline Epistles as a problem in the Ancient Church," in *Neotestamentica et Patristica* (O. Cullmann Festschrift; NovTSup 6; Leiden: Brill, 1962) esp. 266–70.

Against occasional attempts to see Jude as addressed generally to all churches, see R. Bauckham, *Jude, 2 Peter* (Word Biblical Commentary 50; Waco, TX: Word, 1983) 19–20.

2:2, 14; Tit 2:2, 6, 9, 15; 3:1). It should also be noticed that, as in the *Epistle of Peter to James,* this type B(P) characteristic in the Pastorals is combined with foresight of the situation which will prevail after the supposed author's death (see below).

(3) *Type AP5.* 2 Peter is the only NT letter that explicitly addresses readers living not only during the supposed author's lifetime but also after his death (1:12–15). It does so by a careful and deliberate use of the testament genre, which enables Peter to foresee and address a specific situation after his death.[55] Since this literary device so precisely meets the need of the author of a pseudo-apostolic letter to bridge the chronological gap between the supposed author and the real readers, and since there are no known examples of its use in authentic letters, it makes the pseudepigraphal character of 2 Peter at least extremely likely. It is also worth noticing that, whereas the Epistle of Enoch clearly distinguishes the real readers as a generation subsequent to the generation of those who heard Enoch read his testament aloud, 2 Peter does not make such a distinction of generations (cf. 1:12–16; 3:1) but only of periods before and after the apostle's death, probably because in this case the letter was composed not so very long after the apostle's death.

2 Timothy is also a testamentary letter, but is not exactly addressed to readers living after Paul's death. However, Timothy seems to be being instructed with a view to his own conduct (including teaching others) after Paul's death (2 Tim 3:5, 10–4:2, 5), and 1 and 2 Timothy both refer to the period after Paul's death (1 Tim 4:1–3; 2 Tim 3:1–9, 4:3–4). In no other NT letter does the author or supposed author foresee the situation following his death.[56]

(4) *Types AP3 and AP4.* These two types are not always easy to distinguish, but their common characteristic is that they set the supposed readers in a situation analogous to that of the real readers. In one of the cases we have studied *(Epistle of the Apostles)* this situation is clearly but only briefly described (chaps. 1, 7), but in this case of a letter with mainly Gospel content, in which the orientation to a specific situation is more implicit than explicit, the specific character of the situation addressed does not need spelling out at length. In the other cases, where the whole content of the letter is angled to a relatively specific situation (1 Baruch, *2 Baruch* 78–86, *3 Corinthians*), the writers find it necessary to provide quite full details of the supposed historical situation, so as to locate the letter firmly within its historical situation, while at the same time showing that this situation has parallels with the real readers' situation. Even though the context of the

---

[55] For the use of the testament genre in 2 Peter, see Bauckham, *Jude,* 132, 173, 194, 196–97, 199–200, 237–38, 282.

[56] Jude 17–18 is not such a reference, since the prophecy is considered fulfilled in the false teachers active as Jude is writing (v 19).

Baruch letters could have been understood in a general way from the OT, this historical scene-setting was still thought necessary. In all three cases, the scene-setting is achieved largely by placing the letter within a narrative context, which in the case of 3 Corinthians also includes the letter to which Paul's is a reply.

Thus, whereas the authentic real letter can take for granted the situation to which it is addressed, merely alluding to what the addressee(s) do not need to be told, it is characteristic of pseudepigraphal letters of types AP3 and AP4 that they must *describe* the situation of their supposed addressee(s) sufficiently for the real readers, who would not otherwise know it, to be able to recognize it as analogous to their own. Now the large majority of NT letters, both those generally accepted as authentic and some that are often thought to be pseudepigraphal (Colossians, 1 Peter, Jude), take for granted the specific situations to which they are addressed, in the manner of authentic real letters. They do not, in the manner of pseudepigraphal letters of types AP3 and AP4, describe it for the benefit of readers who would not otherwise know it – often to the frustration of modern scholars! No NT letter has a narrative context, like the Baruch letters and *3 Corinthians,* and in no NT letter is there historical scene-setting which clearly goes beyond what could be expected in an authentic letter. Thus, there is no *unambiguous* case of a type AP3 or type AP4 letter in the NT.

The Pastorals seem to show some interest in historical scene-setting, in that the false teachers, supposed to be already active at the supposed time of writing, are described perhaps a little more fully than would be necessary for Timothy and Titus themselves (see esp. 2 Tim 2:17–18), but not decisively so. In the case of 2 Thessalonians it could be argued that 2:2; 3:11 provide all the historical scene-setting that is really necessary in this case, with the additional consideration that 2 Thessalonians could be seen as a kind of pseudepigraphal appendix to the authentic 1 Thessalonians, which thus provides to some degree the historical context for 2 Thessalonians. Thus 2 Thessalonians could be a pseudepigraphal letter of type AP3 or AP4, though it could also be authentic. But Colossians, 1 Peter, and Jude cannot plausibly be regarded as type AP3 or AP4 letters. Like the undoubtedly authentic letters of Paul, they assume a specific situation without having to describe it, because, we must conclude, it was the actual situation of the real readers, not a parallel situation in the past. In other words, they are authentic letters. The same would have to be said of James and Ephesians, *if* they are interpreted as addressing relatively specific situations.

It might be suggested that some NT letters, if pseudepigraphal, could constitute a special case of AP3. If they were composed within a relatively short time after the death of the supposed author and therefore after the supposed time of writing, and if they were written for the actual churches to which they are addressed, then the real readers in those churches could know, without having it described, that the situation in their churches had remained unchanged, in relevant respects, since the supposed time of composition and could therefore read these letters as still relevant to them. However, it should be noticed that such a suggestion would contradict what is frequently regarded as the major argument for pseudepigraphy in these cases, viz., that the situation addressed did not exist during the lifetime of the supposed author. It would in fact leave the hypothesis of pseudepigraphy with no advantage over the hypothesis of authenticity, provided that the latter includes the possibility that a colleague or secretary of the apostle could have composed the letter on his behalf.

It is, of course, a theoretical possibility that NT letters could belong to a type of pseudepigraphal letter not attested among the examples studied in sections II and III. However, such a type would have to have its own way of meeting the problem of writing a didactic pseudepigraphal letter: the problem of the difference between the supposed addressee(s) and the real readers. A pseudepigraphal letter cannot simply ignore this problem, as though an apostle could easily address readers living after his death as if they were his contemporaries. It does not appear that NT writers in fact knew any way of meeting the problem besides those already discussed.

Thus, our criteria derived from the study of indisputably pseudepigraphal letters outside the NT show that 2 Peter can be regarded with very high probability as pseudepigraphal, since it is so clearly designed to meet the problem posed for pseudepigraphal letter writers and does so by means of a genre (the testamentary letter) that had already been used for this purpose. It seems that the Pastorals (which show marked characteristics of type BP and type AP5 letters, as well as possibly also conforming to type AP3 or AP4 letters) could very well be pseudepigraphal, as more detailed discussion in the next section will confirm. In the cases of Ephesians and James (which could be type AP6 letters) and 2 Thessalonians (which could be a type AP3 or AP4 letter), our criteria make pseudepigraphy a possibility, without deciding the issue. As far as our critera go, the question of authenticity remains in these cases an open one which must still be decided on other grounds. But it seems that any other case for pseudepigraphy among the NT letters is by these criteria very implausible indeed.[57]

Finally, it is worth noticing that these results roughly confirm the general tendency of scholarly judgments reached largely on other grounds. 2 Peter and the Pastorals, which our criteria make probably pseudepigraphal, are the NT letters most widely regarded as pseudegraphal. Those which our

---

[57] In the case of the Johannine letters, the real issue, as with Hebrews, is not pseudepigraphy but misattribution.

criteria make possibly pseudepigraphal (Ephesians, James, 2 Thessalonians) are probably the next most popular candidates for pseudepigraphy. Those whose authenticity could be regarded as vindicated by this study (Colossians, 1 Peter, Jude[58]) are those which many scholars still regard as having a reasonable claim to authenticity. None of the letters whose authenticity is universally admitted emerges as even possibly pseudepigraphal by our criteria. This general correspondence with the scholarly consensus suggests that our criteria are reliable and should therefore be given weight in the disputed instances.

V. The Problem of the Pastorals

In the light of the preceding discussion, two characteristics of the Pastorals seem readily *compatible* with pseudepigraphy, a third points rather strongly in the direction of pseudepigraphy, while a fourth will lead to a particular suggestion about the date and authorship of the Pastorals:

(1) The personal details about Paul and Timothy can be paralleled from letters of types AP1 and AP2. If the Pastorals are pseudepigraphal, Timothy and Titus do not have to represent any particular sort of later leader (such as monarchical bishops) but are simply themselves, as historical characters, in the same way that Paul is. The author has thought himself into situations in Paul's ministry and, as many pseudepigraphal letter writers did, has filled out whatever historical information was available to him with historical fiction.

(2) The bulk of the didactic material in the Pastorals is given to Timothy and Titus to *pass on* to the churches and to particular categories of people within the churches. As already mentioned, this is a type BP characteristic,[59] which makes the role of Timothy and Titus comparable with that of the supposed recipients of the *Apocryphon of James*. The resemblance to the *Epistle of Peter to James* is very striking in 2 Tim 2:2.

(3) The treatment of false teachers and heresy. If the Pastorals are considered not only as general teaching, but (as they must be) also as teaching relevant to a relatively specific situation, that situation is really characterized by the threat of false teaching and the evils that flow from it. The false teachers are plainly represented as active at the supposed time of writing. Some of them are named (1 Tim 1:20; 2 Tim 2:17), and these must, of course, be contemporaries of Paul, real or imagined, not contemporaries of the real

---

[58] For the debate about the authenticity of Jude, see R. Bauckham, "The Letter of Jude: An Account of Research," in *ANRW* 2.25.5, pp. 3791–3826.

[59] Of course, it is also a type B characteristic and so is compatible with authenticity as well as with pseudepigraphy.

author. If the Pastorals are pseudepigraphal, this historical situation of the letters must be regarded as an unchanged or typological situation (type AP3 or AP4). Has the author done sufficient scene-setting for this to be possible? The false teachers are fairly fully characterized, probably just fully enough for the author's purpose, provided we assume that he wished to characterize a broad range of false teaching in his own time and therefore could not afford to detail their doctrines too specifically.

However, in addition to the account of false teaching at the supposed time of writing, the picture is complicated by three passages that refer to false teaching and apostasy in the future tense (1 Tim 4:1–3; 2 Tim 3:1–5; 4:3–4). It is noteworthy that two of these passages occur appropriately in the testamentary letter 2 Timothy, where Paul is explicitly instructing Timothy with a view to the period following his impending death (see esp. 2 Tim 4:6). The first two of the three passages *could* be understood as citations of earlier prophecies about the last days which Paul is intending to say are being fulfilled at the time of writing,[60] but this cannot be the case in 2 Tim 4:3–4, and so it is better to take all three passages as really future from the standpoint of Paul when writing the letters.[61] In that case they are very similar to passages in the testamentary letter 2 Peter, where Peter looks into the future after his death, the last days in which false teachers will appear, who are plainly the false teachers of the real readers' own time (2 Pet 2:1–3; 3:1–4). Moreover, the odd phenomenon in 2 Tim 3:1–9, where the future-tense prophecy of the false teachers continues in the present tense (vv 6–8), is also amply paralleled in 2 Peter, where passages prophesying the false teachers alternate with passages describing the same false teachers in the present tense (2 Pet 2:10–22; 3:5, 16).[62]

How are we to understand the combination in the Pastorals of false teaching at the supposed time of writing and false teaching prophesied for the future? The answer must lie in 2 Timothy's indications that Paul is envisaging a situation that, already bad at the time of writing, will get worse in the future (2 Tim 2:16–17; and esp. 3:13). Again this is reminiscent of the *Epistle of Peter to James* (2:17). So it seems that the material about false teaching in the Pastorals, when taken as a whole, amounts to a careful and deliberate attempt to bridge the gap between the situation at the supposed time of writing and the real contemporary situation of the author and his readers.

---

[60] So J. N. D. Kelly, *A Commentary on The Pastoral Epistles* (Black's NT Commentaries; London: A. & C. Black, 1964) 93–94, 192–93.

[61] So M. Dibelius and H. Conzelmann, *The Pastoral Epistles* (Hermeneia; Philadelphia: Fortress, 1972) 64, 115, 120–21.

[62] Note also that 1 Tim 4:1–5, where the prophecy of the false teachers is followed by their refutation, is paralleled by 2 Pet 3:3–10.

(4) If, however, we take seriously the pseudepigraphal implication that the situation Paul foresees after his death is the situation of the real readers, we must also reckon with the fact that Timothy seems to be part of this situation. It seems to be one which follows Paul's death but not Timothy's death. In 2 Timothy, Paul is instructing Timothy how to react to it, most obviously in 3:5, where, after the prophecy of the false teachers in the future tense, Timothy is immediately told, "Avoid *these people*" (τούτους ἀποτρέπου) (cf. also 4:5). Ought we to press the apparent implication that at the real time of writing, the time Paul foresees, Timothy was still alive?

It might be unwise to do so were it not for a confirmatory piece of evidence in 1 Tim 6:14, where, on a natural reading of the text, Paul expects Timothy to survive until the parousia.[63] It is just possible that a pseudepigraphal writer had observed that Paul in his authentic letters tends to write as though his readers will survive till the parousia, and deliberately imitated this way of speaking, but this is not likely.[64] The otherwise attested practice of postapostolic writers is carefully to avoid the implication that the apostles and their contemporaries had expected to see the parousia in their lifetime (cf. *Apocalypse of Peter* [Ethiopic] 1; *Epistle of the Apostles* 34; *Testament of our Lord* 1:2; *Testament of our Lord in Galilee*).[65]

If the Pastorals were written after Paul's death but within Timothy's lifetime, then most probably they were written by Timothy himself. This could also perhaps explain the difference between the letters to Timothy, where we learn a good deal about Timothy, and the letter to Titus, where we learn next to nothing about Titus.[66]

---

[63] So Kelly, *Commentary*. 145. S. G. Wilson denies this, but without offering an alternative explanation of the text (*Luke and the Pastoral Epistles* [London: SPCK, 1979] 16–17). 1 Tim 6:15 may sound a note of caution (especially if there is an allusion to Hab 2:2, the classic text on eschatological delay), but can hardly cancel out the implication of 6:14.

[64] *3 Cor.* 3:3 has Paul write, "the Lord Christ will accomplish his coming quickly" (εἰς ταχεῖαν ποιήσεται ἔλευσιν), but this is less specific (cf. Rev 22:20) and could still be said at the real time of writing, whereas a prediction of the parousia in the lifetime of the generation of the apostles could no longer be valid in postapostolic times.

[65] On these passages, see R. Bauckham, "The Two Fig Tree Parables in the Apocalypse of Peter," *JBL* 104 (1985) 276–77.

[66] I am grateful to members of the Ehrhardt seminar in the University of Manchester, who heard a draft of this article and made useful comments, and especially to Dr. P. S. Alexander, for several discussions about letters in the ancient world, which helped me to formulate and clarify my thoughts.

10. Kainam the Son of Arpachshad in Luke's Genealogy*

In an article in this journal[1], Gert J. Steyn has recently argued that the last part of Luke's genealogy (3,34–38) is dependent on Gen 11,10–32 and Gen 5,1–32 in the LXX version. He regards as the clinching evidence for this the occurrence of the name Καινάμ in Luke 3,37, where Luke agrees with the LXX (Gen 5,9–14: Καινάν; cf. also 10,24, where A has Καινάμ)[2] against the MT and the Samaritan Pentateuch, which do not have this generation at all. Steyn's argument, however, is very unsatisfactory for three reasons: (1) He offers no justification for dealing only with the last part of the genealogy (the generations from Terah to Adam and God). One has to presume that he does not think the earlier parts of the genealogy are dependent on the LXX, but he does not explain why the genealogy should be divided in this way. (2) He does not discuss the significant divergences from the LXX in other parts of the genealogy. (3) Most remarkably, he nowhere refers to the fact that Kainam the son of Arpachshad appears not only in LXX Gen 5,9–14; 10,24 and Luke 3,37, but also in Jubilees 8,1–5.

It is true that in Luke 3,34–38 the only divergences from the LXX are minor differences of spelling (Luke 3,36: Καινάμ/Gen 5,12–13: Καινάν; Luke 3,37: Ἰάρετ/Gen 5,15–20: Ἰάρεδ; Luke 3,37: Καινάμ/Gen 11,9–14: Καινάν), but in the rest of the genealogy they are much more significant. The generations from Nathan to Abraham (Luke 3,31–34) compare with the relevant biblical passages in the LXX as follows:

Luke	LXX	
Ναθάμ	Ναθάν	1 Chron 3,5
Δαυίδ	Δαυίδ	1 Chron 2,15; 3,1
Ἰεσσαί	Ἰεσσαί	1 Chron 2,12–13; Ruth 4,22
Ἰωβήδ	Ὠβήδ (A: Ἰωβήδ)	1 Chron 2,12
	Ὠβήδ	Ruth 4,21–22

---

* First publication: *Ephemerides Theologicae Lovanienses* 67 (1991) 95–103.

[1] G. T. Steyn, *The Ocurrence of "Kainam" in Luke's Genealogy: Evidence of Septuagint Influence?*, in *ETL* 65 (1989) 409–411.

[2] The additional occurrence of the name Καινάν in Gen 10,22 LXX, as a sixth son of Shem, is puzzling. If it is not simply misplaced, it may represent an earlier, distinct attempt to include Καινάν in the descendants of Shem.

Βόος	Βόος	1 Chron 2,11–12; Ruth 4,21
Σάλα	Σαλμών (Α: Σαλμά)	1 Chron 2,11
	Σαλμάν (Α: Σαλμών)	Ruth 3,20–11
Ναασσών	Ναασσών	1 Chron 2,10–11; Ruth 4,20
Ἀμιναδάμ	Ἀμιναδάβ	1 Chron 2,10; Ruth 4,19–20
Ἀδμίν		
Ἀρνί	Ἀράμ (Β: Ἀρράν)	1 Chron 2,9–10
	Ἀρράν (v. 1. Ἀράμ)	Ruth 4,19
Ἑσρώμ	Ἑσερών (Α: Ἑσρώμ)	1 Chron 2,5.9
	Ἑσρών (Α: Ἑσρώμ, Ἑσρών)	Ruth 4,18–19
Φάρες	Φάρες	1 Chron 2,4–5: Ruth 4,18
Ἰούδα	Ἰούδα	1 Chron 2,1–4
Ἰακώβ	Ἰακώβ	
Ἰσαάκ	Ἰσαάκ	
Ἀβραάμ	Ἀβραάμ	

In this list the differences in the form of some of the names is notable. But especially significant is the fact that Luke's genealogy has an additional generation. The sequence of three names Ἀμιναδάμ, Ἀδμίν and Ἀρνί (Luke 3,33) is a point of great confusion in the manuscript tradition, partly because scribes attempted to correct the discrepany with the Old Testament and with Matthew 1,3–4, but these three names in these forms are the best reading[3].

Before Ναθάμ the genealogy has no clear parallels with the Old Testament, except for the two names Ζοροβαβέλ and his father Σαλαθιηλ (Luke 3,27). These represent a notable divergence from 1 Chronicles 3,17–19 (both MT and LXX), according to which Zerubbabel was descended from David not through Nathan but through the royal line, his grandfather being king Jeconiah. (According to 1 Chron 3,19 MT, Zerubbabel was the son not of Shealtiel but of his brother Pedaiah. This discrepancy from the usual OT description of Zerubbabel as son of Shealtiel [Ezra 3,2.8; 5,2 etc] is corrected in 1 Chron 3,19 LXX.). It may be, as has sometimes been argued[4], that a few of the names preceding Ζοροβαβέλ in Luke's genealogy are to be identified with names among the descendants of Zerubbabel in 1 Chronicles 3,19–24, but if so the genealogy is certainly not directly dependent on the text of 1 Chronicles 3,19–24.

In view of these divergences from the LXX, it might be argued that Luke took over from a source a traditional genealogy taking the line of Jesus back to Abraham, as in Matthew 1,1–17, and himself used the LXX of Genesis to

---

[3] Cf. R. Bauckham, *Jude and the Relatives of Jesus in the Early Church*, Edinburgh, T. & T. Clark, 1990, chapter 7: "Additional Note on the Text of the Lukan Genealogy".

[4] A. Hervey, *The Genealogies of our Lord and Saviour Jesus Christ*, Cambridge, Macmillan; London, Hatchard, 1853, pp. 115–120; J. Jeremias, *Jerusalem in the Time of Jesus*, London, SCM Press, 1969, p. 296; G. Kühn, *Die Geschlechtsregister Jesu bei Lukas und Matthäus, nach ihrer Herkunft untersucht*, in ZNW 22 (1923) 212–213.

extend the line back to Adam. In order to argue, to the contrary, that Luke took over the whole genealogy as far as Adam from a source which was probably independent of the LXX, we need to return to Kainam the son of Arpachshad. In Jubilees 8,1–5 he is no mere name in a genealogy, but a figure of some significance:

And on [sic] the twenty-ninth jubilee in the first week, at its beginning Arpachshad took a wife and her name was Rasu'eya, daughter of Susan, daughter of Elam, as a wife [sic]. And she bore a son for him in the third year of that week, and he called him Cainan [Syriac: Kanan; Ethiopic: Kainam][5], (2) and the child grew. And his father taught him writing. And he went forth in order that he might seek a place where he could build a city. (3) And he found a writing which the ancestors engraved on stone. And he read what was in it. And he transcribed it. And he sinned because of what was in it, since there was in it the teaching of the Watchers by which they used to observe the omens of the sun and the moon and stars within all the signs of heaven. (4) And he copied it down, but he did not tell about it because he feared to tell Noah about it lest he be angry with him because of it. (5) And in the thirtieth jubilee in the second week in its first year, he took a wife and her name was Melka, the daughter of Madai, son of Japheth. And in its fourth year he begot a son and he called him Shelah because, he said, "I have certainly been sent out"[6].

The narrative serves to explain how the unlawful teaching of the Watchers, given before the Flood, continued to influence humanity after the Flood. In particular, it traces the origins of Chaldean astrology (11,8) to the Watchers, by contrast to the true astronomical knowledge which Enoch taught (4,17–18). This story about Kainam is therefore closely connected with the traditions about the teaching of the Watchers which are found in the Enoch literature (for their astrological teaching, cf. especially 1 Enoch 8,3). Jubilees had earlier referred to the story of the Watchers (4,15.22; 6,1–11; 7,21–22)[7], but had not in fact mentioned their unlawful teaching (4,15 refers only to their original mission from God to give true teaching, before they sinned).

---

[5] The spelling with a final 'm' recurs remarkable often in reference to the son of Arpachshad. The Ethiopic of Jubilees calls the son of Enosh Kâinân (4,13–14), but the son of Arpachshad Kâinâm (8.1). The Syriac of 8,1 may have assimilated the name of the son of Arpachshad to that of the son of Enosh. In the LXX the son of Enosh is Καινάν (Gen 5,12–16; 1 Chron 1,2); the son of Arpachshad is Καινάν in Gen 11,12–13; but in Gen 10,24 MS A has Καινάμ for the son of Arpachshad. Luke alone calls the son of Enosh, as well as the son of Arpachshad, Καινάμ, but since the latter occurs first in his genealogy he could have assimilated the name of the son of Enosh to it. Thus it is possible that the two names were originally distinct and that the son of Arpachshad was קינם, not קינן.

[6] Translation by O.S. Wintermute, in J.H. Charlesworth (ed.), *The Old Tesament Pseudepigrapha*, vol. 2, London, Darton, Longman & Todd, 1985, p. 71.

[7] For Jubilees' dependence on the Enoch literature, see J. VanderKam, *Enoch Traditions in Jubilees and Other Second-century Sources*, in *SBL 1978 Seminar Papers*, vol. 1, Missoula, MT, Scholars Press, pp. 228–251; ID., *Enoch and the Growth of an Apocalyptic Tradition* (CBQ MS, 16), Washington, Catholic Biblical Association of America, 1984, p. 180.

Thus it seems probable that the story of Kainam's discovery of the inscription belonged to the same cycle of traditions as those about Enoch and the Watchers, to which Jubilees is indebted.

It is likely that Kainam also occurred in a genealogical tradition known to Jubilees. R.H. Charles[8] suggested that Jubilees added Kainam to the line from Shem to Abraham in order to make possible the analogy in 2,23 between the twenty-two kinds of work created on the six days of creation and the "twenty-two chief men from Adam until Jacob". This is not a convincing argument, since if Kainam is ommitted there are twenty-two names, including both Adam and Jacob, from Adam to Jacob, so that it would still be possible to reckon twenty-two. More convincing is the idea that both in Jubilees and in Genesis 11 LXX, Kainam has been added to make ten generations in the line from Shem to Terah, parallel to the ten generations from Adam to Noah[9]. But since Jubilees does not set out these two genealogies in schematic parallel as Genesis does (5,1–32; 11,10–26), it is less plausible that the author of Jubilees added Kainam for this reason than that he found Kainam already in the text of Genesis or in an independent genealogy of the patriarchs. Furthermore, the presence of Kainam in the genealogy cannot be isolated from the question of the various differing chronologies of the generations from Adam to Terah. In the generations from Adam to Shem the age of each patriarch at the birth of his eldest son, as given in Jubilees[10], virtually agree in every case with the figures in the Samaritan Pentateuch, diverging from the MT in the cases where the Samaritan Pentateuch does so[11]. But in the generations from Arpachshad to Terah, where the Samararitan Pentateuch agrees with the LXX in figures which simply add 100 or 50 to those of the MT, Jubilees has a quite different set of figures, higher than the MT's, lower than the LXX's, but unrelated to either[12]. This means that the occurrence of Kainam the son of Arpachshad in Jubilees is not simply paral-

---

[8] R.H. Charles, *The Book of Jubilees or the Little Genesis,* London, A. & C. Black, 1902, p. 66.

[9] For the LXX, cf. R.W. Klein, *Archaic Chronologies and the Textual History of the Old Testament,* in *HTR* 67 (1974) 258.

[10] These ages have to be calculated from the dates Jubilees gives.

[11] Since these agreements with the Samaritan Pentateuch have to be calculated and are not explicitly textual agreements, they are not included in the lists of biblical textual variants in Jubilees and their affinities given by J. VanderKam, *Textual and Historical Studies in the Book of Jubilees* (HSM, 14), Missoula, MT, Scholars Press, 1977, pp. 139–198, but they could be added to his lists B and E and support his case for the affinity of Jubilees' biblical text with the Samaritan.

[12] Discussions of the divergent chronologies in the texts of Genesis in the MT, LXX and Samaritan Pentateuch (e.g. Klein, *Archaic Chronologies,* 253–263; G. Larsson, *The Chronology of the Pentateuch: A Comparison of the MT and LXX,* in *JBL* 102 [1983] 401–409) do not seem to have given due attention to the data of Jubilees or those of Pseudo-Philo, *LAB* (which appears to have yet another distinct chronology, although the transmission of figures in the text of *LAB* is unreliable).

lel to his occurrence in the LXX. In Genesis 11,13 the figures of Kainan's life (130 years to the birth of Shelah, 330 years afterwards) are the same as those of his son Shelah. This duplication, found nowhere else in the genealogy, makes it very probable that Kainan is a secondary addition to it. But this is not the case in Jubilees (where Kainam is 57 at the birth of Shelah, and Shelah 71 at the birth of Eber). In Jubilees the occurrence of Kainam in the genealogy seems to be part of a divergent tradition of the whole genealogy from Arpachshad to Terah.

It is difficult to know whether the author of Jubilees derived this divergent tradition from the text of Genesis he used. VanderKam's meticulous and exhaustive examination of the variant biblical readings in Jubilees shows that Jubilees agrees more frequently with the LXX and the Samaritan than with the MT, and concludes that it depends on an early Palestinian text of the Hebrew Bible which was closer to the *Vorlage* of the LXX than to the MT[13]. However, in this case, Kainam occurs only in LXX and Jubilees, not in other witnesses to a Palestinian type of text (Samaritan; 1 Chronicles 1,18; Pseudo-Philo, *LAB* 4,9), while Jubilees' chronology of the line from Arpachshad to Terah is unparalleled elsewhere. Jubilees may reflect a distinctive tradition of the text of Genesis 11, or it may reflect an independent genealogy which has also influenced the LXX at Genesis 10,24; 11,12–13.

There is additional evidence that a form of the genealogy from Shem to Abraham which included Kainam the son of Arpachshad was already known before Jubilees[14]. This evidence comes from the Enochic Apocalypse of Weeks (1 Enoch 93,3–10; 91,11–17)[15] and thus confirms the suggestion made above that the tradition about Kainam in Jubilees 8,1–5 was connected with the traditions about Enoch and the Watchers which Jubilees knew from the Enoch literature. The Apocalypse of Weeks divides the whole history of the world from Adam to the judgment of the Watchers at the last judgment into ten "weeks". The clear indication of 93,3 (in which Enoch, the seventh in line from Adam, says, "I was born the seventh in the first week") is that the weeks consist of seven generations each. The majority of

---

[13] VanderKam, *Textual and Historical Studies,* pp. 116–138.

[14] The latest full discussion of the date of Jubilees is VanderKam, *Textual and Historical Studies,* chapter 3: he concludes that it must be dated between 163 and 140 B.C.E. The Apocalypse of Weeks has usually been dated just before or during the Maccabean revolt. VanderKam, *Enoch and the Growth,* pp. 142–149, argues for a date between 175 and 167 B.C.E.

[15] This rearrangement of the text, long postulated by scholars, has been shown to be the original form of the Apocalypse of Weeks by the Aramaic fragments from Qumran: see J. T. Milik, *The Book of Enoch: Aramaic Fragments of Qumrân Cave 4,* Oxford, Clarendon Press, 1976, p. 247; F. Dexinger, *Henochs Zehnwochenapokalypse und offene Probleme der Apokalyptikforschung* (SPB, 29), Leiden, Brill, 1977, pp. 102–109; M. Black, *The Apocalypse of Weeks in the Light of 4Q En*ᵃ, in *VT* 28 (1978) 464–469; ID., *The Book of Enoch or I Enoch: A New English Edition* (SVTP, 7), Leiden, Brill, 1985, pp. 287–289, 291–292.

scholars have concluded that the Apocalypse cannot be made to fit a scheme of ten weeks of generations[16], but attempts to understand it as using units other than generations have all failed.[17] In fact, a generational scheme works very well. If we include Kainam the son of Arpachshad, the first five weeks are as follows:

1st week: Adam, Seth, Enosh, Kenan, Mahalalel, Jared, Enoch
End of 1st week: Enoch (93,3)

2nd week: Methuselah, Lamech, Noah, Shem, Arpachshad, Kainam, Shelah
End of 2nd week: Noah's law (93,4)

3rd week: Eber, Peleg, Reu, Serug, Nahor, Terah, Abraham
End of 3rd week: Abraham (93,5)

4th week: Isaac, Jacob, Judah, Perez, Hezron, Ram, Amminadab
End of 4th week: Sinai (93,6)

5th week: Nahshon, Salmon, Boaz, Obed, Jesse, David, Solomon
End of 5th week: Temple (93,7)

Most important events noticed in the Apocalypse happen at the end of each week, i.e. on the sabbath of each week, in the seventh generation. Provided we include Kainam in the generations of the second week, Abraham occurs at the end of the third week, exactly where the Apocalypse indicates. The law made for sinners by Noah, following the growth of iniquity after the Flood (93,4) should probably be identified not with the Noahic covenant of Genesis 9,1–17, but with the testament of Noah found in Jubilees 7,20–39[18]. Jubilees dates this in the jubilee immediately before the birth of Kainam, but the author of the Apocalypse could easily have supposed it to have happened during the lifetime of Shelah, when Noah was certainly still alive. Kainam's sin in connexion with the inscription could then be connected with the renewed growth of iniquity to which 1 Enoch 93,4 refers. If the genealogy continues through the biblical line to Solomon, the thirty-fifth generation, then the giving of the law at Sinai at the end of the fourth week

---

[16] Cf. the discussion, with references to earlier literature, in Dexinger, *Henochs Zehnwochenapokalypse*, pp. 119–120. But C. Kaplan, *Some New Testament Problems in the Light of Rabbinics and the Pseudepigrapha: The Generation Schemes in Matthew I:1–17 and Luke III: 24ff*, in *Bibliotheca Sacra* 87 (1930) 465–471, rightly measures the weeks in generations.

[17] The most detailed alternative reckonings of the weeks are those of R. T. Beckwith, *The Significance of the Calendar for Interpreting Essene Chronology and Eschatology*, in *RevQ* 10 (1980) 167–202, and K. Koch, *Sabbatstruktur und Geschichte: Die sogenannte Zehn-Wochen-Apokalypse (I Hen 93^{1–10}; 91^{1–17}) und das Ringen um die alttestamentlichen Chronologien im späten Israelitentum*, in *ZAW* 95 (1983) 413–420: by comparison with a generational scheme both are very contrived. For the failure of attempts to reckon the weeks, cf. also VanderKam, *Enoch and the Growth*, p. 158.

[18] Dexinger, *Henochs Zehnwochenapokalypse*, pp. 123–124; Black, *The Book of Enoch*, 289–290.

(93,6) is approximately correctly placed and the building of the Temple accurately placed at the end of the fifth week (93,7).

The generational scheme appears to fail after this, because the Apocalypse allows only one week, the sixth, for the whole period of the divided monarchy down to the destruction of the Temple, which it places at the end of the sixth week (93,8). From Rehoboam to Jeconiah there were seventeen generations (1 Chron 3.10–16). This is the main reason why most scholars have rejected the idea that the Apocalypse of Weeks uses a generational scheme. However, the mistake is to suppose that the author would count his generations according to the royal line, in which he shows no interest at all. His interests are priestly interests in the Law and the Temple, and he is much more likely to have followed a priestly genealogy. Since the Old Testament supplies no standard priestly genealogy after Phinehas, we cannot tell what genealogy he would have used. However, if we use, for the sake of illustration, the genealogy given (as that of Ezra) in Ezra 7,1–5, we can see how such a genealogy *could* fit the scheme of the Apocalypse. We need to go back to the fourth week to do so:

4th week: Isaac, Jacob, Levi, Kohath, Amram, Aaron, Eleazar
End of 4th week: Sinai (93,6)

5th week: Phinehas, Abishua, Bukki, Uzzi, Zerahiah, Meraioth, Azariah
End of 5th week: Temple (93,7)

6th week: Amariah, Ahitub, Zadok, Shallum, Hilkiah, Azariah, Seraiah
End of 6th week: Fall of Temple (93,8)

The generation of Eleazar the son of Aaron could be more plausibly than that of Amminadab regarded as the generation of Sinai (Exod 28,1; Num 3,2–4.22). Azariah at the end of the fifth week could be considered contemporary with the building of the Temple (as in 1 Kings 4,2; 1 Chron 6,10) and Seraiah at the end of the sixth week was high priest at the time of the fall of Jerusalem (2 Kings 25,18). This simply shows that the scheme of the Apocalypse could fit a priestly genealogy, which could well record, as this one does, far fewer generations than the line of the kings of Judah. We may also allow for the fact that genealogies were frequently manipulated to fit a numerical scheme. The author of the Apocalypse of Weeks had to cover the monarchical and post-exilic periods in no more than two weeks in order to put his own generation, which received the secrets of Enoch's revelations (93,10), in the key position at the end of the seventh week, since this was the "jubilee" position, the seventh generation of the seventh week. If his scheme fitted so well the recorded genealogies as far as the building of the Temple, we should not be surprised if he stretched it thereafter.

The point of this examination of the Apocalypse of Weeks has been to show how probable it is that its author knew Kainam the son of Arpachshad in the genealogy of the patriarchs. Without this generation, the otherwise precise placings of Abraham and the building of the Temple at the ends of the third and fifth weeks would not be possible. Thus the occurrence of Kainam the son of Arpachshad in the genealogy from Shem to Abraham was not a peculiarity of Jubilees alone, but was more widely known, in the second century B.C. E., in the circles from which the Enoch literature comes.

It remains to demonstrate that the occurrence of Kainam in the Lukan genealogy is more likely to depend on a tradition connected with Jubilees and the Enoch literature than to depend on the LXX. The Lukan genealogy has seventy-seven names from Adam to Jesus[19]. If the order of these is reversed, to follow the usual order of a biblical genealogy, the genealogy can be seen to have been constructed to fit a numerical similar to that of the Apocalypse of Weeks. The names in the seventh, sabbatical position at the end of each week of generations are then as follows:

1st week: Ἐνώχ, *2nd:* Σαλά, *3rd:* Ἀβραάμ, *4th:* Ἀδμίν, *5th:* Δαυίδ, *6th:* Ἰωσήφ, *7th:* Ἰησοῦς, *8th:* Σαλαθιήλ, *9th:* Ματταθίας, *10th:* Ἰωσήφ, *11th:* Ἰησοῦς

Whereas the scheme in the Apocalypse of Weeks correlates Enoch in the seventh generation with the author's own generation in the forty-ninth (seven × seventh) generation, this scheme primarily correlates Enoch in the seventh generation with Jesus in the seventy-seventh generation. This is a Hebraic use of seventy-seven as the fullest extension of seven, as in Genesis 4,24; Matthew 18,22. Enoch, well known to be the seventh generation from Adam (1 Enoch 60,8; 93,3; Jub 7,39; Jude 14; Lev Rab. 29,11), was considered of very special significance for that reason. Jesus as the seventy-seventh generation is thereby shown to be of ultimate significance, the furthest the generations of world history will go, both in number and in significance.

However, we should also note that the Lukan genealogy has the name Ἰησοῦς not only in seventy-seventh place, but also in forty-ninth place, the jubilee position, where the only namesake of Jesus among his ancestors appears (Luke 3,29). Moreover, at the end of each week preceding those in which the name Ἰησοῦς is seventh, stands the name Ἰωσήφ, thus parallelling in the scheme of weeks the position of Ἰωσήφ as the father of Jesus, the seventy-sixth generation immediately before Ἰησοῦς at the end of the list. It looks as though the author who has constructed the genealogy according to this scheme has used the key positions at the ends of the sixth, seventh

---

[19] The seventy-seven names in modern printed editions of the Greek New Testament are found in most but not all MSS. For discussion of the textual questions, see Bauckham, *Jude and the Relatives of Jesus* (n. 3), chapter 7: "Additional Note on the Text of the Lukan Genealogy." Since in a list of this kind it is easier for names to drop out than for names to be added, a name which is lacking in a few MSS should not be rejected without good reason.

and tenth weeks to point forward to the end of the whole line. According to the author's perspective on world history, these positions do not themselves mark turning-points in history, but are significant only as pointing forward to the climax of all history in Jesus the son of Joseph.

Like the scheme in the Apocalypse of Weeks, the Lukan genealogy has Abraham at the end of the third week. But unlike the Apocalypse of Weeks, which places the building of the Temple at the end of the fifth week, the Lukan genealogy ends the fifth week with David. As we have seen the biblical genealogy, if followed, would place Solomon in this position. The Lukan genealogy secures this place for David because, as we have already noticed, it adds a generation to the biblical line of David's descent from Judah: where the Bible has only Ram, it has Ἀρνί and Ἀδμίν. However this extra generation may have originated[20], it serves an important purpose in the genealogical scheme. Unlike the Apocalypse of Weeks, which is not interested in David or the monarchy, the Lukan genealogy is intended to show Jesus' Davidic descent. It therefore highlights David by means of his sabbatical position at the end of a week. The appearance of Σαλαθιηλ (Shealtiel) at the end of the eighth week might also be significant. With this name the line of non-royal descent from David via Nathan rejoins the biblically attested succession to the throne of David (1 Chron 3,17).

If the Lukan genealogy thus resembles the Apocalypse of Weeks in its construction, it differs in having eleven weeks of world history rather than the ten of the Apocalypse. This difference not only gives Jesus the very significant seventh-seventy place. It also shows that the Lukan genealogy is constructed with reference to another part of the Enoch literature: 1 Enoch 10,12 (= 4QEn[b] 1,4,10). The archangel Michael is there instructed to bind the Watchers "for seventy generations under the hills of the earth until the [great] day of their judgment"[21]. From verse 14 it is clear that this day of judgment of the Watchers is *the* day of judgment at the end of world history. The binding of the fallen angels occurred during the lifetime of Enoch's son Methuselah. Thus according to 1 Enoch 10,12 the whole of world history from Adam to the last judgment comprises seventy-seven generations, seven up to and including Enoch, following by a further seventy. For anyone familiar with 1 Enoch 10,12 the Lukan genealogy would clearly designate Jesus the last generation of world history before the end.

These features of the Lukan genealogy, which cannot be coincidental, show it to be constructed according to an apocalyptic world-historical

---

[20] See Jeremias, *Jerusalem* (n. 4), p. 293, for a suggestion that it originated by scribal error.

[21] Translation of the Ethiopic from M. Knibb, *The Ethiopic Book of Enoch*, vol. 2, Oxford, Clarendon Press, 1978, p. 789, but with 'great' supplied from the Aramaic in 4QEn[b] 1,4,10.

scheme inspired by the Enoch literature. I have discussed the nature and origin of the genealogy in more detail elsewhere[22]. For the present purpose, we can now draw three conclusions: (1) The generations from Adam to Abraham are integral to the structure of the whole genealogy and cannot be considered without reference to the rest. (2) The structure of the genealogy is only clear when it is seen as a descending genealogy, beginning with Adam and ending with Jesus. It is probable therefore that Luke found it in this form in a source, reversed it to form an ascending genealogy, in order to accommodate it to his narrative, and at the same time added the reference to God at the end, for his own theological purpose. But he made no other changes. (3) It cannot be completely excluded that the author of the genealogy referred to the LXX. But since the genealogy shows striking independence of the LXX in the generations between Abraham and David, it is most likely not dependent on the LXX for the generations between Adam and Abraham. An author as familiar with the Enoch literature as this author was would probably have known of Kainam the son of Arpachshad from Jubilees, and may well have known other genealogical traditions in related literature not known to us. He may even have known a Hebrew text of Genesis in which Kainam the son of Arpachshad appeared.

---

[22] Bauckham, *Jude and the Relatives of Jesus* (n. 3), chapter 7.

11. The List of the Tribes of Israel in Revelation 7*

In a recent article in this journal,[1] Christopher R. Smith has offered an ingenious explanation of the anomalous features of the list of the twelve tribes of Israel in Rev. 7.5–8. The list, he claims, is 'a systematic reworking of a paradigmatic list of the sons of Israel grouped by maternal descent, whose otherwise perplexing features are clearly explained by the author's design of portraying the church as the New Israel'.[2] He suggests that an original list (see Fig. 1) was transformed by the author of Revelation into the list he gives by making three changes, for the following reasons:

(1) Judah is moved from fourth place to first, because Christ, the head of the church, was of that tribe;

(2) Dan is omitted and Manasseh substituted, in order to assimilate the list to that of the twelve apostles, in which Judas was removed and Matthias substituted. The choice of Dan as the tribe to be omitted is said to be 'because of that tribe's longstanding association with idolatry, and because of the Jewish tradition that the antichrist would come from the tribe of Dan'.[3]

(3) The sons of the handmaids are moved up, as a group of four, from the end of the list to follow Reuben near the top. This is partly because they were tribes living in 'Galilee of the Gentiles', the focus of Christ's early ministry, but more especially so that the nullification of privilege based on difference of birth might represent the inclusion of Gentiles in the church. Reuben retains his place as first-born, however, to represent the inclusion of believing Israelites in the church.

The first of these three arguments is plausible, but the others are unconvincing for the follow reasons;

(1) The tradition that Antichrist would come from the tribe of Dan is first found in Irenaeus, *Adv. Haer.* 5.30.2 and Hippolytus, *De Antichristo* 14; it is found in no Jewish text and is very unlikely to be pre-Christian. The

---

* First publication: *Journal for the Study of the New Testament* 42 (1991) 99–115.
[1] C.R. Smith, 'The Portrayal of the Church as the New Israel in the Names and Order of the Tribes in Revelation 7.5–8', *JSNT* 39 (1990), pp. 111–18.
[2] *Ibid.*, pp. 115–16.
[3] *Ibid.*, p. 115.

Figure 1

	Original list	Judah moved up; Manasseh for Dan	Handmaids' sons moved up
(Leah)	Reuben	Judah	Judah
	Simeon	Reuben	Reuben
	Levi	Simeon	
	Judah	Levi	Gad
	Issachar	Issachar	Asher
	Zebulun	Zebulun	Naphtali
			Manasseh
(Rachel)	Joseph	Joseph	
	Benjamin	Benjamin	Simeon
			Levi
(Zilpah)	Gad	Gad	Issachar
	Asher	Asher	Zebulun
		– Dan	
(Bilhah)	Dan	Naphtali	Joseph
	Naphtali	+ Manasseh	Benjamin

'Antichrist' figures of Jewish apocalyptic are always Gentiles.[4] It is true that *Testament of Dan* 5.4–6 predicts the apostasy of Dan, but 5.9–13 envisages the tribe's restoration and participation in the eschatological salvation of Israel. In any case, even if there had been such a tradition, it is incomprehensible that the author of Revelation, whose Antichrist is the imperial power of Rome, should have made use of it.

(2) The replacement of Dan by Manasseh is hardly a convincing parallel to the replacement of Judas by Matthias. Manasseh frequently appears in lists of the tribes of Israel, but always along with Ephraim in place of Joseph. What needs explaining is not the appearance of Manasseh in this list, but the appearance of Manasseh along with Joseph, rather than Ephraim.

(3) The tribes whose territory was included in Galilee in New Testament times were Naphtali, Zebulun and Issachar, two of which are actually moved down the list by the alleged rearrangement. The tribes actually associated with 'Galilee of the Gentiles' in Isa. 9.1, cited in Mt. 4.15, are Naphtali and Zebulun. Gad, Asher, and Manasseh were not Galilaean tribes.

(4) The idea that the rearrangement of the list nullifies the difference of birth depends on assuming that the Leah and Rachel tribes were normally

---

[4] W. Bousset (*The Antichrist Legend* [London: Hutchinson, 1896], pp. 171–74] argues for the pre-Christian origin of the tradition, but can adduce only Christian sources. Besides the influence of Gen. 49.17, Jer. 8.16, and the omission of Dan from Rev. 7.5–8, the Christian tradition that Antichrist will be a Danite may have originated as an ant-Jewish interpretation of the common expectation of an Antichrist from the East, beyond the Euphrates, which was where the ten tribes were believed to be.

given priority over the Bilhah and Zilpah tribes. In fact, few Old Testament lists arrange the tribes in this way (only Gen. 35.23–26; Exod. 1.2–4; Num. 1.5–15), while, as we shall see later, in New Testament times there seem to have been two standard ways of listing the tribes, one of which gives the sons of the wives priority over the sons of the handmaids, but the other of which places the Rachel tribes at the end of the list where they belong in the order of birth. Though John's list conforms to neither of these standard patterns, it is not at all clear that it would have been recognized as reordering precedence among the tribes.

(5) It is in any case hard to see how a revision of the order of precedence among the tribes of Israel could represent the inclusion of Gentiles in the New Israel.

More generally, Smith's argument fails to consider adequately the relation between the 144,000 of the tribes of Israel (7.4–8) and the great multitude (7.9–17). He merely answers Feuillet's arguments that the two groups must be different, but fails to consider whether the juxtaposition of the two may not assist the understanding of the first. Here I must summarize an argument I have presented in detail elsewhere.[5]

Literary links and parallels suggest that the vision of the 144,000 and the innumerable multitude in ch. 7 should be seen as a parallel to the vision of the Lion and the Lamb of 5.5–14.[6] In 5.5 John hears that victory has been won by the Lion of the tribe of Judah, the Root of David. These two messianic titles, alluding to Gen. 49.9 and Isa. 11.1–5, both classic texts for Jewish messianic hopes in the first century CE,[7] evoke the image of the messiah as a new David who wins a military victory over the enemies of Israel. But after *hearing* this description of the victorious messiah, John *sees* the slaughtered Lamb (5.6), whose blood has ransomed a people from every tribe, language, people and nation (5.9). By juxtaposing these images, John gives his Jewish Christian interpretation of Jewish messianic hopes. The conquering Davidic messiah is not repudiated,[8] but his victory is shown to be by sacrifice, not military conflict, while the people he delivers are not

---

[5] R. Bauckham, 'The Book of Revelation as a Christian War Scroll', *Neotestamentica* 22 (1988), pp. 17–40.

[6] For this paragraph see also R. Bauckham, 'The *Figurae* of John of Patmos', in A. Williams (ed.), *Prophecy and Millenarianism: Essays in Honour of Marjorie Reeves* (London: Longman, 1980), pp 107–25.

[7] For allusions to both passages together, see 4QPBless; 1QSb 5.20–29; *4 Ezra* 12.31–32; and for the Shoot of David, see 4QFlor 1.11–12; 4QpIsa frag. A; *Pss. Sol.* 17.24,35–37; *1 Enoch* 49.3; *4 Ezra* 13.10; *T. Jud.* 24.4–6.

[8] For Revelation's emphasis on the fulfilment of Old Testament Davidic promises in Christ, see J. Fekkes, 'Isaiah and Prophetic Traditions in the Book of Revelation: Visionary Antecedents and their Development' (unpublished PhD thesis, University of Manchester, 1988), pp. 153–54.

only Israelites, but from all the nations. Moreover, the second image, the slaughtered Lamb, is just as scriptural as the first: there is probably an allusion to Isa. 53.7 and certainly to the Passover lamb,[9] whose blood effects the new Exodus and redeems the eschatological people of God (5.9–10, alluding to Exod. 19.6). By juxtaposing the two scriptural images of the conquering messiah and the slaughtered Lamb, John builds the notion of a messiah who conquers by sacrificial death.

In ch. 7, John *hears* the number of those sealed from the tribes of Israel, but he *sees* the innumerable multitude from all nations. Just as he has deliberately juxtaposed the contrasting images of the messiah in 5.5–6, so he has deliberately juxtaposed contrasting images of the messiah's followers in 7.4–9. The contrast is obvious in two respects: the 144,000 are counted, whereas the great multitude cannot be counted; the 144,000 are from the twelve tribes of Israel, whereas the great multitude are from all nations, tribes, peoples and languages.[10] The contrasting images are parallel to those of 5.5–6: the 144,000 are the Israelite army of the Lion of Judah, while the international multitude are the followers of the slaughtered Lamb. The purpose of the contrast is the same as in 5.5–6: to give a Christian interpretation of an element of Jewish messianic expectation. Moreover, just as in 5.6 the image which conveys John's Jewish Christian interpretation of Jewish hopes is a scriptural one, so in 7.9 the image of the innumerable multitude from all nations is a scriptural allusion. It echoes God's promise to the patriarchs that their descendants would be innumerable (Gen. 13.16; 15.5; 32.12; Hos. 1.10; *Jub.* 13.20; 14.4–5; Heb. 11.12; cf. Gen. 22.17; 26.4; 28.14; *Jub.* 18.15; 25.16; 27.13; *Lad. Jac.* 1.10). By contrast with some contemporary Jewish expectations that this promise would be fulfilled by the growth of the exiled ten tribes to vast numbers in the lands of their exile,[11] John has probably understood it in terms of the other form of the promise to the patriarchs: that their descendants would be a multitude of nations (Gen. 17.4–6; 35.11; 48.19; cf. Rom. 4.16–18; Justin, *Dial.* 119–120). Unlike the twelve tribes which can be numbered, the great multitude is innumerable because it is international, drawn not only from Israel but from all the nations.

Less obvious than the contrast between the fixed number of Israelites and the innumerable multitude from all nations is the contrast between the 144,000 as an *army* called to military service in the messianic war, and the

---

[9] Fekkes ('Isaiah', pp. 154–59) rejects Isa. 53.7 in favour of the paschal lamb as John's Old Testament source here.

[10] 5.9 and 7.9 are the first two occurrences in Revelation of this fourfold expression, which John uses five more times, always varying the order or terms: 10.11; 11.9; 13.7; 14.6; 17.15.

[11] Evidence in Bauckham, 'Revelation as a Christian War Scroll', p. 25.

innumerable multitude as victors who have won their victory by following the Lamb in his sacrificial death. That the multitude are the martyrs in
heaven, who have conquered by their suffering witness as a participation in
the Lamb's own sacrificial death, becomes clear only in 7.14, which must
be read in connection with later passages such as 12.11 and 15.2.[12] That the
144,000 are an Israelite army is implicit in the fact that 7.4–8 is a *census* of
the tribes of Israel. In the Old Testament a census was always a reckoning
of the *military* strength of the nation, in which only males of military age
were counted.[13] Accordingly, it later becomes apparent from Rev. 14.4 that
the 144,000 are adult male Israelites: those eligible for military service.[14]
The only divinely commanded censuses in the Old Testament were those
in the wilderness (Num. 1; 26). It looks as though the repeated formula of
Rev. 7.5–8 (ἐκ φυλῆς…) is modelled on that of Numbers (1.21, 23; etc.: ἐκ
τῆς φυλῆς…). A possible link with the census of Numbers 1 is of particular
interest, since the account of the organization of the military camp of Israel
in the wilderness which this census introduces considerably influenced
the Qumran War Rule (1QM). Israel, organized in the wilderness for the
conquest of the promised land, was readily treated as a model for the eschatological Israel who would come from the wilderness (1QM 1.2–3) to
reconquer the promised land in the messianic war.[15]

Of course, the number 144,000 has symbolic appropriateness, which in
Revelation reappears in the dimensions of the New Jerusalem (21.16–17).
But it would be natural to think of an army of all Israel, assembled for the
messianic war, as composed of twelve equal tribal contingents. The small
force which Moses sent against Midian was 12,000 strong, composed of
1,000 from each of the tribes (Num. 31.4–6; cf. Philo, *Mos.* 1.306). Moreover, not only was the return of the ten tribes and the reunion of all Israel
a strong traditional element in the eschatological hope,[16] so that the list of
equal numbers from the twelve tribes in Rev. 7.4–8 would readily suggest to
any Jewish Christian reader the eschatological restoration of the people of

---

[12] For this interpretation, see Bauckham, 'Revelation as a Christian War Scroll',
pp. 27–28.
[13] Num. 1.3, 18, 20, etc.; 26.2, 4; 1 Chron. 27.23; cf. 2 Sam. 24.9; 1 Chron. 21.5.
[14] Hence also the sexual abstinence of the 144,000 (14.4) is to be explained according
to the requirement of ritual purity for soldiers in the holy war: Bauckham, 'Revelation as
a Christian War Scroll', p. 29.
[15] For the influence of Num. 1–3, 10 on 1QM, see P. R. Davies, *1QM, the War Scroll
from Qumran: Its Structure and History* (BibOr, 32; Rome: Biblical Institute Press, 1977),
pp. 28, 30–31; Y. Yadin, *The Scroll of the War of the Sons of Light against the Sons of Dark-
ness* (Oxford: Oxford University Press, 1962), pp. 39, 42–48, 54–56; J. van der Ploeg, *Le
Rouleau de la Guerre* (STDJ, 2; Leiden: Brill, 1959), pp. 27–28.
[16] Isa. 11.11–12, 15–16; 27.12–13; Jer. 31.7–9; Ezek. 37.15–23; Sir. 36.11; Tob. 13.13;
2 Bar. 78.5–7; *T. Jos.* 19.4; cf. Mt. 19.28; *m. Sanh.* 10.3; *j. Sanh.* 10.6.

God.[17] There is also evidence for the expectation that the ten tribes would return specifically to take part in the messianic war of liberation (*Sib. Or.* 2.170–76; Commodian, *Carmen apol.* 941–86).[18] The army in 1QM, modelled on Numbers 1–2, is organized according to the traditional division of Israel into twelve tribes.[19]

It follows that we should not look, as Smith does, for a Christian interpretation of the list of twelve tribes *within* 7.4–8. This image as such is a traditional Jewish image of the people of God called to military service in the messianic war. The Christian interpretation comes in 7.9–14, which shows the same people celebrating their victory in heaven, but shows them to be an innumerable multitude of martyrs from all the nations. Smith is right in thinking that John does not list the twelve tribes in order to represent Jewish Christians only, but intends to reinterpret the twelve tribes as the new international people of God. He does this, however, precisely by means of the *contrast* between 7.4–8 and 7.9.

We return to the names and order of the tribes. Smith has failed to consider whether we have evidence for the way Jewish writers of the first century CE listed the tribes. It so happens that we have such evidence: in Josephus and in Pseudo-Philo's *Liber Antiquitatum Biblicarum (LAB)*. (The five lists in Pseudo-Philo[20] are given in Fig. 2.) We may also take into account the lists in *Jubilees,* the Qumran Temple Scroll,[21] and the *Testaments of the Twelve Patriarchs.*

---

[17] Cf. A. Geyser, 'The Twelve Tribes in Revelation: Judean and Judeo-Christian Apocalypticism', *NTS* 28 (1982), pp. 388–99.

[18] For Commodian's dependence on a Jewish apocalyptic source, see Bauckham, 'Revelation as a Christian War Scroll', p. 23; M.R. James, *Apocrypha Anecdota* (TextS, 2/3; Cambridge: Cambridge University Press, 1893), pp. 90–94; M.R. James, *The Lost Apocrypha of the Old Testament* (London: SPCK, 1920), pp. 103–106; F. Schmidt, 'Une source essénienne chez Commodien', in M. Philonenko, J.-C. Picard, J.-M. Rosenstiehl and F. Schmidt, *Pseudépigraphes de l'Ancien Testament et manuscrits de la Mer Morte,* I (Cahiers de la RHPR, 41; Paris: Presses Universitaires de France, 1967); J. Daniélou, *The Origins of Latin Christianity* (London: Darton, Longman & Todd, 1977), pp. 116–19.

[19] 1QM 2.2–3.7; 3.13–14; 14.16; 5.1–2; 6.10; and cf. Yadin, *Scroll,* pp. 79–83. 1QM 1.2–3 may indicate that the first six years of the war will be fought by the three tribes of Levi, Judah and Benjamin, who will then be joined by the lost tribes for the remainder of the forty years' war.

[20] There is a sixth list in *LAB* 10.3, but it is not of the same kind: the tribes are divided into three groups of four according to their response to the situation at the Red Sea. On this passage, see my discussion in 'The *Liber Antiquitatum Biblicarum* of Pseudo-Philo and the Gospels as Midrash', in R.T. France and D. Wenham (eds.), *Studies in Midrash and Historiography* (Gospel Perspectives, 3; Sheffield: JSOT Press, 1983), pp. 44–46.

[21] As well as the list in 11QT 24, which will be discussed here, the tribes are also listed in 11QT 39–41, 44–45, in connection with the gates and rooms allotted to the tribes in the Temple. For the way in which they are arranged, see J. Maier, *The Temple Scroll* (JSOT-Sup, 34; Sheffield: JSOT Press, 1985), pp. 112–12, 114.

Figure 2

LAB 8.6	8.11–14	26.10–11	25.4	25.9–13
Reuben	Reuben	Reuben	Judah	Judah
Simeon	Simeon	Simeon	Reuben	Reuben
Levi	Levi	Levi	Simeon	
Judah	Judah	Judah	Levi	Levi
Issachar	Issachar	Issachar	Issachar	Issachar
Zebulun	Zebulun	Zebulun	Zebulun	Zebulun
Joseph	Dan	Dan		Dan
Benjamin	Naphtali	Naphtali		Naphtali
Dan	Gad	Gad	Gad	Gad
Naphtali	[Asher]	Asher	Asher	Asher
Gad	Joseph	Joseph	Manasseh	Manasseh
Asher	Benjamin	Benjamin	Ephraim	Ephraim
			Benjamin	Benjamin

The first of Pseudo-Philo's lists, in *LAB* 8.6, lists all the Leah and the Rachel tribes before the Bilhah and Zilpah tribes. This is a matriological list (i. e. arranged according to the mothers of the patriarchs), which gives precedence to the sons of the two wives of Jacob over the sons of the two handmaids. The senior wife Leah has precedence over Rachel, but Rachel's maid Bilhah precedes Leah's maid Zilpah, presumably because Bilhah bore her children before Zilpah bore hers (Gen. 30.1–13). (Alternatively the arrangement could be understood as chiastic: Leah–Rachel–Rachel's maid–Leah's maid.) In *LAB* 8.6 the list is simply copied from Gen. 35.23–26, the passage which Pseudo-Philo is following at this point in his work. For the same reason this list is found also in *Jub.* 33.22. More significant is the fact that Josephus uses this list in *Ant.* 2.177–83, where the biblical passage he is following, Gen. 46.8–27, has a different order (sons of Leah, sons of Zilpah, sons of Rachel, sons of Bilhah: see Fig. 3). This matriological order makes a lot of sense in Genesis: the sons of Leah's maid follow Leah's own because they are in a sense hers, and the sons of Rachel's maid similarly follow Rachel's. But Josephus rearranges it in order to give both wives precedence over the handmaids. That this was the order he regarded as standard is confirmed by *Ant.* 1.344, where he indicates the same order (though without naming the tribes themselves). It is worth noticing, however, that when he mentions the order in which the names of the tribes appeared on the stones of the high priest's breastplate, he says that the order was that of birth (*Ant.* 3.169). Since this is not the order he himself prefers, he must be reporting what was well known.

Figure 3

Gen. 29–30 (order of birth)	Gen. 46	11QT 24
Reuben	Reuben	Levi
Simeon	Simeon	Judah
Levi	Levi	
Judah	Judah	Benjamin
	Issachar	Joseph
Dan	Zebulun	
Naphtali		Reuben
	Gad	Simeon
Gad	Asher	
Asher		Issachar
	Joseph	Zebulun
Issachar	Benjamin	
Zebulun		Gad
	Dan	Asher
Joseph	Naphtali	
Benjamin		Dan
		Naphtali

At this point we may mention the unique list in 11QT 24.10–16 (see Fig. 3), which gives the order in which burnt offerings for the twelve tribes are to be offered on the six days of the Wood Festival (hence the grouping of the tribes in pairs). This list is best understood as a modification of a matriological list, which was like that preferred by Josephus but more logically places the Bilhah tribes last, after the Zilpah tribes. The author has moved to the top of the list the three tribes which composed the southern kingdom and made up the majority of Jews in his day, and his own levitical interests dictate the precedence: Levi, Judah, Benjamin. But this precedence also assures that a matriological arrangement still obtains, in that the first pair of tribes are Leah tribes. To ensure that the next pair are also of the same mother, Joseph has had to be moved up the list also along with Benjamin. Then follow the remaining four Leah tribes, the Bilhah tribes, and the Zilpah tribes. The list is of interest in illustrating how strong the matriological principle of ordering was, even when another principle was also employed.

The second of Pseudo-Philo's lists occurs in 8.11–14 and the same list reappears in 26.10–11. The genealogical section 8.11–14, which lists all the children and grandchildren of Jacob, is closely dependent on Gen. 46.8–27. *Jub.* 44.11–34, also closely dependent on Gen. 46.8–27, follows its order, but, as we have just seen, Josephus finds this order unsatisfactory and rearranges it. Pseudo-Philo also rearranges the list, but differently from Josephus. Pseudo-Philo has gone to some trouble to rearrange the genealogical information so that the patriarchs appear in this order: sons of Leah, sons of

Zilpah, sons of Bilhah, sons of Rachel.[22] He must have regarded this order as a normative one and attached some importance to it, despite the fact that it nowhere appears in the Old Testament. When Pseudo-Philo uses it again in 26.10–11, it is in connection with the twelve precious stones from paradise which are given to Kenaz so that he can place them on the ephod alongside the twelve precious stones Moses placed on the breastplate of the high priest (cf. 26.4, 12). They are so described as to resemble closely the stones on the breastplate.[23] Like the stones on the breastplate (Exod. 28.21; 39.14), these twelve stones have the names of the twelve tribes of Israel engraved on them. They are carefully listed in order ('first…second…', etc.).

The remaining lists in *LAB* (25.4; 25.9–13) are, as we shall see, modifications of this list in 8.6 and 26.10–11. Nor is this list a peculiarity of Pseudo-Philo: it also occurs in *Jub.* 34.30, and is the order in which the testaments of the patriarchs appear in the *Testaments of the Twelve Patriarchs*. Moreover, it is also found, as the order in which the names of the tribes appeared on the stones of the high priest's breastplate, in two of the Targums (*Fragm. Tg.* Exod. 28.17–20; *Tg. Neof.* Exod. 28.17–20; 39.10–13) and in *Midrash Rabbah* (*Exod. R.* 38.8–9; *Num. R.* 2.7).[24] This must be evidence of a strong tradition of the normative status of this particular order of the tribes.

The order, as we have noticed, is not found in any Old Testament list of the tribes. It is in fact a modification of the order of birth of the patriarchs (as given in Gen. 29.31–30.24; 35.16–18: see Fig. 3), obtained by moving Issachar and Zebulun, the fifth and sixth sons of Leah, who were born after the sons of the handmaids, up the list to follow the first four sons of Leah. In this way the order of birth is modified so as to keep the sons of each of the four mothers together. We see once again the strength of the matriological principle of ordering.

However, this modification of the order of birth is treated in the *Testaments of the Twelve Patriarchs* actually *as the order of birth* of the patriarchs. Issachar calls himself Jacob's fifth son (*T. Iss.* 1.2), and Gad calls himself Jacob's ninth son (*T. Gad* 1.2). We recall also Josephus's statement that the tribs appeared on the breastplate of the high priest in the order of birth (*Ant.* 3.169). *Targum Pseudo-Jonathan* (to Exod. 28.17–20; 39.10–13) lists the tribes on the breastplate in the order of birth as given in Genesis 29–30, but the other texts which give the order on the breastplate agree with

---

[22] In the text as it stands, the name Asher is missing, but comparison with Gen. 46.16–17 shows that a section of text has been lost in *LAB* 8.13.

[23] The list is probably based on a list of the stones on the breastplate: cf. W. R. Reader, 'The Twelve Jewels of Revelation 21:19–20: Tradition History and Modern Interpretations', *JBL* 100 (1981), p. 446.

[24] In *Num. R.* 2.7, the positions of Gad and Naphtali are reversed. Reader ('Twelve Jewels', pp. 440–44) gives the lists in the Targums and *Exodus Rabbah*, but not that in *Numbers Rabbah*.

Pseudo-Philo's list in *LAB* 26.10–11. It looks very much as though the universally accepted tradition was that the tribes were named on the breastplate in the order of the birth of the patriarchs, and that *Targum Pseudo-Jonathan* merely differs from other traditions as to what the order of birth was.

Thus it would seem as though the reason why the list in *LAB* 8.11–14 and 26.10–11 was widely given normative status, and regarded as the order in which the tribes appeared on the stones of the breastplate, is that it was treated as the order of birth. This need not have been in disregard of Genesis. It could have been based on an interpretation of Genesis which, because Gen. 30.9 says that Leah had stopped bearing children, concluded that the story of Leah's bearing of Issachar, Zebulun and Dinah in 30.14–21 must actually have happened before 30.9.

Thus there seem, in the first century CE, to have been two standard ways of listing the tribes. Both were matriological, grouping all the sons of each mother together. One, preferred by Josephus, gave precedence to the sons of the wives over the sons of the handmaids. The other, which seems to have been more popular, was a matriological modification of the order of birth, and seems to have been treated as the order of birth. On this latter list Pseudo-Philo also has two variations: in 25.4 and 25.9–13. Both these lists occur in the story of Kenaz's discovery of the sinners among the tribes, and so the two lists should correspond. Both include both Manasseh and Ephraim, rather than Joseph, as is natural in a narrative involving the actual tribes of the Old Testament, but the first list omits Dan and Naphtali, whereas the second list omits Simeon. As a result the first list has only eleven tribes, the second twelve. If both lists were originally of twelve tribes, omitting one name to achieve the number twelve, then they were inconsistent. If both lists were originally the same, they must have been of thirteen tribes. It is impossible to be sure of the original text, but at least the problem illustrates the difficulty encountered by any one listing the tribes, not as names of the patriarchs but as actual tribes: Israel was supposed to have had twelve tribes, but in fact had thirteen.

However, both these lists agree on another variation from what we have called the normative order: Judah appears first. The reason is clear: the tribes are led by Kenaz, whose own tribe was Judah (25.9). Kenaz, whom Pseudo-Philo glorifies as the first and greatest of the judges, is depicted by him as a kind of forerunner of David (cf. 21.4–5; 49.1) and probably as a prototype of the future messianic deliverer of Israel from the Gentiles.[25] Thus *LAB* 25.4 and 25.9–13 are clear disproof of Smith's claim that in a first-century vision of the literal twelve tribes of Israel and their spiritual future, one must

---

[25] I hope to argue this in detail elsewhere.

expect Levi rather than Judah to head the list.[26] The place of Judah in the list in Rev. 7.4–8 is entirely explicable in terms of Jewish Davidic messianism, with which, of course, John's own belief that Jesus fulfilled the hope of a messiah of David coincided.

Comparing the lists I have discussed with the list of Revelation 7, the most anomalous feature of the latter is the position of Manasseh, since this is such a complete and apparently pointless breach of the matriological principle. If we could amend the text to read Dan instead of Manasseh, the tribes would at least be grouped in matriological pairs, as they are in 11QT 24. We could then understand the list as an attempt to list the tribes in an intelligible order which failed owing to faulty memory[27] (whereas no Jew who knew the Scriptures as well as John did would, simply from faulty memory, associate Manasseh with Naphtali, rather than with Joseph and Benjamin). Amending the text in this way would also eliminate the other great anomaly in the list: the presence of Manasseh along with Joseph (rather than Ephraim). It is therefore tempting to amend the text, as others have suggested. But if the present text is accepted, the following is an attempt to explain it.

In Fig. 4 I suggest how the list in Revelation 7 could have resulted from the order which was widely accepted as standard at the time of writing, the order found in *LAB* 8.11–14; 26.10–11; and the *Testaments of the Twelve Patriarchs*. Column 1 gives this normative order. Column 2 is the result of the following changes: (a) The order of the Bilhah and Zilpah tribes is reversed. this could easily happen in reproducing the list from memory.[28] (b) Judah is moved to the head of the list, as in *LAB* 25.4 and 25.9–13. (c) Manasseh and Ephraim appear as two tribes, again as in *LAB* 25.4 and 25.9–13. (d) Dan is omitted in order to keep the number to twelve. Column 3 is the list in Rev. 7.5–8. It is the result of two changes: (a) Ephraim is renamed Joseph. (b) Two blocks of four tribes (Levi–Zebulun; Gad–Manasseh) have changed places.

This account of the origin of the order in Revelation 7 can explain the very odd place of Manasseh without supposing it to be a textual error. If it is not a textual error, then the order of the list must result from copying a written list like that in column 2 and either deliberately or carelessly moving a block of four tribes to a different position. Such a change of position could be made if a list which was deliberately ordered were copied by a writer who did not really care in what order he listed the tribes.

But hardest of all to explain is the inclusion of *Joseph,* rather than Ephraim, along with Manasseh. This is unparalleled in any extant list of the

---

[26] Smith, 'Portrayal of the Church', p. 114.
[27] Note that the last four names correctly follow the Genesis order of birth.
[28] Cf. the variation in *Num. R.* 2.7, noted above.

Figure 4

Normative order		Rev 7
Reuben	Judah	Judah
Simeon	Reuben	Reuben
Levi	Simeon	
Judah	Levi	*Gad*
Issachar	Issachar	*Asher*
Zebulun	Zebulun	*Naphtali*
		Manasseh
Dan	Gad	
Naphtali	*Asher*	Simeon
		Levi
Gad	*Naphtali*	Issachar
Asher		Zebulun
	Manasseh	
Joseph	Ephraim	Joseph
Benjamin	Benjamin	Benjamin

tribes. However, there is one *apparent* parallel which *might* explain it.[29] In the account of the census in Numbers 1, on which I have already suggested Rev. 7.4–8 may be partly modelled, the repeated formula introducing the number of each tribe is varied once. Whereas for every other tribe, it begins: 'for the sons of Reuben...', 'for the sons of Simeon...', etc. in the case of Ephraim it begins: 'for the sons of Joseph, for the sons of Ephraim...' (Num. 1.32).[30] If this is why John or his source called the tribe of Ephraim Joseph, he did not, however, follow the order of the tribes in Numbers 1. That order is a unique one, related to the places of the tribes in the camp (Num. 2). It may have suggested to John or his source that the order of tribes in a military census should not be the normative order of the tribes, so that he rearranged the normative order to form an anomalous order of his own. A more plausible explanation may yet be discovered![31]

---

[29] In Bauckham, 'Revelation as a Christian War Scroll', p. 24, I drew attention instead to Ezek. 37.16, 19, where the name Joseph has been glossed with references to Ephraim in such a way that a reader might think 'Joseph' was being used as a name for the tribe of Ephraim. Since this is an account of the reunion of the twelve tribes in the messianic kingdom, 'Joseph' might therefore seem a suitable name for Ephraim in a list of the tribes of the eschatological, reunited Israel.

[30] 'For the sons of Joseph' should really be understood as a rubric which covers both the reference to the sons of Ephraim which immediately follows and the reference to the sons of Manasseh in v. 34.

[31] After completing this article, I came across another recent attempt to explain the order of the tribes in Rev. 7: R.E. Winkle, 'Another Look at the List of Tribes in Revelation', *AUSS* 27 (1989). pp. 53–67. The key point in Winkle's argument is a novel explanation of the omission of Dan: that the tribe was associated with Judas Iscariot. However,

Abstract

The anomalous features of the list of the tribes of Israel in Rev. 7.5–8 are not satisfactorily explained by the arguments of C.R. Smith (*JSNT* 39 [1990], pp. 111–18). He misunderstands the relationship between the 144,000 (7.5–8) and the great multitude (7.9–14): the former is a traditional Jewish image which is given a Christian interpretation only in 7.9–14. Smith also neglects the many lists of the twelve tribes to be found in Jewish literature of the New Testament period. From these it appears that a list in the order of the birth of the patriarchs, but modified by the matriological principle, was widely regarded as normative. The list in Rev. 7 can be understood as derived, by changes partly intentional and partly unintentional, from this normative list.

---

this association is known only from Christian sources several centuries later than the New Testament.

12. The Parting of the Ways: What Happened and Why*

The problem of the 'parting of the ways' between Judaism and Christianity (to use the increasingly popular term for a currently popular subject) is in part a problem of finding an appropriate conceptual model with which to interrogate the evidence. Recent discussion of the issue seems to indicate that one conceptual model, which used to be dominant, has now been widely, though not entirely, discredited, while another is becoming popular, if not dominant.

The older model thought of Judaism as essentially a constant and Christianity as a new development which grew out of Judaism to become a new religion. Curiously this view suited the old confessional approaches of both Jewish and Christian scholarship. It could legitimate rabbinic Judaism as the legitimate heir of the religion of the Hebrew Bible, or it could legitimate Christianity as the fulfilment and successor of the religion of Israel, leaving the Judaism of the Christian era as a kind of unfulfilled, fossilized anachronism. But this model can accommodate a good deal of modern insight into variety and development within Judaism. Second Temple Judaism may be conveived as highly diverse, and rabbinic Judaism may be seen as the result of a considerable development in the post-70 period, but nevertheless all these forms of Judaism are Judaism, whereas Christianity is something else. There is one religion which continued (Judaism) and another which broke away (Christianity).

This model is silently endorsed by nearly all the modern textbooks on Second Temple Judaism, which do not consider even early Palestinian Jewish Christianity part of their subject, studiously ignoring Jewish Christianity as though there were no reason even to raise the question whether Jewish Christianity was also a form of Judaism.[1] The first treatment of Second Temple Judaism to pass over Jewish Christianity in complete silence was Josephus' *Antiquities,* the latest is E. P. Sanders' *Judaism: Practice and Belief.*[2]

---

* First publication: *Studia Theologica* 47 (1993) 135–151.
[1] An exception is H. Jagersma, *A History of Israel from Alexander the Great to Bar Kochba,* tr. J. Bowden (London: SCM Press, 1985).
[2] E. P. Sanders, *Judaism: Practice and Belief 63 BCE – 66 CE* (London: SCM Press/ Philadelphia: Trinity Press International, 1992).

For the new, increasingly popular model a particularly outspoken advocate is the Italian scholar Gabriele Boccaccini, in his recent book *Middle Judaism*.[3] As well as proposing a new name, 'Middle Judaism,' for what was once called Late Judaism and has more recently been called Early Judaism, Boccaccini's book is notable for its attempt to treat early Christianity consistently as one form of Judaism among others – or, more precisely and to use his own terminology, as one Judaism among others. Middle Judaism, according to Boccaccini, is the genus, while the various Judaisms of the period (Pharisaism, Essenism, Christianity and so on) are species.[4]

According to Boccaccini, the first century C.E. was a highly pluralistic phase of the history of Judaism, in which the most diverse Judaisms coexisted. By the end of the century, however, this diversity was largely reduced to the two Judaisms which from now on would be dominant, Christianity and rabbinic Judaism: 'After having tried long and hard to convince one another of their own conviction that they represented the true Israel, the Christian and Pharisaic roads grew further apart, finally reaching a reciprocal estrangement. A pluralistic Judaism had generated two much less pluralistic and tolerant but more homogeneous Judaisms.'[5] Boccaccini's insistence that Christianity remains a Judaism and should be called such (even down to the present day) in the classification of religions is unusual, but his basic model is currently quite influential: that from the diversity of pre-70 Judaism two forms of Judaism survived, defining themselves in opposition to each other, and becoming two religions: Christianity and rabbinic Judaism. This model has the merit of seeing the distinction between Christianity and rabbinic Judaism as resulting as much from the development of rabbinic Judaism as from the development of Christianity. It is probably preferable to the first model, but it is also too simple, as we shall now see.

As far as the post-70 developments go, this model tends to attribute too much power and influence too quickly to rabbinic Judaism as compared with non-rabbinic forms of non-Christian Judaism. We do not know how quickly rabbinic Judaism became the overwhelmingly dominant form of non-Christian Judaism. The rabbis at Yavneh set out to delegitimize all other kinds of Judaism, including Jewish Christianity (this was the purpose of the Birkat ha-Minim). They probably did not succeed fully in *Palestine* until the third century, in the Diaspora much more slowly and not fully

---

[3] G. Boccaccini, *Middle Judaism: Jewish Thought 300 B. C. E. to 200 C. E.* (Minneapolis: Fortress Press, 1991).

[4] Boccaccini, *Middle Judaism*, 18–21. He lists the various Judaisms as 'Pharisees, Sadducees, Zealots, followers of Jesus, apocalyptics, Essenes, Judeo-Hellenists, and so forth' (p. 214).

[5] Boccaccini, *Middle Judaism*, 215.

until the early middle ages.[6] The opposition of the rabbis to Jewish Christianity was important for the fate of Jewish Christianity in Palestine, but it is unlikely to have been the major factor in the estrangement of Jews and Christians in the Diaspora. We have to envisage a different process whereby most Diaspora synagogues, largely independently of the rabbis at Yavneh, came to regard Jewish Christianity as not a legitimate form of Judaism. If we are not to exaggerate the influence of rabbinic Judaism, we have to say that by the end of the first century not just rabbinic Jews but most non-Christian Jews placed Jewish Christians outside the community of Israel.

As far as pre-70 Judaism goes, we need to look more closely at the nature of diversity in Judaism and at Christianity's place within that diversity. The currently fashionable talk emphasizes the diversity by talking of Judaisms in the plural.[7] I think this usage is misleading, for several reasons: (a) It encourages one to think of the varieties of Second Temple Judaism as rather like Christian denominations. Just as (at least until recently) every Christian was either a Baptist or a Lutheran or a Roman Catholic or a Syrian Jacobite or something of the kind, so every Jew belonged to one of the so-called Judaisms. But this was not in fact the case at all. The groups to which we can give names (the four parties defined by Josephus, Jewish Christianity, some other much more obscure pietist groups) were a small minority of Jews. These groups advanced a specific interpretation of Judaism, self-consciously distinct from other interpretations. But the vast majority of Jews, both in Palestine and in the Diaspora, did not adhere to such a group and did not think of themselves as following any particular interpretation of Judaism. They were just Jews.

J. D. G. Dunn, in his *The Partings of the Ways,* comes close to recognizing this problem but evades it: 'Second Temple Judaism to a large extent, latterly at least, consisted of a range of different interest groups.' He lists the four parties from Josephus, postulates others, and adds: 'Not to mention the mass of the people, the people(s) of the land *(am[me] ha'arets)*..., and the large proportion of Jews who lived outside the land of Israel, that is, the diaspora.'[8] But these two categories of Jews were not 'interest groups' in the way that Pharisees and Essenes were. The mass of the people who did not belong to a party cannot be regarded as another party alongside the others.

---

[6] See P. S. Alexander, "'The Parting of the Ways' from the Perspective of Rabbinic Judaism," in J. D. G. Dunn ed., *Jews and Christians: The Parting of the Ways A. D. 70 to 135* (WUNT 66; Tübingen: Mohr [Siebeck], 1993) 20–21.

[7] Besides Boccaccini, see also J. Neusner, W. S. Green and E. Frerichs ed., *Judaisms and Their Messiahs at the Turn of the Christian Era* (Cambridge: Cambridge University Press, 1987), especially Neusner on pp. ix–xii.

[8] J. D. G. Dunn, *The Partings of the Ways: Between Judaism and Christianity and their Significance for the Character of Christianity* (London: SCM Press/Philadelphia: Trinity Press International, 1991) 18.

(b) The talk of many Judaisms (like the corresponding talk of many Christianities in the New Testament) moves too easily from the different interpretations of Judaism in the literature to postulating distinct groups of Jews, each holding one of these interpretations. The logic of this approach is to divide Judaism into as many different Judaisms as there are extant texts from the period, since virtually every text has its own emphasis or interests which distinguish it from other texts. But numerous parallels from religious history show that somewhat differing interpretations of a religion can easily coexist within a single, even a strongly unified community, and can even be preached from the same pulpit to the same congregation without the congregation consciously perceiving the differences. The fact that much of the extant literature of Second Temple Judaism cannot easily be assigned to a specific group should not lead us to invent such groups, but rather to recognize that such literature, whoever wrote it, belonged like the Bible to common Judaism. Pseudo-Philo's *Biblical Antiquities,* for example, does, of course, have its own theological perspectives and emphases, but there is no reason why Pharisees, Essenes, Zealots, Christians and mere Jews should not have read it with interest and profit, without identifying it as belonging to a Judaism not their own.

(c) Very importantly for our purposes, the talk of many Judaisms obscures the distinction between variety and separation or schism. The distinction between Pharisees and Sadducees is not of the same order as the distinction between Jews and Samaritans. If we are to speak of more than one Judaism, it may be better to reserve that terminology, before the rise of Christianity, for the two Judaisms that resulted from the Samaritan schism. This is a point to which we shall return. It does, however, suggest that all those Jews who regarded Samaritans as not Jews at all but did not, even at their most polemical, say the same of each other, recognized a common Judaism which they shared but which the Samaritans did not. It may also help us to understand how they could come to think the same of Christians.

(d) The final point may be another way of putting the same point. It is that the model of many Judaisms, while it makes it easy to locate Christianity as one more Judaism among the other pre-70 Judaisms, also makes it impossible to trace any roots of the parting of the ways before 70, in case there may be such roots. Dunn, for one, does want to trace such roots, and is therefore not content with the model of many Judaisms, though he uses it, but goes on to define 'a common and unifying core for Second Temple Judaism, a fourhold foundation on which all these more diverse forms of Judaism built, a common heritage which they all interpreted in their own ways.'[9] The thesis of his book is that Christians also inherited the same

---

[9] Dunn, *The Partings of the Ways,* 18.

common heritage (what Dunn calls 'the four pillars of Judaism') in their own way, but did so in such a distinctive way that other Jews saw it not as interpretation but as denial. The four pillars were thus each an occasion for various 'partings of the ways', before and after 70, of which the final parting was the cumulative result.

Dunn's 'four pillars of Second Temple Judaism' are monotheism, election, torah and temple. This is an accurate and useful classification of what virtually all Jews had in common. But unfortunately, because it is still an account of what various Judaisms had in common, it still sounds like an account of what, say, Eastern Orthodox, Roman Catholics, Calvinists and Pentecostalists have in common. In that case the parting of the ways – or Dunn's partings of the ways – lacks reality. We might imagine a new and very distinctive form of Christianity arriving on the scene of denominational Christianity – a form so distinctive most Christians come to doubt its right to be called Christianity. Mormonism might be an example. But the analogy rapidly breaks down. Nothing resembling the parting of the ways described by Dunn occurs.

It is much better to change the model, as E. P. Sanders does in his *Judaism: Practice and Belief*. What Dunn regards as the common denominator of all the Judaisms, Sanders regards as 'common Judaism', which for most Jews (those who did not belong to the parties) simply was Judaism. Because he sees it as focused on the temple, he says it is 'what the priests and the people agreed on.'[10] However, the merit of Sanders' account of common Judaism is that this notion actually means more than what, as it happens, Jews agreed about. Sanders shows how the temple and shared religious practices gave Jews a real sense of commonality with all other Jews.[11] At one of the great pilgrim festivals at the temple, attended by Jews from all parts of the world (even if not from Qumran), what they concretely and emotively shared was not simply what different forms of Judaism had in common, but what gave them their own ethnic-religious identity as Jews. Common Judaism – the temple, the torah, the one God who was worshipped in the temple and obeyed in following the torah, election as his covenant people to whom he had given temple and torah – this common Judaism gave Jews common identity in very concrete ways. This common Judaism makes the parting of the ways a real issue, as the model of many Judaisms does not.

To put it another way, Sanders' model makes it meaningful to ask what could exclude a group of Jews from this common Judaism, in the eyes of other Jews. From this point of view, there are two groups with whom the position of Christians vis-a-vis common Judaism might usefully be

---

[10] Sanders, *Judaism*, 47.
[11] E. g. Sanders, *Judaism*, 256–257.

compared. The first is the Samaritans, whom Sanders ignores, presumably because their exclusion from common Judaism can be taken for granted in his period. But the position of the Samaritans is in fact very instructive.[12]

The prevalent contemporary scholarly view is that Samaritanism was a form of Judaism.[13] Although the terminology is odd (in that it does not correspond to ancient usage), it indicates that Samaritanism was not simply a continuation of the pre-exilic religion of Northern Israel, but a schismatic form of post-exilic Judaism. Samaritans claimed descent from the patriarch Joseph, worshipped the God of Israel as the one and only God, kept the law of Moses rigorously, practised circumcision as a sign of the covenant, understood themselves to be the faithful part of the elect people of God. But most Jews regarded them as outside the covenant people, more or less on a par with Gentiles. The key issue was the disagreement over the true site of the one sanctuary of the God of Israel prescribed in Deuteronomy.[14] As the Samaritan woman in the Fourth Gospel puts it, 'Our ancestors worshipped on this mountain [Mount Gerizim], but you [Jews] say that the place where people must worship is in Jerusalem' (4:20). This account of the issue between Jews and Samaritans was, it should be noted, still entirely accurate when John's Gospel was written, even though no temple then stood on either mountain.

Jews also regarded Samaritans as Gentile by race, or at best of dubious ancestry, but it is doubtful if this issue would have carried much weight were it not for the issue of the temple. (Other Gentiles who were circumcised and kept the law were included in the covenant people, not excluded.) Of course, the mutual antipathy of Jews and Samaritans had centuries-old roots, but in the late Second Temple period it was focused on the Samaritan rejection of the Jerusalem Temple, not just as a matter of theological debate, but as a matter of deeply felt, highly emotive popular sentiment. Galilean pilgrims

---

[12] Cf. F. Dexinger, 'Limits of Tolerance in Judaism: The Samaritan Example,' in E. P. Sanders ed., *Jewish and Christian Self-Definition*, vol. 2 (London: SCM Press, 1981) 88–114.

[13] For a survey of the issue, see J. D. Purvis, 'The Samaritans and Judaism,' in R. A. Kraft and G. W. E. Nickelsburg, ed., *Early Judaism and Its Modern Interpreters* (Atlanta, Georgia: Scholars Press, 1986) 81–98.

[14] Cf. E. Bickerman, quoted in Dexinger, 'Limits of Tolerance,' 109: 'The whole controversy between Jews and Samaritans was now subordinated to the questions: Which place was chosen by God for His habitation, Zion or Gerizim?' Whether the temple at Leontopolis was the object of a similar controversy is uncertain, since we do not really know how either its own priests or the Jerusalem temple authorities regarded it. Although Josephus attributes its foundation to a desire to rival the Jerusalem sanctuary, in the sense of attracting worshippers who would otherwise have gone to Jerusalem (*War* 7:431), it is unlikely that its priesthood claimed it as *the* single, divinely-ordained place of Yahweh's presence on earth, as was claimed for Zion and Gerizim. The mere fact that it was not in Palestine must have greatly reduced its significance as a rival to the Jerusalem temple.

travelling through Samaria on their way to the temple in Jerusalem risked not only being refused hospitality, as Jesus was (Luke 9:52–53), but even their lives (as in a famous incident recorded by Josephus, *War* 2:232–246; *Ant.* 20:118–136), not because they were Jews but because they were Jews on their way to the rival sanctuary.

The case of the Samaritans illustrates a number of points. In the first place, it shows how central the temple was to Jewish identity (as also to Samaritan identity). That Samaritans and Jews shared all other features of common Judaism in no way mitigated the effect of the difference over the place of God's earthly presence with his people. This alone was sufficient, in Jewish eyes, to put Samaritans as definitively outside the covenant people as uncircumcised Gentiles were. Secondly, the case of the Samaritans shows how a Jewish group's self-identity could remain completely at odds with other Jews' identification of them. Samaritans asserted their identity as Israel just as strongly as Jews denied it to them.

Thirdly, such a conflict over identity can produce confusion over terminology, as used by outsiders as well as by the groups immediately concerned. Samaritan called themselves Israelites, as Jews did.[15] But Jews called them Samaritans, when not using the more polemically abusive term Cutheans. Gentiles, who never normally called anyone Israelites, seem not to have called Samaritans Jews but adopted the Jewish term: Samaritans (Josephus, *Ant.* 9:290). But the relation between Samaritans and Jews was not unequivocally clear to outsiders.[16] Hegesippus includes Samaritans in his list of the seven Jewish parties (*apud* Eusebius, *Hist. Eccl.* 4.22.7),[17] but Justin, himself a Gentile native of Samaria, does not include them in his similar list (*Dial.* 80.2).

With such a conflict of terminology it is worth comparing the book of Revelation's description of the synagogues at Smyrna and Philadelphia, as 'those who say they are Jews but are not' (2:9; 3:9). No doubt this description throws back at non-Christian Jews what non-Christian Jews said about Christian Jews. Such polemic suggests at least incipient schism of the Jew-

---

[15] The Samaritan community on Delos called themselves, no doubt in order to distinguish themselves from Jews, 'the Israelites on Delos who pay firstfruits to sacred Gerizim' (οἱ ἐν Δήλῳ Ἰσραηλῖται οἱ ἀπαρχόμενοι εἰς ἅγιον Ἀργαριζείν): inscription quoted in E. Schürer, revised by G. Vermes, F. Millar and M. Goodman, *The History of the Jewish People in the Age of Jesus Christ (175 B.C.–A.D. 135)*, vol. 3/1 (Edinburgh: T. & T. Clark, 1986) 71.

[16] The difficulty Samaritans would have had in explaining to Gentiles that they were Israelites but not 'Jews' may well lie behind Josephus' statement in *Ant.* 9:291, which, as it stands, is adapted to Jewish anti-Samaritan polemic and cannot be true.

[17] Strictly speaking, however, Hegesippus himself calls these the 'various opinions among the circumcision, the children of Israel,' while Eusebius calls them the 'Jewish parties.'

ish/Samaritan kind, rather than mere diversity, and it suggests two groups, like Jews and Samaritans, both understanding their self-identity as Jewish, while denying Jewish identity to the other.

The second group whose relation to common Judaism is worth considering for comparison with that of Christians is the Qumran community. Sanders treats them as the only Jewish group which can properly be called a sect rather than a party since they excluded themselves from common Judaism by not participating in the worship of the temple.[18] Decisive for their relation to common Judaism was not their distinctive halakhah or their eschatological consciousness, but their withdrawal from temple worship, constituting themselves a temporary substitute for the temple.[19] We do not really know what other Jews thought of them. (Since Josephus' account of the Essenes' relation to the temple [*Ant.* 18:19][20] is so obscure, it is impossible to tell whether he is thinking of Essenes who withdrew completely from temple worship or of Essenes who, though critical, continued to participate to some degree.) The Qumran community must have been perceived as a marginal group, but their non-participation in temple worship probably did not put them outside Israel, since unlike the Samaritans their opposition to the temple was contingent (resulting from their disapproval of the practice of the priests). They strongly believed that the God of Israel should be worshipped in Jerusalem and would be again in the future.

The examples of the Samaritans and the Qumran community suggest the heuristic model that Christianity began as a party, like the Pharisees, within common Judaism, and became either a group marginal to common Judaism, like the Qumran community, or a community definitively separated from common Judaism, like the Samaritans.[21] That alternative leaves appropriate scope for variation and indeterminateness. Not all non-Christian Jews at one time (say, in the early second century) need have seen Christianity in precisely the same terms, not all need have been very clear about the status of Christianity, not all Christian groups need have been in precisely the same relationship to common Judaism. My suggestion is not, of course, that the Pharisees or the Qumran community or the Samaritans could be

---

[18] Sanders, *Judaism*, 352. According to Sanders, the Qumran community, represented by 1QS and related documents, was a sect, while other Essenes, represented by CD, were an 'extremist party'.

[19] Sanders, *Judaism*, 362.

[20] For discussion see T. S. Beall, *Josephus' description of the Essenes illustrated by the Dead Sea Scrolls* (SNTSMS 58; Cambridge: Cambridge University Press, 1988) 115–119.

[21] This proposed model is not, as stated, an explicitly sociological one, but it could be developed with the aid of sociological insights: cf. the discussion of the move from reform movement to sectarian group as a sociological model for Christianity's break with common Judaism in P. F. Esler, *Community and Gospel in Luke-Acts* (SNTSMS 57; Cambridge: Cambridge University Press, 1987) 51–53.

precise parallels to Christianity's relation to common Judaism. But the model may enable us to identify, by comparison, both the similarities and the differences.

One implication of the model is to direct our attention to the temple. The cases of Qumran and the Samaritans show how central the temple was to Jewish self-identity. The temple was not so exclusively important to the parting of the ways between common Judaism and Christianity. In general Dunn is right to argue that all four of his 'pillars of Judaism' featured in the process that separated Christianity from common Judaism: i.e. (1) the temple (we shall explicate the difference over the temple below); (2) the covenant people, in that Christians redefined the covenant people so as to include Gentiles; (3) the torah, in that Gentile Christians included in the covenant people were not obligated to keep the whole law as Jews were; (4) monotheism, in that Christians redefined monotheism to include Christology. On all four points, which were basic to Jewish self-identity, Christians *interpreted* what all Jews had in common in a way that other Jews eventually considered un-Jewish, unrecognizable as common Judaism. But the rest of this article will focus on the temple. There are several reasons why this will prove a useful focus: (a) the role of the temple in 'the parting of the ways' has been comparatively underplayed in the literature on this issue. This is true even of Dunn's work, although he does regard the temple as the first of the four pillars that occasioned a parting of the ways,[22] while Maurice Casey's recent analysis of Jewish identity and the process of Christian departure from it omits the temple altogether.[23] (b) It was in relation to the temple that there was *precedent* for schism between Jews and Jews, which could have provided non-Christian Jews with a category to apply to Christianity. (c) The Christian view on this point is closely connected with the Christian view of the other three pillars, in a way that is not sufficiently recognized. (d) The Christian view of the temple enables us to understand the inner dynamic which moved Christianity from being a party within common Judaism to being a community separated from common Judaism.

We must first return to the centrality of the temple for the self-identity of common Judaism. Why was this so? Fundamentally, the temple was

---

[22] Dunn, *The Partings of the Ways*, chapters 4–5.

[23] M. Casey, *From Jewish Prophet to Gentile God: The Origins and Development of New Testament Christology* (Cambridge: James Clarke/Louisville: Westminster/John Know, 1991) chapter 2. In this chapter Casey lists eight 'identity factors' which provide an 'identity scale' for measuring whether people would have regarded themselves as Jewish. This methodological approach is useful and illuminating, but its application to the parting of the ways in the rest of the book is less satisfactory. For example, Casey recognizes that a person's or group's self-identification and the perception of their identity by others may conflict (p. 12), but he fails to make full use of this insight in his later discussion of Jews and Christians.

the place where God's covenant people had access to his presence.[24] It was where Israel's privileged relationship to God took place. The importance of the temple in this respect by no means necessarily depended on an individual Jew's ability to visit it, important though it was to do this if possible. Whether or not they could offer their own sacrifices by attending the temple, all Jews everywhere offered, in a sense, the daily burnt offerings every morning and evening, because these were paid for by the temple tax which all Jews paid and offered on behalf of Israel by the priests. The assiduity and enthusiasm with which Diaspora Jews paid their temple tax were not just because the temple tax was a symbolic expression of their allegiance to the religious centre of their nation; it was also actually the means by which the sacrifices offered in the temple enabled their own access to God. Also, of course, the ritual of the day of atonement effected atonement for all Jews without their having to be present. We should not underestimate the importance of the temple for Diaspora Jews even apart from pilgrimage to Jerusalem.[25]

As the temple was God's gracious means of presence with his covenant people, so it defined the covenant people in distinction from others: Gentiles, who were debarred from access to his presence in the temple. The temple was the greatest, the most meaningful boundary-marker between Jew and Gentile. However fluid the distinction between Jew and Gentile might seem in a Diaspora synagogue, where Gentiles who kept some Jewish laws but stopped short of conversion attended, in the temple the distinction was dramatically absolute. On pain of death, no Gentile could pass from the outer court into the sacred precincts proper.[26] In this way the temple made clear the real meaning of all the other boundary-markers – such as circumcision, food laws and Sabbath – which Jews sensitive to Jewish distinction from Gentiles stressed.

With regard to Christian views of the temple, it is important to recognize, though this is rarely stressed, that the early Jerusalem church already had a highly distinctive attitude to the temple. What we know about its attitude amounts to the following three points: (1) Christians continued to partici-

---

[24] For the presence of God in the Second Temple, see G. I. Davies, 'The Presence of God in the Second Temple and Rabbinic Doctrine,' in W. Horbury ed., *Templum Amicitiae: Essays on the Second Temple presented to Ernst Bammel* (JSNTSS 48; Sheffield: JSOT Press, 1991) 32–36.

[25] Diaspora Jews had at least partial substitutes for some of the temple's functions – forms of ritual purification, prayer regarded as a substitute for sin- and guilt-offerings – but these were peripheral to the temple's continuing centrality both in its sacrificial effectiveness and its symbolic significance.

[26] It is noteworthy that this rule and its sanction presuppose a clear, workable, accepted definition of what made one a Jew and not a Gentile. This is neglected by those who emphasize the fluidity of definitions of Jewishness in the Second Temple period.

pate in temple worship. Evidence for this is in fact extremely sparse, but, as well as the evidence of Acts (2:46; 3:1; 5:42), we should probably also count as evidence Matthew 5:23, a saying of Jesus which takes for granted that its hearers offer sacrifice in the temple. Although this saying is preserved by Matthew at a time when certainly no Christians continued to offer sacrifices, if only because the temple no longer existed, it is difficult to imagine that it would have been initially preserved in the earliest church had the earliest Jewish Christians not continued to offer sacrifice. (2) The earliest Jerusalem church must have preserved Jesus' prophecy of the destruction of the temple. Since this occurs in nearly all strands of the Gospel tradition in a variety of forms (Matt 23:38; 24:2; 26:61; 27:40; Mark 13:2; 14:58; 15:29; Luke 13:35; 19:44; 21:6; John 2:19; GThom 71; cf. Acts 6:14), it must have been current in the earliest community. Therefore they must have viewed the temple as a doomed institution, in which they participated while it lasted, but which they did not expect to last long. (3) The early Jerusalem church saw *itself* as the new, eschatological temple of God. This is made probable by the fact that the concept of the Christian community as the eschatological temple is very widespread in early Christian literature.[27] It is found in Paul (1 Cor 3:16–17; 2 Cor 6:16), Jude (20),[28] 1 Peter (2:5; 4:17), Ephesians (2:20–22), Hebrews (13:15–16), Revelation (11:1–2),[29] the Didache (10:2), Barnabas (4:11; 6:15; 16), Ignatius (*Eph.* 9:1) and Hermas (*Vis.* 3; *Sim.* 3),[30] and throughout this literature it is regularly taken for granted, not argued. It must therefore stem from an early stage of Christian history. But that it stemmed from the early Jerusalem church is made even more probable by Paul's reference to James, Peter and John as those who were 'regarded as pillars' of the new temple (cf. Rev 3:12).[31]

---

[27] On the general theme, see R. J. McKelvey, *The New Temple: The Church in the New Testament* (Oxford: Oxford University Press, 1969).

[28] For the temple image here, see R. Bauckham, *Jude, 2 Peter* (Word Biblical Commentary 50; Waco, Texas: Word Books, 1983) 112–113.

[29] For the temple as an image of the church in this passage, see R. Bauckham, *The Climax of Prophecy: Studies in the Book of Revelation* (Edinburgh: T. & T. Clark, 1993) 266–273.

[30] Other instances of the frequently used metaphor of 'building' the Christian community are probably also evidence of the widespread currency of the image of the church as the eschatological temple: see Matt 16:18; Acts 9:31; 15:16; 20:32; Rom 14:19; 15:2, 20; 1 Cor 8:1; 10:23; 14:3–5, 12, 17, 26; 2 Cor 10:8; 12:19; 13:10; Gal 2:18; Eph 4:12, 16; Col 2:7; 1 Thess 5:11; Polycarp, *Phil.* 3:2; 12:2; *Odes Sol.* 22:12.

[31] C. K. Barrett, 'Paul and the 'Pillar' Apostles,' in: J. N. Sevenster and W. C. van Unnik ed., *Studia Paulina* (FS J. de Zwaan; Haarlem: Bohn, 1953) 1–19. For an alternative interpretation, see R. Aus, 'Three Pillars and Three Patriarchs: A Proposal Concerning Gal 2:9,' *ZNW* 70 (1979) 252–261 (comparing the Jewish tradition that Abraham, Isaac and Jacob were the three pillars on whom the world was supported). But the idea of pillars in the eschatological temple was current (1 Enoch 90:28–29; JosAsen 17:6; Hermas, *Vis.* 3:8:2) and

That the early Jerusalem church understood itself in this way is a re-markable fact.[32] The concept of the temple as a community, not a building, is found outside Christianity only at Qumran.[33] (This is surely the most impressive of all parallels between Qumran and early Christianity.) At Qumran it was connected precisely with the community's sectarian status vis-a-vis common Judaism, in that, withdrawing from the Jerusalem temple, they saw themselves as a substitute for the temple. In the Jerusalem church, the idea of the community as temple was evidently not accompanied by withdrawal from the Jerusalem temple. Unlike the Qumran community, they did not regard the temple service as invalid. And so by this criterion they remained fully part of common Judaism. Why then was it believed that the community constituted the eschatological temple? This must have expressed the conviction that in the Christian community, through the mediation of the exalted Christ, God's promised eschatological presence in the midst of his people was taking place. The place of God's eschatological presence – the new temple – was the church.

Compared with Qumran, this Christian view was, in different ways, both less radical and more radical. Unlike the Qumran community, Christians did not regard worship in the Jerusalem temple as defiled and illegitimate, and so they could continue to participate in it. But whereas for the Qumran community the identification of the temple with the community was only an interim situation, to be succeeded by the new temple to be built by God in Jerusalem in the eschatological age, the temple envisaged in the New Jerusalem text from Qumran,[34] the early Jerusalem church seems to have regarded itself as *the* eschatological temple. Nowhere in early Christian literature is there any trace of an expectation of an eschatological temple still to come in the future: this common Jewish expectation was evidently

---

coheres best with other early Christian imagery. On Rev 3:12, see also R. H. Wilkinson, 'The Στῦλος of Revelation 3:12 and Ancient Coronation Rites,' *JBL* 107 (1988) 498–501.

[32] Dunn, *The Partings of the Ways,* 60, recognizes but underestimates the significance of this fact. While denying that the Jerusalem church's view of the Christian community as the new temple had any implications for their attitude to the Jerusalem temple, he in-consistently concludes from Paul's expression of the same idea that 'the Temple no longer functioned for him as the focus of God's presence' (75).

[33] For the community as temple at Qumran, see B. Gärtner, *The Temple and the Com-munity in the Qumran Scrolls and the New Testament* (Cambridge: Cambridge University Press, 1965) 16–46; D. Juel, *Messiah and Temple: The Trial of Jesus in the Gospel of Mark* (SBLDS 31; Missoula, Montana: Scholars Press, 1977) 159–168; H. Lichtenberger, 'Atone-ment and Sacrifice in the Qumran Community', in W. S. Green ed., *Approaches to Ancient Judaism,* vol. 2 (Brown Judaic Studies 9; Chico, California: Scholars Press, 1980) 159–171; G. J. Brooke, *Exegesis at Qumran: 4QFlorilegium in its Jewish Context* (JSOTSS 29; Shef-field: JSOT Press, 1985) 178–193.

[34] For an argument that this text is a product of the Qumran community and envisages the eschatological temple, see F. Garcia Martinez, *Qumran and Apocalyptic: Studies on the Aramaic Texts from Qumran* (STDJ 9; Leiden: Brill, 1992) 180–213.

replaced from the beginning of Christianity by the belief that the community itself *was* the eschatological place of God's presence. Such a view in effect relativizes the Jerusalem temple more radically than the Qumran view. Whatever the value of the temple, it was highly provisional and soon to be replaced by that eschatological presence of God to which the church already had access in its own fellowship.

The importance of this view for our purposes is that it explains *both* how the Jerusalem church could remain a party within common Judaism *and* how other Christian groups could move to a more marginal position from a common Jewish standpoint. From this view of the community as the eschatological temple it was possible to conclude *either* that Christians should (or at least could) continue to take part in the worship of the Jerusalem temple while it still stood (until, that is, God himself removed it), *or* that, since the temple was already superseded by the community as the new temple, Christians should not participate in the temple worship. The Jerusalem church seems to have taken the former view and by its praxis with regard to the temple maintained its standing in the Jewish community, even if with some difficulty. The author to the Hebrews is the only Christian voice from before 70 C.E. who clearly takes the latter view.[35] Paul is often supposed to have taken this view, but the evidence is lacking. More likely the temple no longer mattered to Paul,[36] it was in principle superseded by the Christian community,[37] but Paul did not actually oppose participation in temple worship, while his principle of becoming as a Jew in order to win Jews (1 Cor 9:20) makes his behaviour according to Acts 21:26 entirely credible.[38]

Thus a common early Christian premise – that the church constitutes the eschatological temple – had varied consequences with regard to Christianity's relation to common Judaism. Some Christian Jews remained regular participants in temple worship, others neglected the temple, others specifically opposed participation in temple rituals. Where Christians were

---

[35] For the view that the argument of Hebrews presupposes that the Second Temple still stood, see B. Lindars, 'Hebrews and the Second Temple,' in Horbury ed., *Templum Amicitiae*, 410–413.

[36] It is surely significant that in fourteen years (Gal 2:1) Paul only visited Jerusalem once.

[37] But Dunn, *The Partings of the Ways*, 70, 77–79, concludes much too readily that Paul's understanding of the death of Christ as a sacrifice made the sacrificial cult of the temple redundant. Such an argument would apply only to sin-offerings. It would leave the greater part of the sacrificial cult – for example, the regular daily morning and evening burnt-offerings – unaffected. Although the argument of Hebrews focuses on the death of Christ, the developing Christian sense of the redundancy of the temple cult must have had a broader christological basis in the sense of Jesus Christ as the way of access to God in the messianic age.

[38] See J.P.M. Sweet, 'A House Not Made With Hands,' in Horbury ed., *Templum Amicitiae*, 368–369, especially 388–390.

perceived to be treating the temple in the way Samaritans did, nothing was more calculated to categorize them as sectarian, schismatic and a threat to Jewish identity. Hence controversy about the temple was evidently the occasion for the first major persecution of Christians (Acts 6–8).[39] Conversely, non-Christian Jewish suspicions about Christianity could best be allayed by Christians demonstrating their loyalty and reverence for the temple. Hence the Jerusalem church elders' advice to Paul in Acts 21:20–25. (We shall see below why it was not successful in Paul's case.)

The issue of the temple did not disappear after 70 c.e., because the temple did not cease to be central to Jewish identity. Few Jews would have expected the loss of the temple to be permanent. The temple had been destroyed before – and rebuilt before, significantly after a period more or less the length of the period between 70 c.e. and the Bar Kokhba revolt. Consequently, in Christian literature of this period, between the two Jewish revolts, the temple issue is alive and well precisely in texts in which the schism between Christianity and common Judaism is clear and painful: the Gospel of John, the Epistle of Barnabas.[40]

For Palestinian Jewish Christianity the effect of 70 c.e. was paradoxical. Jesus' prophecy of the destruction of the temple was vindicated. As a messianic movement, but a non-militant messianic movement dissociated from the disastrous consequences of the revolt, and a movement, virtually unique among Jewish groups, for which the loss of the temple was no kind of problem, Jewish Christianity must have had some appeal and probably enjoyed some success in Palestine between the two revolts.[41] But the destruction of the temple also had an unfortunate consequence for Palestinian Jewish Christians. While the temple stood they could maintain their place in common Judaism by worshipping in it. But once the temple was destroyed, what they could not do was participate in any movement to rebuild the temple. Such a movement was Bar Kokhba's revolt. The attempt to build the temple was the principal raison d'être of the revolt and the main reason it gained such widespread support.[42] Probably it was because Bar Kokhba

---

[39] However, I am not convinced that Stephen and the Hellenists took the radically antitemple position that is now commonly attributed to them. But the issue cannot be discussed here.

[40] For the view of the temple in Barnabas, see M.B. Shukster and P. Richardson, 'Temple and Bet Ha-midrash in the Epistle of Barnabas,' in S.G. Wilson ed., Anti-Judaism in Early Christianity, vol. 2 (Studies in Judaism and Christianity 2; Waterloo, Ontario: Wilfrid Laurier University Press, 1986).

[41] Cf. R. Bauckham, Jude and the Relatives of Jesus in the Early Church (Edinburgh: T. & T. Clark, 1990) 116, 375.

[42] B. Isaac and A. Oppenheimer, 'The Revolt of Bar Kokhba: Ideology and Modern Scholarship,' JJS 36 (1985) 47–49; L. Mildenberg, The Coinage of the Bar Kokhba Revolt (Aarau/Frankfurt am Main/Salzburg: Sauerländer, 1984) 31–48.

looked like succeeding in this aim that he was widely regarded as Messiah.[43] Christians could not regard him as Messiah (cf. Justin, *1 Apol.* 31.6), but even more significantly they could not join a movement to restore the temple. Their non-participation in the Bar Kokhba revolt[44] probably sealed their exclusion from common Judaism and removed the rabbis' main rivals for dominance in Palestinian Judaism.

However, we must now return to a much earlier point in the story, in order to notice the most radical implication of the common early Christian view of the eschatological temple. The identification of the Christian community as itself the new temple was, of course, an expression of the eschatological consciousness of the earliest church. The messianic age was dawning, and God was newly, eschatologically present in the midst of his people, the Christian community which constituted the core of the renewed covenant people. Another expression of this eschatological consciousness was the inclusion of Gentiles in the Christian community, fulfilling those remarkably universalistic prophecies from the post-exilic period which predicted the inclusion of the nations in the covenant people of God.[45] On the basis of these prophecies, Christian could justify the inclusion of Gentiles as Gentiles, without their becoming Jews. The arrival of the messianic age made possible the Pauline, but by no means only Pauline, vision of the eschatological people of God as continuous with Israel but no longer bounded by the observances which distinguished Jew from Gentile. However, such a people of God could not have the Jerusalem temple as its temple, its place of access to the covenant God. The Jerusalem temple embodied, as the principle of its sanctity, the exclusion of Gentiles from the covenant and from access to the God of the covenant. The point is vividly made by the account in Acts 21:17–36, in which Paul's attempt to demonstrate his loyalty to common Judaism by taking part in temple rituals fails disastrously. It does so because visiting Jews from Ephesus make a natural mistake (21:27–29). To them Paul was notorious for insisting that Gentiles were included as Gentiles, without becoming Jews, in the covenant people of God. They naturally assume that the logic of such a position must be that Paul's Gentile converts should be admitted to the temple, and they jump to

---

[43] Against some recent doubts that Bar Kokhba was regarded as Messiah, see A. Rheinhartz, 'Rabbinic Perceptions of Simeon bar Kosiba,' *JSJ* 20 (1989) 171–194.

[44] For the Apocalypse of Peter as evidence of Palestinian Jewish Christian attitudes to the revolt at the time of the revolt, see R. Bauckham, 'The Two fig Tree Parables in the Apocalypse of Peter,' *JBL* 104 (1985) 269–287; idem, 'The Apocalypse of Peter: An Account of Research,' in W. Haase ed., *Aufstieg und Niedergang der römischen Welt* II.25/6 (Berlin/New York: de Gruyter, 1988) 4738–4739.

[45] On the continuation of this tradition of expectation in post-biblical Second Temple Judaism, see T. L. Donaldson, 'Proselytes or 'Righteous Gentiles'? The Status of Gentiles in Eschatological Pilgrimage Patterns of Thought,' *JSP* 7 (1990) 3–27.

the conclusion that Paul actually has defiled the sanctity of the temple by taking Trophimus the Ephesian into the court of the Israelites.

The inclusion of Gentiles in the covenant people was actually possible only because the eschatological covenant people had its own *new* temple, the community itself, in which Gentiles could have access to God equally with Jews. The connexion between the image of the community as temple and the inclusion of Gentiles in the covenant is explicit in Ephesians 2:11–22 and 1 Peter 2:4–10, but already implicit in 2 Corinthians 6:16–7:1. But it was certainly not the Gentile mission that gave rise to the idea of the community as temple. The reverse was the case.

From this point of view it is of great significance that the early Jerusalem church, under James's leadership, already saw itself as the temple of the messianic age. This made possible what happened at the Jerusalem conference recounted in Acts 15, when those members of the Jerusalem church who opposed the inclusion of Gentiles as Gentiles were marginalized and the Pauline mission approved, with the qualifications stated in the so-called Apostolic Decree (Acts 15:29–29). This was given its required scriptural basis by James' quotation of Amos 9:11–12 (Acts 15:16–17): 'After this I will return and I will rebuild the tent of David [i. e. establish the new temple of the messianic age]... *so that* the rest of humanity, the Gentiles over whom my name has been called [i. e. Gentiles included as Gentiles in the covenant people of God], may seek the Lord [i. e. seek God's presence in his temple, the Christian community].'[46]

Once again, the parallel and contrast with Qumran is illuminating. In both cases the community's consciousness of access to God independently of the Jerusalem temple effectively relativized the latter. But the Qumran community, who thought the Jerusalem temple ritually defiled by the practice of the priests, constituted themselves a temple so pure as to require even more strictly restricted access than the Jerusalem temple had. As 4QFlorilegium puts it, this is 'the house to which shall not come even to the tenth generation and for ever, Ammonite nor Moabite nor bastard nor stranger nor proselyte for ever, for his holy ones are there' (1:3–4). The careful selection and interpretation of OT prohibitions (Deut 23:2–3; Ezek 44:6–9)[47] are designed to exclude any kind of Gentile, even the issue of mixed marriages and even proselytes. By contrast the effect of the Christian community's understanding of itself as temple was to break out of the restriction embodied in the Jerusalem temple in a quite unprecedented way. The relativizing

---

[46] For this interpretation of Acts 15:16–17 and for the argument of the paragraph in detail, see my article: 'James and the Gentiles (Acts 15:1.21),' in B. Witherington III ed., *The Acts of the Historians: Acts and Ancient Historiography* (Cambridge University Press, 1994).

[47] See Brooke, *Exegesis at Qumran*, 180–181.

of the Jerusalem temple enabled both communities to redefine the covenant people, but whereas the Qumran sect did so by taking to an extreme the emphasis of Second Temple Judaism on purity and differentiation from Gentiles,[48] the Christian community did so in a way quite opposite to this emphasis.

Therefore, even though the earliest church's praxis with regard to the temple maintained its place within common Judaism, its view of itself as the new temple, its eschatological consciousness of access to God independently of the Jerusalem temple, already contained the dynamic of the process which increasingly differentiated Christianity from common Judaism. The Christian reinterpretation of one of the 'four pillars' of Judaism (the temple) made possible the Christian reinterpretation of the three other pillars (election, torah and monotheism) in ways which were in the end decisive for the parting of the ways.[49] We have already seen how this happened with respect to election, i. e. the belief that Israel was the chosen covenant people of God. The reinterpretation of the temple made possible the inclusion of Gentiles in the covenant people of God. Along with this went a new Christian attitude to the torah. Since Gentiles, as Gentiles, were now included in the covenant people and had access to the covenant God in his new temple equally with Jews, the specifically Jewish requirements of the law of Moses no longer constituted the boundary of the covenant people. These were Christian interpretations of election and torah which common Judaism rejected as denials of Jewish identity.

Finally, the reinterpretation of the temple was not unrelated to the specifically Christian interpretation of Jewish monotheism. The church's eschatological sense of access to God independently of the Jerusalem temple was connected with the christological understanding of Jesus as the eschatological presence of God with his people, which led to that inclusion of Jesus in the definition of the one God of Israel which common Judaism rejected as a denial of Jewish monotheism. It is no accident that the two New Testament books with the highest Christologies – the Fourth Gospel and the Book of Revelation – both include Jesus in the definition of the one

---

[48] Note also how sacrifices made by Gentiles, a traditional practice in the temple, were prohibited in 66 c.e., as one of the first acts of the revolt (Josephus, *War* 2:409–421).

[49] On universalism, torah and monotheism as the issues between Christianity and Judaism, see, besides Dunn, *The Partings of the Ways,* also A. F. Segal, *Rebecca's Children: Judaism and Christianity in the Roman World* (Cambridge, Massachusetts/London: Harvard University Press, 1986). Note also the mid-second-century Jewish characterization of Christianity (preserved by Justin, *Dial.* 17.1; 108.2) as 'a godless ad lawless sect' (αἵρεσίς τις ἄθεος καὶ ἄνομος: *Dial.* 108.2), discussed by G. N. Stanton, 'Aspects of Early Christian-Jewish Polemic and Apologetic,' *NTS* 31 (1985) 383–384.

God of Jewish monotheism,[50] and both give a new, christological twist to the theme of the eschatological temple: it is Jesus himself who replaces the Jerusalem temple as the place of God's presence with his covenant people (John 1:51, 2:19–22; Rev 21:22).

---

[50] For Revelation, see R. Bauckham, *The Theology of the Book of Revelation* (Cambridge: Cambridge University Press, 1993) chapter 3; idem, *The Climax of Prophecy*, chapter 4.

13. The Messianic Interpretation
of Isaiah 10:34*

Isaiah 11:1–5 was probably the most popular text of Davidic messianism in early Judaism. Modern readers usually assume that this prophecy begins at Isaiah 11:1 and do not connect the preceding verses with it.[1] Ancient Jewish exegesis, however, frequently sought the connexions between adjacent passages of Scripture. In this article we shall examine evidence that a Jewish exegetical tradition which appears in the Dead Sea Scrolls and in the Syriac Apocalypse of Baruch not only connected Isaiah 10:33–34 closely with the following verses, but also found a reference to the Messiah in Isaiah 10:34. This tradition of messianic interpretation of Isaiah 10:34 will then be shown to inform the preaching of John the Baptist, as it appears in the Gospels, with the implication that, contrary to many interpretations of John's message, he did expect the coming of the Davidic Messiah.

Dead Sea Scrolls

The texts

4QpIsaᵃ (4Q161) fr. 8–10, lines 2–9:[2]

ונוקפו ס]ו[בכי [היער] בברזל ולבנון באדיר	2
יפול פשרו על הכ]תיאים אש[ר] יפ[לו] ביד ישראל וענוי	3
כ]ול הגואים וגבורים יחתו ונמס ל[בם	4
ורמי] הקומה גדועים המה גבורי כת]יאים	5

---

* First publication: *Dead Sea Discoveries* 2 (1995) 202–216.

[1] But see O. Kaiser, *Isaiah 1–12* (London: SCM Press, 1972) 156–162, for an exegesis which treats 10:33–11:9 as a unit, and connects the tree imagery of 10:33–34 with that of 11:1.

[2] These fragment numbers and line numbers are those used in the *editio princeps:* J. M. Allegro, *Qumrân Cave 4: I (4Q158–4Q186)* (DJD 5; Oxford: Clarendon Press, 1968)13–14. M. P. Horgan, *Pesharim: Qumran Interpretations of Biblical Books* (CBQMS 8; Washington, D. C.: Catholic Biblical Association of America, 1979) 75–76, renumbers the section as fragments 7–10 (column 3), lines 6–13. The text given here follows Allegro with modifications adopted from J. Strugnell, 'Notes en marge du volume V des "Discoveries in the Judaean Desert of Jordan,"' *RQ* 7 (1970) 185, and Horgan, *Pesharim,* 83–85. (I have not

ר] ונוקפו סובכי [ה]יער בברזל ה[מה   6

ם] למלחמת כתיאים ולבנון בא]דיר   7

ה[כתיאים אשר ינת]נו[ביד נדולו]   8   יפול

ים בברחו מלפ]ני יש[ראל]   9

2 *and the th]ickets of [the forest will be cut down] with an axe, and Lebanon by a*
powerful one

3 *shall fall (Isa 10:34)*. Its interpretation concerns the Ki]ttim, wh[o] will fa[ll] by
the hand of Israel. And the poor ones of

4] all the nations, and the warriors will be dismayed, and [their]
he[arts] will melt

5 *and the tall] in stature will be hewn down (Isa 10:33)*. They are
the warriors of the Kitt[im

6] *and the thickets of [the] forest will be cut down with an axe*. Th[ey are

7] for the battle of the Kittim. *And Lebanon by a pow[erful one*

8 *shall fall.*   the] Kittim who will be gi[ven] into the hand of his
great one [

9] when he flees from befo[re Is]rael [

4Q285, fr. 5:[3]

ישעיהו הנביא ונוק]פו סובכי היער [1

בברזל ולבנון באדיר י]פול ויצא חוטר מגזע ישי]   2

צמח דויד ונשפטו את]   3

והמיתו נשיא העדה צמ]ח דויד]   4

ם] ובמחוללות וצוה כוהן]   5

ח]ל[ל]י[כתיים]ל[6

1] Isaiah the prophet: [*and the thickets of the forest]will be cut [down*

2 *with an axe, and Lebanon by a powerful one shall f]all. And there shall come forth*
a shoot from the stump of Jesse (Isa 10:34–11:1) [

3] the Branch of David and they will enter into judgment with [

4] and the Prince of the Congregation, the Bran[ch of David] will kill him [

5] and by wounds. And a priest [   ] will command [

6   the s]lai[n] of the Kitti[m

Discussion

There are two Qumran texts which preserve the messianic interpretation
of Isaiah 10:34. The first is 4QpIsa[a] (4Q161), which is a continuous pesher
on Isaiah 10:22–11:5 and interprets this whole section of Isaiah as prophetic
of the eschatological war against the Kittim, conducted and won by the

---

indicated doubtful letters.) Note especially that in line 3 I have preferred Horgan's reading
יפ]לו[ביד to Allegro's ביה יכח]ו[י. The translation is indebted to Allegro and Horgan.

[3] Text and translation from G. Vermes, 'The Oxford Forum for Qumran Research on
the Rule of War from Cave 4 (4Q285),' *JJS* 43 (1991) 88. (I have not indicated doubtful
letters.) In R. H. Eisenman and M. Wise, *The Dead Sea Scrolls Uncovered* (Shaftesbury,
Dorset: Element, 1992) 28–29, this is numbered fragment 7.

Davidic Messiah, who is called both the Prince of the Congregation[4] and the Branch of David.[5] The second text is the only recently published 4Q285, fragment 5, made famous in 1991 by the claim of Robert Eisenman and Michael Wise that it describes the Davidic Messiah as put to death. The group of fragments to which it belongs has affinities with the War Scroll[6] and evidently represent a text which, like the War Scroll and 4QpIsaᵃ, concerned the eschatological victory over the Kittim. As a seminar of the Oxford Forum for Qumran Research showed,[7] precisely these parallels with other Qumran texts make the interpretation of fragment 5 by Eisenman and Wise quite implausible. Fragment 5 is especially close to 4QpIsaᵃ, since it is itself a pesher on Isaiah 10:34–11:1a, the verses which are quoted in its first two lines and then interpreted. These two texts (4QpIsaᵃ and 4Q285 fr.5) are so closely parallel that there can be little doubt they share the same interpretation of Isaiah 10:34. Both are fragmentary, but what is not quite clear in one can be clarified by the other.

Isaiah 10:34 is taken in both texts to describe the defeat of the Kittim. 4QpIsaᵃ reads the whole of the preceding passage of Isaiah as an account of the war of the sons of Light, led by the Prince of the Congregation, the Davidic Messiah, against the Kittim.[8] Isaiah 10:28–32 seems to be understood to describe the Messiah's victorious campaign which leads to his confrontation with the Kittim at Jerusalem.[9] Isaiah 10:33–34 are then taken to refer to the final battle in which the Kittim are destroyed. The Messiah described in Isaiah 11:1–5 is therefore the one whose victory over the Kittim has already been described at the end of chapter 10.

However, we must examine the more detailed interpretation of Isaiah 10:33–34. 4QpIsaᵃ interprets the tall trees of Isaiah 10:33, the 'tall in stature' (ורמי הקומה) who are to be hewn down, as 'the warriors of the Kittim' (גבורי כתיאים),[10] and although the specific interpretation of v 34a ('and the thickets of the forest will be cut down with an axe') has not been preserved,[11] most likely 'the thickets of the forest' (סבכי היער) are taken to be the Kittim

---

[4] 5–6:3 [Allegro] = 2–6:19 [Horgan]

[5] 8–10:17 [Allegro] = 7–10:22 [Horgan]

[6] Vermes, 'Oxford Forum,' 86, 89–90; J. T. Milik, '*Milkî-ṣedeq et Milkî-resaᶜ* dans les anciens écrits juifs et chrétiens,' *JJS* 23 (1972) 143.

[7] Vermes, 'Oxford Forum,' 88–90.

[8] Note the parallel between 5–6:2 [Allegro] = 2–6:18 [Horgan] and 1QM 1:3.

[9] So J.M. Allegro, 'Further Messianic References in Qumran Literature,' *JBL* 75 (1956) 181; idem, 'Addendum to Professor Millar Burrow's Note on the Ascent from Accho in 4QpIsaᵃ,' *VT* 7 (1957) 183. This is also how Tg. Isaiah understands vv 28–29 (following its statement in v 27: 'the Gentiles will be shattered before the Messiah'), though the later verses of the chapter are applied to Sennacherib.

[10] 8–10:5 [Allegro] = 7–10:9 [Horgan].

[11] See 8–10:6–7 [Allegro] = 7–10:10–11 [Horgan].

in general, who 'fall by the hand of Israel.'[12] בברזל, which in the context of the image of felling a forest must mean 'with an axe,' could easily have been understood, in the Qumran interpretation with reference to a battle, as 'with a sword,' as it is in the LXX (πεσοῦνται ὑψηλοὶ μαχαίρᾳ).

The precise interpretation of v 34b ('and Lebanon will fall by a powerful one') is again not entirely clear in either text, but careful attention to both texts reveals that probably 'by a powerful one' (באדיר) is understood to refer to the Prince of the Congregation and 'Lebanon' to the king of the Kittim. In 4QpIsaᵃ the interpretation of this half-verse begins: '[Its interpretation concerns the] Kittim who will be given into the hand of his great one (גדולו).'[13] אדיר, which often in the Hebrew Bible refers to those with power in society – nobles or princes, is here paraphrased by גדול, which can have the same sense, and the suffix (גדולו) makes it clear that the reference is to God's great one, his Messiah. An interpretation of אדיר as the Messiah would have been assisted by the fact that this word is used of the messianic ruler in Jeremiah 30:21.

This messianic reading of Isaiah 10:34b is confirmed by 4Q285, fr. 5, which quotes v 34 along with at least the first half of 11:1, and presumably interprets both verses together in the fragmentary text (lines 3–5) about 'the Prince of the Congregation, the Branch of David.' Here it is said that the Branch of David 'will kill him' (והמיתו).[14] The singular masculine object of the verb can only be the king of the Kittim (cf. 1QM 15:2).[15] But if the statement is meant to be an interpretation of the Isaianic text quoted, then 'Lebanon' in Isaiah 10:34b must have been understood to refer to the king of the Kittim.[16] At first sight this may appear to be a difference from 4QpIsaᵃ, since

---

[12] 8–10:3 = 7–10:7 [Horgan]. This reading is the one suggested by Horgan, *Pesharim*, 83–84.

[13] The word could be read as גדולו or גדולי ('the great ones of'), but the text being interpreted (Isa 10:34b) gives a reference for 'his great one' (באדיר), not for 'great ones.' Horgan, *Pesharim*, 84, fails to recognize this.

[14] Eisenman and Wise, *Dead Sea Scrolls*, 29, translate: 'and they will put to death the Leader of the Community, the Bran[ch of David].' This translation is the basis of their view that the text refers to a slain Messiah. While this translation is possible (despite the absence of את before נשיא העדה), it does not fit the context of an interpretation of Isa 10:34–11:1, and the parallels with 4QpIsaᵃ and 1QM make it improbable: see Vermes, 'Oxford Forum,' 88–89.

[15] So Vermes, 'Oxford Forum,' 89.

[16] It is likely that Isa 10:34 LXX reflects a similar interpretation of Lebanon as the king of Assyria. LXX Isa 10:33–34 removes almost entirely the MT's metaphor of a forest, turning all the MT's trees into people, slain by the sword in a battle, but it retains the word Lebanon: 'Lebanon shall fall with the lofty ones' (ὁ δὲ Λίβανος σὺν τοῖς ὑψηλοῖς πεσεῖται). Since ὑψηλοῖς here are not trees but people, the reference is presumably to the king with his military leaders. Note also that the reference in Isa 2:13 to 'all the cedars of Lebanon' appears in the Targum as 'all the kings of the Gentiles.' Other instances of the interpretation of Lebanon as 'kings' in the Targums are assembled in G. Vermes, *Scripture and*

the beginning of the interpretation of v 34 b in the latter can be understood as identifying Lebanon with the Kittim,[17] but this interpretation also apparently includes the words: 'when he flees before Israel' (בברחו מלפ[נ]י יש[ר]אל).[18] Again, the singular can scarcely refer to anyone but the king of the Kittim, who is presumably envisaged as fleeing, after the defeat of his army, and then being apprehended, brought before the Prince of the Congregation, condemned and executed. Another fragment of 4Q285 (fr.4)[19] presumably refers to the same events when it says that 'they will bring him before the Prince of [the Congregation]' (יביאוהו לפני נשיא [העדה]).

2 Baruch

Among explicit interpretations of Isaiah 10:34 in extant Jewish literature, these two Qumran texts are unique in taking באדיר as a reference to the Messiah. Both the LXX of Isaiah 10:33–34 and the Targum to these verses interpret them as referring to a battle in which the enemies of Israel are defeated and slain, but neither understands באדיר as the Messiah. A different interpretation, attributed in rabbinic literature to Yohanan ben Zakkai, takes Isaiah 10:34 b to refer to the destruction of the Temple in 70 c.e.: Lebanon is interpreted as the Temple, following a widely attested exegetical tradition of understanding Lebanon in many biblical texts in this way,[20] and באדיר is understood to refer to the emperor Vespasian, through whom the temple fell (Lam. R. 1:5:31; b. Gitt. 56 a–56 b). A development of this tradition concluded, by understanding 10:34 and 11:1 in close connection, that the Messiah was born at the time when the temple was destroyed (j. Ber. 2:5 a). This exegesis shares with 4Q285 and 4QpIsaᵃ the practice of reading 10:34 in close connexion with 11:1, but it does not take באדיר to refer to the Messiah.

We might therefore have to conclude that the specifically messianic interpretation of Isaiah 10:34 was a peculiarity of the Qumran community, were it not for a passage in the Syriac Apocalypse of Baruch which, while it is not explicitly an interpretation of Isaiah 10:34, is certainly implicitly such.[21] In 2 Baruch 36–40 Baruch is given a vision and its interpretation. The vision is a prophecy of the way in which the fourth kingdom (2 Bar 39:5),

---

Tradition in Judaism (SPB 4; Leiden: Brill, 1961) 27; cf. also R. P. Gordon, 'Appendix 2: The Interpretation of "Lebanon" and 4Q285,' in Vermes, 'Oxford Forum,' 93.

[17] So Vermes, 'Oxford Forum,' 89.

[18] This reading is Strugnell's correction of Allegro: Strugnell, 'Notes,' 185.

[19] Numbered fragment 6 in Eisenman and Wise, *Dead Sea Scrolls*, 28–29.

[20] Vermes, *Scripture*, 26–39.

[21] I had independently noticed the correspondence between 4Q285, fr.5, and 2 Bar 36–40, before noticing that this correspondence was also pointed out by W. Horbury at the Oxford Forum seminar: Vermes, 'Oxford Forum,' 89–90.

i. e. the Roman empire, will be destroyed and succeeded by the rule of the Messiah. The Roman empire is symbolized by a large forest surrounded by high mountains (40:2); the Messiah and his kingdom are symbolized by a vine and a fountain (40:3; 39:7). The fountain comes to the forest and submerges it, uprooting all the trees and levelling the mountains (40:4–5). Only one cedar is left, which is felled and then brought to the vine, who denounces it for its evil rule and condemns it to be reduced to ashes like the rest of the forest (40:6–11). According to the interpretation, the cedar is the last ruler, i. e. the last Roman emperor, who, when his army is destroyed, will be bound and brought to the Messiah on Mount Zion. The Messiah will convict him of his wickedness and put him to death (39:8–40:2). The Messiah's peaceful and prosperous rule follows (37:1; 40:3).

With the help of the Qumran texts we have examined, we can see that this vision is based on an interpretation of Isaiah 10:34 very similar to that found in 4Q285 and 4QpIsaᵃ. The whole vision can be explained as resulting from an exegesis of Isaiah 10:34 in its immediate context and in close connexion with a number of other passages which have been exegetically linked with it. The forest is the forest of Isaiah 10:33–34 a. When the account of the vision says that 'the height of the forest became low' (36:5), there is an echo of Isaiah 10:33 b: 'the tall in stature will be hewn down, and the lofty will be brought low.' The fact that the forest seems to be first uprooted (36:4–6) and then burned to ashes (36:10) is probably due to the fact that the phrase 'the thickets of the forest' (סבכי היער) occurs not only in Isaiah 10:34 a, where the thickets are said to be cut down, but also in Isaiah 9:17 (EVV 18), where they are said to be burned. (The phrase is found nowhere else in the Hebrew Bible.) The fact that the emperor is portrayed in 2 Baruch as a cedar is due to the fact that he is the 'Lebanon' to which Isaiah 10:34 b refers. The fact that the cedar is first thrown down (36:6), and then judged, sentenced and executed by the vine (the Messiah), may well be due to a sequential interpretation of Isaiah 10:34 a–11:4. First, Lebanon falls by the Messiah (10:34 b); then the Messiah, acting as righteous judge (11:3–4), kills the wicked one (רשע) with the breath of his lips (11:4; note the stress on the cedar's wickedness in 2 Bar 36:7–8; 40:1). The fact that the cedar is finally destroyed by burning (36:10; 37:1) may result from an exegetical link between the reference to Lebanon in Isaiah 10:34 b and the prophecy that Lebanon will burn in Zechariah 11:1. Alternatively, it may derive from Daniel 7:11, since the cedar has been identified as 'the fourth kingdom' (2 Bar 39:5), which is the fourth beast in the vision of Daniel 7.[22]

Other features of the vision can also be explained by exegetical links between Isaiah 10:33–11:1 and other passages of scripture. The vision's symbol

---

[22] This point was suggested to me by George W. E. Nickelsburg.

of the Roman empire is not only the forest which is thrown down but also the high mountains which are levelled: 'the height of the forest became low, and that top of the mountains became low' (36:5). This is probably due to Isaiah 2:12–14:

> For the LORD of hosts has a day against all that is proud and lofty (ורם),
> against all that is lifted up; and it shall become low (ושפל);
> against all the cedars of Lebanon, lofty (הרמים) and lifted up;
> and against all the oaks of Bashan;
> against all the lofty (הרמים) mountains, and against all the high hills.

Not only the reference to Lebanon links this with Isaiah 10:34, but also other verbal links associate it with Isaiah 10:33 b: 'and the tall (ורמי) in stature will be hewn down, and the lofty will become low (ישפלו).'[23] One thinks also of Isaiah 40:4: 'every mountain and hill shall become low (ישפלו).'

The messianic shoot (חטר) or branch (נצר) of Isaiah 11:1 (usually in the Scrolls called צמח דויד, following the use of צמח in Isa 4:2; Jer 23:5; 33:15; Zech 3:8; 6:12) has been interpreted as a vine, perhaps under the influence of Psalm 80, but more probably by association with Ezekiel 17:6–8, where the twig which symbolizes a scion of the royal house of Judah is said to have 'sprouted (ויצמח) and become a vine' (17:6), and is later described as a 'noble (אדרת) vine' (17:8). The use of אדיר links this vine with the messianic interpretation of Isaiah 10:34 b (באדיר). Finally, the use of a fountain to symbolize the royal power of the Messiah[24] may owe something to Song 4:15 (where a fountain is associated with Lebanon), but probably more to 'the waters of Shiloah that flow gently' (Isa 8:6), interpreted with the aid of a messianic interpretation of Shiloh (Gen 49:10)[25] as a reference to the kingdom of the Messiah. The emphasis on the peace and tranquillity of, first, the fountain (2 Bar 36:3), and then the vine with the fountain (36:6), which is surprising in view of their destruction of the forest and the cedar, may be due not only to the statement that 'the waters of Shiloah flow gently' (Isa 8:6) but also to an association of the name Shiloah (שלח) with שלה (to be quiet, tranquil) or שלום (peace).

Baruch's vision is constructed from a detailed exegesis of Isaiah 10:33–11:5, including the messianic interpretation of 10:34, in association with several other scriptural passages. This kind of exegetical basis for a vision is by no means unique. For example, the pair of visions of the harvest and the vintage in Revelation 14:14–20 are based on Joel 4:13 (EVV 3:13) in association with

---

[23] Cf. also Ezek 17:24.

[24] 2 Bar 39:7 is not clear as to the distinction between the fountain and the vine, but from the whole account of the vision and its interpretation it is clear that the vine is the Messiah in person and most likely the fountain is his dominion or royal power.

[25] This interpretation is attested in the Targums, rabbinic literature, and probably the LXX.

other passages, especially Daniel 7:13–14 and Isaiah 63:3. Abraham's dream of the cedar and the palm tree in 1QapGen 19:14–19 is probably based, rather more loosely, on Psalm 92:13 (which was applied to Abraham and Sarah because of v 15; cf. Gen. R. 41:1).

John the Baptist

2 Baruch 36–40 demonstrates that the messianic interpretation of Isaiah 10:34 was not confined to the Qumran community, but must have been more widely known and accepted in the New Testament period. This means that, in arguing, as I shall now do, that it is also presupposed in the preaching of John the Baptist I do not need to lay any weight on the possibility, which has been frequently suggested, of an association between John and Qumran, though others may find in my argument a further support for postulating such an association.

The preaching of John the Baptist, as recorded in the Gospels, contains two allusions to Isaiah 10:34. The first is in Matthew 3:10 = Luke 3:9:

ἤδη δὲ [Luke: καὶ] ἡ ἀξίνη πρὸς τὴν ῥίζαν τῶν δένδρων κεῖται· πᾶν οὖν δένδρον μὴ ποιοῦν καρπὸν καλὸν ἐκκόπτεται καὶ εἰς πῦρ βάλλεται.

The image of trees cut down by an axe, as an image of divine judgment, is found in the Hebrew Bible in Isaiah 10:34; Jeremiah 46:22–23; Ezekiel 31:12; and Daniel 4:10 (EVV 13), but only the first two of these passages explicitly mention the axe (Isa 10:34) or the axes (Jer 46:22), and in any case it is clear that only Isaiah 10:34 is a suitable text for allusion in this saying of John. Unlike the others it is easily susceptible to the interpretation John seems to give it, as referring not to the judgment of Gentile kings, armies or nations, but to the judgment of those within Israel who do not repent in response to John's message. The tall trees of Isaiah 10:33, especially when associated with Isaiah 2:12–13, can readily be taken to symbolize the proud and arrogant who, priding themselves on their descent from Abraham (Matt 3:9 = Luke 3:8), refuse to admit their need of repentance. If, then, the saying alludes to Isaiah 10:34, it understands that verse differently from the texts we have already discussed: the forest is not the Roman army and Lebanon is not the Roman emperor. However, John's interpretation does have one further point in common with that in 2 Baruch 36–40: he expects the trees to be not only felled but also burned. No doubt this agreement results from the use of the same exegetical procedure: the association of the two passages (Isa 9:17 [EVV 18] and 10:34) which use the highly distinctive phrase 'the thickets of the forest' (סבכי היער).

The saying in itself cannot tell us whether John adopted a *messianic* interpretation of Isaiah 10:34. The axe might be wielded by the Davidic Messiah, understood to be the אדיר of Isaiah 10:34 b. But, in the light of Isaiah 10:33, it could be wielded by God himself coming in judgment. Identifying an allusion to Isaiah 10:34 does not immediately settle the much debated issue of the identity of the figure John expected to come. However, we can initially make two points. First, the reference to the axe probably does make implicit reference to a figure who wields it. The opening words of our saying, in which John envisages the imminent judgment so vividly[26] that he sees the axe already positioned to chop down the trees,[27] are parallel to the opening of another of John's sayings, which uses a different image of judgment and similarly envisages the instrument of judgment already poised for action: 'His winnowing shovel[28] is in his hand...' (Matt 3:12 = Luke 3:17). The figure implicit in the first saying becomes explicit in the second.[29] Secondly, it seems most likely that, if John adopted the image of Isaiah 10:34 as an especially significant image of the imminent eschatological judgment, this was because of its connexion with the well-known messianic prophecy that follows in 11:1–5. As we have seen, there was an exegetical tradition of reading Isaiah 10:33–11:5 as a unit. Thus we should expect that John's allusion to Isaiah 10:34 indicates some connexion between his message of imminent judgment and the expectation of the Davidic Messiah.

The problem of the identity of the one who wields the axe can be resolved by attending to a second allusion to Isaiah 10:34 in the reported sayings of the Baptist. Unlike the allusion in Matthew 3:10 = Luke 3:9, which has sometimes been recognized, at least as a possibility,[30] the second allusion seems not to have been noticed before. It occurs in the best attested saying of John:

---

[26] For a similar image of the immediacy of judgment, cf. Jas 5:9.

[27] The blade of the axe is 'placed against the lowest point of the exposed trunk (i. e. the root) in order rightly to judge the first swing of the felling operation': J. Nolland, *Luke 1–9:20* (WBC 35A; Dallas, Texas: Word Books, 1989) 147; so also R. L. Webb, *John the Baptizer and Prophet: A Socio-Historical Study* (JSNTSS 62; Sheffield: JSOT Press, 1991) 301.

[28] For this translation, rather than the usual 'winnowing fork,' see Webb, *John the Baptizer*, 296–298.

[29] This point is oddly neglected by Webb, *John the Baptizer*, who in his discussion of the identity and activities of the figure John expected (chapters 7–8) gives much attention to the image in Matt 3:12 = Luke 3:17, but none to the image in Matt 3:10 = Luke 3:9.

[30] E.g. by J.A. Fitzmyer, *The Gospel According to Luke (I–IX)* (New York: Doubleday, 1981) 469. If the saying is an authentic saying of John, then the fact that Matthew and Luke use ἀξίνη, while Isa 10:34 MT has ברזל and Isa 10:34 LXX has μάχαιρα, is no reason to hesitate about the allusion, as Fitzmyer thinks. ברזל in this context certainly means 'axe' (as in Deut 19:5; Eccles 10:10), and ἀξίνη is a good translation. The LXX uses μάχαιρα because it replaces the image of felling trees with that of slaughter in battle.

Mark 1:7: ἔρχεται ὁ ἰσχυρότερός μου ὀπίσω μου...
Matthew 3:11: ὁ δὲ ὀπίσω μου ἐρχόμενος ἰσχυρότερός μου ἐστιν...
Luke 3:16: ἔρχεται ὁ ἰσχυρότερός μου...
John 1:15: ὁ ὀπίσω μου ἐρχόμενος ἔμπροσθέν μου γέγονεν...
John 1:30: ὀπίσω μου ἔρχεται ἀνὴρ ὃς ἔμπροσθέν μου γέγονεν...

These five versions probably derive from three distinct traditions of the saying: Markan, Q (represented here by Matthew rather than Luke) and Johannine. There are two significant variations among the versions. The first is between, 'There is coming after me the one who is more powerful than I / ranks ahead of me,' and 'The one who is coming after me is more powerful than I / ranks ahead of me.' This variation occurs not only between Mark and Q(Matthew), but also between the two Johannine forms of the saying (1:30 agreeing with Mark, 1:15 agreeing with Matthew). Which is the more original we need not decide here. The second variation is between the Synoptic expression ἰσχυρότερός μου and the Johannine ἔμπροσθέν μου. This should probably be regarded as a translation variant.

Even without the Johannine addition (ὅτι πρῶτός μου ἦν) to the saying in both its occurrences (John 1:15, 30), which serves to interpret it in terms of a preexistence Christology, the Johannine versions of the saying are characteristically loaded with paradox and double meaning. There is the apparent temporal paradox: 'The one who comes after me is before me.' And there is the apparent paradox of status: 'The one who is following me [= is my disciple] has taken precedence over me.' But the basic meaning must be: 'The one who is coming after me ranks ahead of me' (1:15) or 'After me is coming a man who ranks ahead of me' (1:30). With this meaning, the two Johannine versions of the same saying are equivalent to the Synoptic versions, provided that ἔμπροσθέν μου can be regarded as equivalent to ἰσχυρότερός μου. At first sight this does not seem possible, because ἰσχυρότερός μου is commonly understood to mean that the expected figure is stronger than John.[31] In fact, however, the expression must refer, not to physical strength, but to the power associated with high social status. This is clear from the way the saying continues in the Synoptic versions, with John's declaration that he is not worthy to untie (Mark, Luke; cf. also Acts 13:25) or to carry (Matthew) the expected figure's sandals.[32] In other words, the figure is so much more eminent than John that John is unworthy even to act as slave

---

[31] Thus, when Webb, *John the Baptizer*, chapter 7 (and cf. 303), looks for parallels to this feature of John's expectation in figures of Jewish eschatological expectation, he looks for references to their strength.

[32] The Johannine parallel is in John 1:27. John seems to have split the traditional saying of the Baptist in two, using part of it in 1:15, 30 and part in 1:27. This division is made partly to make possible the interpretation in terms of preexistence which the Fourth Evangelist adds in 1:5, 30. But it seems that he does not intend to report the Baptist's utterance of the saying itself: in 1:15 and 1:30 the Baptist refers back to what he had said

to him. In this way John indicates a difference of status greater than any in human society. The phrase ἰσχυρότερος μου does not make a different point, but is John's initial statement of the expected figure's preeminence over him; he then explains just how great this preeminence is by means of the statement about the sandals.[33]

There is no difficulty in taking ἰσχυρότερος in this sense, but we may wonder why John should have spoken of the expected figure in this way. The answer may lie in the messianic interpretation of באדיר in Isaiah 10:34. אדיר, used as a substantive, refers to a person of powerful status in society, a prince or noble or military leader. In this sense, the LXX sometimes translates it by ἰσχυρός (Judg 5:13, 25; Jer 37:21 [= 30:21 MT]), as well as by μεγιστάν (Jer 14:3; Nah 2:5; Zech 11:2), δυνάστης (Nah 3:18) and δυνατός (2 Chron 23:20). If John, speaking in Aramaic, referred to the expected figure as אדיר מני, the Synoptic ἰσχυρότερος μου would be a natural translation, but, in the context of John's saying, which goes on to emphasize the figure's eminence rather than his power as such, the Johannine ἔμπροσθέν μου would be even more appropriate.

Like the tradition of exegesis we have traced in the Dead Sea Scrolls and 2 Baruch, the Baptist, it seems, read Isaiah 10:33–34 as referring to a divine judgment executed by the Messiah (באדיר), i.e. by the Davidic Messiah whose rule is described in Isaiah 11:1–5. Unlike that tradition, however, John was not concerned with victory over the Gentiles. The judgment he envisaged was closely connected with his own ministry of calling Israel to repentance. It was a judgment on Israel – a discriminatory judgment on the arrogant and unrepentant within Israel. These are the forest which the Messiah will fell with his axe and burn.[34] The reason why John did not

---

previously, while in 1:27 the traditional saying is not reproduced, but echoed in order to make a further point about the one who is coming after him (1:26b).

[33] J. D. Crossan, *The Historical Jesus* (Edinburgh: T. & T. Clark, 1991) 235, is the latest of many who have understood this saying to refer to God rather than to a messianic figure. A decisive objection to this view is that of C. H. Kraeling, *John the Baptist* (New York/London: Scribners, 1951) 54: 'It is a pronouncement about one who can be and is being compared to *[sic]* John, albeit to the latter's disadvantage. The fact of the comparison shows that the person in question is not God, for to compare oneself with God, even in the most abject humility, would have been presumptuous for any Jew in John's day.' Cf. also Webb, *John the Baptizer,* 284–286.

[34] The parallel image of the threshing-floor (Matt 3:12 =Luke 3:17) does not portray the Messiah as winnowing the grain, but rather as acting after the winnowing has taken place, to clear the threshing-floor by shovelling the wheat into the barn and by burning up the chaff (see Webb, *John the Baptiser,* 292–300). Presumably it is John's preaching which achieves the winnowing, i.e. it separates the wheat from the chaff, the repentant from the unrepentant. The Messiah, portrayed as the owner of the threshing-floor, then deals appropriately with each. If there is a scriptural source for this image, it is most likely Mal 3:19 (EVV 4:1), which not only provides an image of the burning of the chaff (as distinct from the more common image of the chaff blown away by the wind) but also relates (from

refer to the Messiah as the Lord's Messiah or the Branch of David or by some other clear reference to the Davidic Messiah of Isaiah 11:1–5 will be that such terms were so predominantly associated with the messianic role of defeating the Gentiles. In order not to distract attention from the theme of a judgment hanging over the heads of his Jewish hearers, which they urgently needed to avoid by responding to John's message, John only hinted at the messianic identity of the figure who would execute this judgment.[35] He carefully chose and spelt out the meaning of a scriptural term for the Messiah – אדיר – which had not acquired associations from common usage, but which, as he expounded it, said what needed to be said about the figure whose coming he predicted: that he is the preeminent one whose authority surpasses all earthly rulers and judges.

If this hypothesis about John's interpretation of Isaiah 10:34 is correct, several other implications for interpreting the Gospel traditions about the Baptist may be drawn. First, since it is now clear that John did expect the Messiah described in Isaiah 11:1–5, it may be that John's prediction that the one who comes after him will baptize with the Holy Spirit (Mark 1:8; John 1:33) and or with the Holy Spirit and with fire (Matt 3:11; Luke 3:16) derives from exegesis of Isaiah 11:4: 'with the breath of his lips he will kill the wicked.' Interpreting this text, the vision of the Messiah in 4 Ezra 13:9–11 reads: 'he neither lifted his hand nor held a spear or any weapon of war; but I saw only how he sent forth from his mouth as it were a stream of fire, and from his lips a flaming breath, and from his tongue he shot forth a storm of sparks. All these were mingled together, the stream of fire and the flaming breath and the great storm, and fell on the onrushing multitude which was prepared to fight, and burned them all up…' (cf. the interpretation given in 13:37–38).[36]

---

its context in 3:17–20) to the the theme of differentiating the righteous from the wicked in Israel, which seems to have been John's conception of his ministry.

[35] In this sense, Jesus' reticence with regard to his messianic role, avoiding the usual titles and terms associated with the expectation of the Davidic Messiah, is continuous with John's preaching.

[36] The figure in this vision in 4 Ezra 13 is not only the Messiah of Isaiah 11:1–5 but also the 'one like a son of man' of Daniel 7 (see 4 Ezra 13:2). This identification of the Davidic Messiah of Isaiah 11 with the Danielic figure 'like a son of man' is also made, not only in the Parables of Enoch, but also in 2 Baruch 35–40 (cf. 39:5; 40:3, with Dan 7:23, 27). (For this tradition of interpretation, see G. W. E. Nickelsburg, 'Son of Man,' *Anchor Bible Dictionary*, vol. 6 [New York: Doubleday, 1992] 138–142). The possibility therefore arises that John the Baptist shared with 2 Baruch not only the messianic interpretation of Isaiah 10:34 but also the identification of the Messiah of Isaiah 10:34–11:5 with the 'one like a son of man' of Daniel 7. George Nickelsburg points out to me, in this connexion, that in Matthew 13:30, 40–41, imagery very close to that used by the Baptist in Matthew 3:12 is interpreted as eschatological judgment by 'the Son of Man.' However, there is no unequivocal evidence that the Baptist made use of Daniel 7. His interest in judgment on

Secondly, it may be that the peculiarly Johannine claim that the Baptist recognized Jesus to be the Messiah when he saw the Spirit descend and remain on him (μένον ἐπ' αὐτόν: John 1:33) should be allowed more historical plausibility than it usually is. The statement probably alludes to Isaiah 11:2 ('The Spirit of the Lord shall rest on him [ונחה עליו]'), and means that John saw Jesus anointed with the Spirit by God and so knew him to be the Messiah of Isaiah 11:1–5.

Thirdly, another feature peculiar to the Fourth Gospel's account of the Baptist is that it represents him as identifying himself by quoting Isaiah 40:3 (John 1:23). In the Synoptics, this quotation is applied to John (Matt 3:3; Mark 1:3; Luke 3:4–6[37]), but not attributed to him. That the quotation does in fact go back to John himself becomes plausible when we remember how 2 Baruch associates the image of felling of tall trees in Isaiah 10:33–34 with that of levelling mountains. The association is easily made on the basis of Isaiah 2:12–14, the more so for John the Baptist who thought of judgment coming on the arrogant within Israel, which is the theme of Isaiah 2:12–14 in its context. Thus John could have understood Isaiah 40:4, which predicts that 'every mountain and hill shall be made low,' as a prophecy parallel to Isaiah 10:33–34, and therefore as one which made clear, in verse 3, his own role as a voice calling for repentance in view of the coming judgment.

Israel, rather than on the Gentiles, would make Daniel 7 less appropriate for the Baptist's use than for the authors of 2 Baruch, 4 Ezra and the Parables of Enoch.

[37] Luke quotes the whole of Isaiah 40:3–5 a.

14. The Relevance of Extra-Canonical Jewish Texts to New Testament Study*

Introduction

Jesus was a Galilean Jew whose ministry took place almost entirely within Jewish Palestine. The earliest Christian churches were composed of Palestinian Jews (including some Jews from the diaspora who were resident in Jerusalem). When Christianity spread outside Palestine, it was among Jewish communities in the diaspora that it first made converts. Even when large numbers of Gentile converts entered the church in the course of the New Testament period, the leadership of the churches still remained largely in the hands of Jewish Christians. Most of the writers of the New Testament were Jews. The Hebrew Bible in Greek translation became the Bible of Gentile Christians, and, although they read it from the perspective of their faith in Jesus, they also read it within the Jewish traditions of interpreting Scripture which they learned from Jewish Christians. Furthermore, even Jewish religious literature which they did not regard as canonical Scripture must have been read and valued by Gentile Christians. It is a very striking fact that, apart from the Hebrew Bible itself and apart from the Dead Sea Scrolls and a few other Jewish documents which have been recovered by archaeologists in recent times, almost all of the Jewish literature which has survived from the period before 200 c.e. was preserved, not by Jews, who ceased to use it, but by Christians. Even Jewish works which were not written until the Christian church was already well established and most of the New Testament writings were already written, such as the apocalypses of Ezra (4 Ezra or 2 Esdras) and Baruch (2 Baruch and 3 Baruch), were appropriated by Christians.

These facts clearly suggest, not only that first-century Judaism was the principal religious context of Christian origins, but also that the character of early Christianity was decisively determined by these origins, so much so that, in terms of the history of religions, the Christianity of the New Testament period must be seen, not as something quite different from Judaism,

* First Publication: Joel B. Green ed., *Hearing the New Testament* (Grand Rapids: Eerdmans/Carlisle: Paternoster, 1995) 90–108.

but as a distinctive form of Judaism. The fact that by the end of the first century probably the majority of Christians were Gentiles who had not adopted the full observance of the law of Moses does not contradict this description, though it is one of several reasons why Christianity was coming to be seen by most non-Christian Jews as not a legitimate form of Judaism. Yet even this 'parting of the ways' between Christianity and Judaism was essentially a dispute between divergent interpretations of a common religious heritage.

All this is not to deny that both Jews and Christians were strongly influenced by the culture of the Greco-Roman world. Both Jews and Christians shared, in many respects, a common cultural world with their pagan neighbours. It would be a serious mistake to isolate the Jewish context of early Christianity from the wider Greco-Roman context. Nevertheless Jews of this period had a strong sense of their religious distinctiveness and the necessity to preserve it, and Christians, by worshipping the God of Israel, retained the core of this distinctiveness, while relaxing its strict connexion with observance of the law of Moses. In recent decades of New Testament study older theories which attributed a determinative influence on early Christianity to non-Jewish religious cults or ideas, such as the mystery cults or pre-Christian Gnosticism, have largely lost credibility (though very recently the parallels between the Gospel traditions and Cynicism, which was not a religious cult, but a school of Greco-Roman philosophy, have attracted fresh attention). The thoroughly Jewish character of the New Testament literature has been constantly demonstrated by the intensive study of this literature in relation to relevant Jewish literature.

Moreover, such study has taken place in a period in which the study of early Judaism and its literature has itself blossomed. New discoveries, especially the Dead Sea Scrolls, serious study of works which have long been known but largely neglected, such as many of the so-called Pseudepigrapha, properly critical work on the extent to which traditions of the New Testament period may be preserved in the Targums and the rabbinic literature, and major works of historical analysis and synthesis, such as Martin Hengel's influential work on the hellenization of Palestinian Jewish culture,[1] have transformed the study of early Judaism. The resources now available to the New Testament student and scholar for understanding the Jewish context of early Christianity are abundant. There are introductory textbooks and major reference works. Editions, translations, commentaries and studies of texts make them available and more accurately usable than ever before. At

---

[1] M. Hengel, *Judaism and Hellenism* (ET; London: SCM Press, 1974); *Jews, Greeks and Barbarians* (ET; London: SCM Press, 1980); *The 'Hellenization' of Judaea in the First Century after Christ* (ET; London: SCm Press, 1989).

the same time, there is much to be done. Important texts still await editing. Some have still been very little studied. Major issues of interpretation are highly debated. Students of the New Testament who take the Jewish context of early Christianity seriously cannot expect to find simply uncontroversial facts and agreed conclusions. They will encounter major debates between the leading scholars, such as that over the character of Pharisaism in the first century. They will have to learn that, as in the study of the New Testament, the textbooks sometimes make unqualified assertions, for example about the date of a work, which in fact rest on the slenderest of evidence and are highly debatable. They will find themselves trying to understand puzzling texts without the kind of help that is readily available in the commentaries for interpreting difficult New Testament texts. They will have to realise the uncertainties involved in relying, for example, on an English translation of a badly transmitted Old Slavonic version of a no longer extant Greek text which might have been translated from a Semitic original.

This may make the use of non-canonical Jewish literature in New Testament study seem a dauntingly difficult task. It is! The study of early Judaism is a complex and constantly developing field of study, in reality composed of a variety of highly technical and specialized disciplines. Advanced students who wish to make original contributions to this aspect of New Testament study will have to gain some understanding of the skills and tools of these disciplines, even if only to understand the way they are deployed by the scholars they read. In fact, many New Testament researchers who have turned to Jewish texts for the sake of comparing them with the New Testament have found themselves involved in major projects of interpretation of the Jewish texts for their own sake. Some such firsthand work on Jewish material should now be virtually a prerequisite for competent historical research in New Testament studies. But students who are only beginning New Testament study or have no expectation of doing original work in the field should not be deterred from reading Jewish texts of the period along with the excellent introductory literature now available. They cannot in any case avoid the extensive references to Jewish parallels and discussions of the Jewish context in virtually all literature about the New Testament. Even a small degree of firsthand acquaintance with the Jewish texts will make a considerable difference to their appreciation of such references and discussions.

Using the Literature

The general usefulness of the extra-canonical Jewish literature for NT interpretation is obvious. Insofar as the context of Jesus, the early church and the NT writings was Jewish, these writings provide us with most of what we know about that context (along with archeological evidence and some references to Judaism and Jewish history in pagan literature). Of course, we must understand the historical context here in the most comprehensive sense. It involves not only the religious, but (insofar as the distinctions are valid in a religious culture) the political, social, economic and cultural life of the Jews in Palestine and in the western diaspora. To take a very simple example, we should not know who the 'king Herod' of Acts 12:1 was, we might well confuse him with the tetrarch Herod of Luke's Gospel, and we might accuse Luke of inaccuracy in attributing to him authority in Jerusalem at this time, if we did not have Josephus' indispensable political history of first-century Jewish Palestine.

However, since most of the surviving Jewish literature is religious in purpose and content, as is the NT, it will not be surprising if the religious dimension of life (including the religious dimension of political, social, economic and cultural life) predominates in the value of the former to illuminate the context of the latter. To take a much less simple example, every serious student of the Gospels wants to know who the Pharisees were, since, although the NT offers some indications (e. g. Acts 26:5), for the most part it refers to them without explaining who they were. The Gospels are interested solely in the Pharisees' interaction with Jesus, and so, even if their account of the Pharisees were entirely accurate, it could still be very incomplete and onesided. But the Gospels could also be suspected of having polemically distorted their picture of the Pharisees, or of having retrojected onto pre-70 Pharisaism concerns belonging to the late first century. Unfortunately, the other main sources of information about the Pharisees – Josephus and rabbinic traditions about the Pharisees – are also problematic: Josephus because he had his own agenda which made him very selective and (some would say) not wholly accurate in what he records about the Pharisees; the rabbinic evidence because the selection, preservation and redaction of rabbinic traditions about the Pharisees was controlled by the concerns of the post-70 rabbinic movement. It is not surprising, therefore, that reconstructing the nature of Pharisaism in the NT period is a complex historical task with no fully agreed conclusions, but one of vital importance to NT scholarship. One important methodological point for NT interpretation is that clearly it will not do for NT scholars simply to plunder the Jewish evidence to illustrate what the various NT texts say about the Pharisees. Of course, it is true that, for example, Matthew 19:3 can be greatly illuminated by the rabbinic traditions about the debate between the schools of Hillel and Shammai over the grounds for divorce. But if we are to discuss the relationship of Jesus or the early Christians to the Pharisees in broader terms, we need as rounded and accurate an understanding of the Pharisees as a Jewish religious movement as we can gain. For this purpose, we cannot allow the NT material to control the agenda, but must study the Pharisees for their own sake, with the full range of evidence available, problematic though it is. Having said that, of course, it should not be forgotten that the NT is, among other things, itself evidence of early Judaism, including Pharisaism. If the Gospels are problematic as evidence for Pharisaism, so are the other sources.

What is true of the Pharisees, is true of the whole subject. The NT student and scholar must use the Jewish literature in the first place to understand Judaism. Only someone who understands early Judaism for its own sake will be able to use Jewish texts appropriately and accurately in the interpretation of the NT. The famous warning issued by Samuel Sandmel against 'parallelomania' in NT studies[2] has its most general application here. Someone who knows the Jewish literature only in the form of isolated texts selected for the sake of their apparent relationship to NT texts will not understand those texts in their own contexts (literary and otherwise) and so will not know whether they constitute real or only apparent parallels and, even supposing they are real parallels, will not be able to use them properly. A principle which NT students and even NT scholars rarely take to heart is that, for the sake of a balanced view of the relationship of Christianity to early Judaism, it is just as important to study Jewish texts which are least like anything in the NT as it is to study those with which the NT writings have most affinity.

Of course, it would be a mistake to wait until one has mastered the broad picture – whether of early Judaism or of early Christianity's relationship to Judaism – before studying the detailed ways in which Jewish texts can illuminate specific NT texts. In this as in most fields of study, one's understanding of the general will be enhanced by study of particulars, and the two will be constantly interrelating. What is important in the study of particular Jewish parallels to particular NT texts is never to forget that the former have a context which is essential to their meaning and relevance. This context will need to be explored in a variety of ways. The theme may need to be traced in other Jewish texts, or related to other themes. A particular word or expression or image may have to be traced in a variety of texts before the significance of its occurrence in one can be evaluated. It is usually also important to know as a whole the particular Jewish work which is being used. (Compared with modern books, all ancient Jewish works are short,

---

[2] S. Sandmel, 'Parallelomania,' *JBL* 81 (1962) 1–13.

most extremely short. It does not take long to read one through!) No NT student would quote a verse from a Pauline epistle, without further ado, as evidence of early Christianity in general, because Paul was a highly individual and creative thinker, and even what he shared with other Christians, which was certainly a great deal, would not have been shared equally with all Christians. But early Jewish writers were also individual and creative writers, and early Judaism was more diverse than early Christianity. Precisely in what sense a Jewish text constitutes evidence of the Jewish context of early Christianity needs to be more carefully considered than it often is.

It is extremely probable that all of the NT writers read some extra-canonical Jewish literature and that some of them were very familiar with some such literature. (In addition, many of them would have known Jewish oral traditions, such as the legal traditions of the Pharisees and the exegetical traditions of the synagogues.) However, it is very rarely possible to prove that a particular NT writer knew a particular Jewish writing that we know. The letter of Jude, which not only explicitly quotes (Jude 14) from part of that collection of Enoch literature we know as 1 Enoch, but can also be shown to make several allusions to parts of the Enoch literature, is very unusual. In most cases we cannot treat the Jewish literature as sources the NT writers used, but must see them as evidence of the ideas and terminology with which NT writers were familiar. But at this point we must raise two problems.

One is the kind of Judaism of which a particular Jewish writing is evidence. In the unusual case of the Dead Sea Scrolls, we know at least that these writings all belonged to the library of the Qumran community. Some of the literature was written within the community and is unlikely to have been known outside it, except by other Essenes, but clearly the community also read extra-canonical religious literature which was not peculiarly its own and had either a wide or limited circulation among other Jews. These categories cannot always be easily distinguished. In the case of most other pre-rabbinic Jewish literature we do not know who wrote or read it. For a text to be relevant to NT interpretation, we need to be able to suppose (from various kinds of evidence, including the NT) either that Christianity was influenced by (or, in relevant cases, opposed) the particular kind of Judaism represented by the text, or that in relevant respects what text says was not peculiar to the group that produced and read it, or that the writing in question was not restricted to a particular Jewish group but circulated widely. Such judgments cannot be made in isolation from current discussion of the extent of variety in early Judaism. The current trend to emphasize diversity to such an extent as to speak of 'Judaisms' in the plural[3] has rightly

---

[3] E. g. J. Neusner, W. S. Green and E. Frerichs ed., *Judaisms and their Messiahs at the Turn of the Christian Era* (Cambridge: Cambridge University Press, 1987); G. Boccaccini,

been challenged by E. P. Sanders' claim that it makes sense to speak of a 'common Judaism' which most Jews shared and in which even those Jews who belonged to the parties, such as the Pharisees, participated.[4] Much of the literature that has survived may well have circulated quite widely and have been read by Jews who differed from each other on some issues. Even literature which belonged rather exclusively to particular groups, such the Qumran community's own writings, can be shown to share many themes, traditions and concerns with wider Jewish circles. This makes virtually all the literature of the period potentially relevant to NT interpretation, but it does not enable us to shirk the difficult questions about the extent to which a particular text in any particular case is representative or idiosyncratic.

However, the reference in the last sentence to 'literature of the period' raises the second problem: that of the date of the literature. In the past, many scholars made rather indiscriminate use of evidence from the rabbinic literature (all of which was written two centuries or more after the NT) as evidence for pre-70 Judaism, influenced by a misleading historical model, according to which Pharisaism was 'normative Judaism' and later rabbinic Judaism essentially a continuation of Pharisaism. This model, along with the uncritical acceptance of all ascriptions of traditions to early rabbis in the literature, is no longer credible. In reaction, some NT scholars are reluctant to admit the relevance of any Jewish literature which cannot be shown to have been written before the NT. But this seeming methodological stringency is a spurious kind of purism. Judaism changed after 70 CE, but not in such a way as to destroy all continuity with its past. Many of the Targums, though of uncertain date, can be shown to preserve exegetical traditions from the NT period. Their evidence must be used with care, but it is not unusable. Similarly, many of the so-called Old Testament Pseudepigrapha are of very uncertain date – and not a few included in the now standard collection edited by J. H. Charlesworth[5] are much later than the NT and even of Christian origin – but that they preserve early Jewish traditions can often be argued. They cannot be used in the same way as those which are certainly pre-Christian in date, but they are not unusable. Sometimes a striking parallel between the NT and a later Jewish work can itself show (since the influence of Jesus or Christian literature on the Jewish work is

---

Middle Judaism: Jewish Thought 300 B. C. E. to 200 C. E. (Minneapolis: Fortress Press, 1991).

[4] E. P. Sanders, *Judaism: Practice and Belief 63 BCE–66 CE* (London: SCM Press / Philadelphia: Trinity Press International, 1992). For this issue, see also R. Bauckham, 'The Parting of the Ways: What Happened and Why,' *ST* 47 (1993) 135–139 (= chapter 12 above).

[5] J. H. Charlesworth ed., *The Old Testament Pseudepigrapha*, 2 vols. (London: Darton, Longman & Todd, 1983, 1985). For discussion of some of the problems created by the scope of this collection, see R. Bauckham, 'The Apocalypses in the New Pseudepigrapha,' *JSNT* 26 (1986) 97–117 (= chapter 8 above).

not, in such cases, usually plausible) that the Jewish work here preserves an old tradition. The use of Jewish sources later than the NT for NT interpretation requires careful and informed historical judgment by a scholar well acquainted with the literature, but it cannot be ruled out.

Sometimes parallels are instructive irrespective of date. This is sometimes the case, for example, in one of the most important areas of relationship between NT writings and Jewish literature: exegesis of the Jewish scriptures. Evidence from early writings, especially the Qumran *pesharim* (commentaries on scripture), shows that, despite some important differences, many of the techniques of exegesis known from rabbinic midrash and the Targums were already in use in the NT period. A later Jewish writing may therefore be able to illuminate the way in which a Jewish exegete is likely to have read a particular OT text, even if we cannot be confident that it preserves an ancient piece of exegesis. But this too is a field where it is important to go beyond parallels to an understanding of how Jewish exegetes worked and thought. Sometimes NT writers and the Christian exegetical traditions they used followed Jewish traditions of exegesis of particular texts, as we can demonstrate from parallels, but sometimes their exegesis was original. In the latter cases, however, they were still engaged in a Jewish kind of exegesis, with Jewish exegetical presuppositions and methods. In these cases, it is not particular parallels, but real understanding, gained from study of Jewish exegesis, of how Jewish exegesis was done, which will enable us to understand the NT texts in their Jewish context.

Example: James 4:13–5:6

The question of how the letter of James is related to Jewish religious traditions is an important issue in determining the character of this New Testament writing. Some scholars have stressed its affinities with and indebtedness to wisdom traditions, and have therefore seen James as a Christian wisdom writing. Others have pointed out its resemblance to prophetic-apocalyptic material (especially in 5:1–8). Interpretation of the law of Moses also has a significant place in the letter (especially in 2:8–13). Study of the passage 4:13–5:6 in the light of Jewish literary parallels will enable us to see how these three elements coexist and cohere within the letter.

This passage is in two sections, introduced by the two parallel addresses in 4:13; 5:1, denouncing in turn two different categories of wealthy people: merchants (4:13–17) and landowners (5:1–6). Not only are the two categories of people distinct: they are also condemned in quite different terms. The merchants are denounced for their arrogant self-confidence, treating their lives as though they were entirely within their own control, without